277

PLUMBING
INSTALLATION and REPAIR

By
H. P. MANLY
Technical Editor
ENGINEERING TRADE MANUALS

DRAKE PUBLISHERS

Published in 1974 by
Drake Publishers Inc.
381 Park Avenue South
New York, New York 10016

Library of Congress Data

Manly, Harold Phillips, 1887-
    Plumbing, installation and repair.

    1. Plumbing.

TH6122.M35   1957   696.1   57-59174
ISBN 0-87749-706-0

Printed in the United States of America

FOREWORD

This book is intended for use by those having no previous training in plumbing practice, nor special knowledge of the requirements, but who wish to plan, install and maintain simple plumbing systems in accordance with good practice and without violating the rules and regulations generally in force.

It would be incorrect to say that the material is arranged only for plumbers, mechanics, trade schools, or home owners; because good plumbing depends not on who does the work, but on how it is done. The rules are no different for one person than another. In fact, a building owner who installs plumbing is subject to the same rules as the professional plumber, and to the same penalties for not obtaining permits or inspections, or for failure to comply with local regulations.

Recommended methods, sizes, lengths, and types of fixtures and connections given in this book represent generally accepted practice or minimum requirements, but do not necessarily apply in all localities. In every case the local codes and ordinances should be consulted before doing extensive work. However, it is felt that one becoming acquainted with the methods here outlined will need to make only minor adjustments for any local conditions.

The material presented applies primarily to residences, small apartment buildings, small stores, offices and shops, and to kitchen equipment in restaurants and hotels. Much of the instruction applies as well to buildings of any size and type.

The object is to enable the user of this book to install plumbing with the least labor and lowest cost for material, while at the same time obtaining an installation that will prove durable, suffer only slow depreciation, and give the least possible trouble. In carrying out this ideal, preference always is given to the simplest systems and designs.

The book is devoted chiefly to the practical side of plumbing, although hydraulic and pneumatic principles are explained briefly when they materially assist in understanding why and how certain things happen, and why certain methods are to be preferred over others. Knowing only the practice might lead to unintentional violation of safety rules, and certainly would limit one's ability to reason out problems which do not conform in every detail to established rules.

The aim has been to exclude individual or unsupported opinions, possibly biased in favor of certain methods, and to substitute therefor a cross section of the advice and suggestions of competent authorities in the field.

Most of the rules and recommendations have been taken from or adapted from the Recommended Minimum Requirements for Plumbing (the basis of most codes) issued by the Building Code Committee, from the Plumbing Manual issued by the Central Housing Committee on Research, Design and Construction, and from other bulletins of the United States Bureau of Standards. Material specifications follow in general the several Federal Standard Stock Catalogs. Many of the application and structural details and methods are adapted from bulletins of the United States Department of Agriculture, and from others issued by the National Committee on Wood Utilization. Much material pertaining to work with tubing and special types of material has been obtained from publications of the manufacturers and their associations.

CONTENTS

CHAPTER 1

THE PLUMBING SYSTEM

A plumbing installation includes parts which handle three principal requirements. One group of parts includes all the water supply and distributing pipes such as shown in Fig. 1. These pipes bring

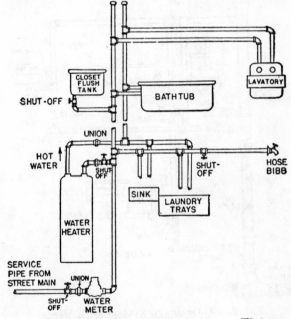

Fig. 1.—Piping for Water Distribution to Fixtures.

water from the street main to the building and carry it to the various points in the building at which water is used.

The second part of the plumbing installation includes all the fixtures which allow occupants of the

9

building to use the water. The fixtures shown in Fig. 1 include on the upper floor a water closet, a bathtub and a lavatory, and on the lower floor a sink and two laundry trays, which often are called laundry tubs.

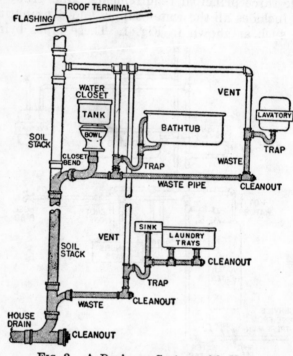

FIG. 2.—A Drainage System with Vents.

The Drainage System.—The third part of the plumbing installation is shown in Fig. 2, which shows also the fixtures. This third part is called the drainage system. The purpose of the drainage system is to carry away from the fixtures all wastes and human excreta which may contain disease-producing bacteria. Although the drainage system is highly important from the standpoint of health, it often is the part least understood.

The drainage system consists of two chief classes of piping and fittings. In the first class are all the portions which carry away water, other liquids, and water-borne waste matter. These parts include drain pipes, waste pipes, and the lower portion of the soil stack. They are shown shaded in Fig. 2. In this class are also the traps, which contain a water seal that prevents air passing from the sewer and drainage system back through the fixtures into the building.

The second class of pipes and fittings in the drainage system consists of the parts which carry only air. Here we find all the vent pipes, vent stacks, and the upper part of the soil stack. A vent is defined as any pipe which allows flow of air to or from the drainage pipes, or any pipe providing circulation of air within the drainage system. This flow and circulation of air through the vents prevents water from being forced out of the trap seals by siphon action or by back pressures.

The traps are downwardly looped sections of pipe, in the lower part of which remains a quantity of water. This water forms a seal that prevents sewer air and gases from entering the building through the fixture drain openings. In general, each fixture must be fitted with a trap. However, there are a few exceptions to this rule. One exception is shown on the lower floor in Fig. 2, where two laundry trays and a sink drain through the same trap. The water closet has its own trap built into the closet bowl.

Naming the Pipes.—Fig. 3 shows in a simple line diagram the names given to many of the pipes according to their position and purpose in the drainage system. The names and functions of these pipes will become familiar when investigating the details of installations later on, but it is well here in the beginning to become acquainted with as many plumbing terms as possible.

A *drain pipe* is any pipe which carries water or water-borne wastes in the building drainage system. A *fixture drain* is the portion of a drain line between the trap of a fixture and the point at which

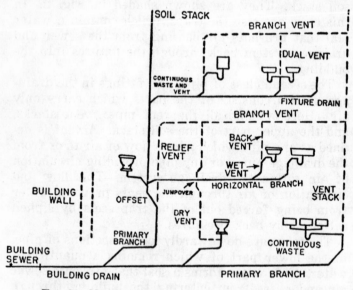

Fig. 3.—Names of Pipes in the Drainage System.

this drain joins any other drain pipe. The term *waste pipe* should be applied only to drains which receive the discharge from fixtures other than water closets, urinals, and other fixtures receiving human excreta. Thus we have waste pipes from sinks, lavatories, bathtubs, laundry trays, and similar fixtures.

The *soil pipe* or *soil stack* is the largest line of pipe in the installation. Its lower end connects to the building drain or house drain. The *building or house drain* is the pipe which leads outside the building to the *building sewer* or *house sewer,* which leads in turn to the street sewer or other place at which sewage is discharged. The soil stack runs in a straight line, or as nearly so as possible, right through the roof, where the upper end is open to outside air.

A *main* is any principal pipe to which are connected drain pipes and waste pipes, either directly or through branches. The word *stack* is a general name given to any vertical main in the drainage system. The soil stack, also any horizontal soil pipe, carries the discharge from water closets, urinals, and fixtures of similar purpose, and may carry also the discharge from any other fixtures. In addition to soil stacks we may have *waste stacks* which carry the discharge only from fixtures other than water closets and urinals, and also *vent stacks* which are vertical mains in the vent system.

Other pipes shown by Fig. 3 are defined as follows, following from the top toward the bottom of the diagram:

A *branch vent* is a vent pipe which connects from a branch in the drainage system to the vent stack. A *dual vent* connects to the point at which two fixture drains come together, and provides a vent for both drains. A *continuous waste-and-vent* consists of a vent pipe and a waste pipe which are in a straight line.

A *relief vent* is connected between a branch from the vent stack and the soil stack or a waste stack, primarily for the purpose of allowing air to circulate between the two stacks to which connected. A *back vent* is any vent which allows air to enter a waste pipe so that water will not be drawn out of the fixture traps by siphon action. A *wet vent* is any portion of a waste pipe that acts also as a vent for other fixtures on the some line.

A *horizontal branch,* often called a *lateral,* is a drain pipe that extends from the soil stack, waste stack, or building drain and receives the discharge from one or more fixtures. The branch may include vertical portions as well as those which are horizontal. An *offset* is a combination of fittings which carries a pipe line to one side or the other, then continues the line parallel with its original direction. A *jumpover* or *double offset* consists of two offsets by means of which the pipe is returned to its original line. A *dry vent* is a vent which at no time carries water or water-borne wastes. A *continuous vent* is a waste pipe running from two or more fixtures into a single trap.

The building sewer or house sewer connects to the building drain or house drain at a point five feet outside the inner surface of the building wall. A *primary branch* of the building or house drain is a connection from the base of a stack to the main building drain.

Importance of Venting.—As shown by Figs. 2 and 3, the vent pipes are installed in such manner that from the sewer side of each trap there is a continuous open connection through the vents to the upper part of the soil stack or the vent stack, and through the tops of the stacks to the open air. The vent pipes equalize air pressure on both sides of the water in the trap seals. They allow the same air pressure to reach the sewer side of the seal as reaches the other side through the fixture drain opening. With the pressures thus balanced there is no tendency for water to be forced out of the trap in either direction.

Were vents not provided, suction effects on the trap for one fixture when water is discharged from other fixtures might draw enough water out of the trap to destroy the seal. Again, unless relieved through the vents, there might be excessive pressure on the sewer side of a trap, which would force sewer air through the trap and out of the fixture into the building.

At times when the drainage pipes are carrying no discharges, there is free travel of air from the building drain through the soil or vent stack, the wastes, and the vents to the roof terminal. This circulation reduces the slime formed in drainage pipes and helps retard corrosion of the pipes themselves.

The drainage systems shown in Figs. 2 and 3 carry away liquids which might, directly or indirectly, be injurious to health. Therefore, these are called *sanitary drainage* systems. The plumbing installation may include also a separate *storm water* drainage system to carry away rain water and other water not used directly by occupants of the building.

CHAPTER 2

PLUMBING FIXTURES

A plumbing fixture is any receptacle which receives water and discharges any water, liquid, or water-borne waste into the drainage system. Fixtures most commonly used include bathtubs and shower baths, water closets and urinals, lavatories or wash stands, sinks of many types, laundry trays, and drinking fountains.

All fixtures are made with smooth non-absorbent surfaces, and of such shapes as to have no concealed surfaces which may become foul or which may not be readily cleaned. Fixtures commonly are made of enameled cast iron or enameled pressed steel, of vitreous (glass-like) china, of solid porcelain, and often of metals such as stainless steel, nickel silver, Monel metal, and copper. Occasionally we find fixtures made of slate or soapstone, and even of concrete.

All types of fixtures are made in such great variety of style and size that there is space here to mention only some of the more important classifications and their characteristics. Detailed information is available from catalogs of houses selling this equipment.

Bathtubs.—The bathtub of lowest cost is the leg type which stands free from the floor on four legs. It is difficult to clean underneath and behind such tubs. A better style is the base type which rests upon a rectangular base extending around the bottom of the tub and enclosing the space between tub bottom and floor. The more modern built-in bathtubs are shown by Fig. 4. The recessed tub is built into the floor, and into the walls at its two ends and the back. The corner tub is built into the floor and into the walls at one end and the back. This and the other styles come with the water supply and drain either at the right-hand end, as shown, or at the left-hand end. The pier tub is built into the floor, and

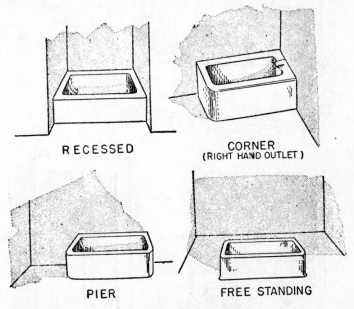

FIG. 4.—Types of Bathtubs.

into the wall only at its back. The free-standing tub is built only into the floor, being free from the walls on all sides.

Shower Baths.—The most generally used shower arrangement is the over-tub type, often called a wall shower, as shown in Fig. 5. Such showers may use the tub supply valves with extra valves to transfer the water flow to the shower head, they may use two separate valves connected only to the shower head,

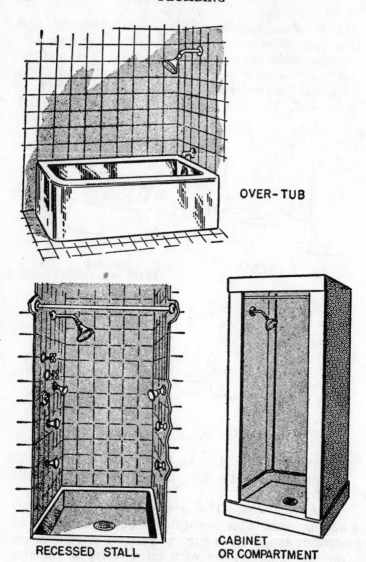

OVER-TUB

RECESSED STALL

CABINET OR COMPARTMENT

Fig. 5.—Types of Shower Baths.

or they may have a type of mixing valve that changes the proportions of hot and cold water by means of a single handle.

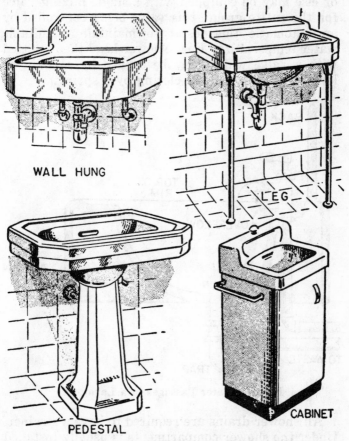

WALL HUNG

LEG

PEDESTAL

CABINET

Fig. 6.—Types of Lavatories.

The stall type shower may be recessed as shown, or may have side partitions built out from a wall. The cabinet type or compartment shower stall may be installed as a complete self-contained unit. Gang showers, consisting of several shower units in one group, may have the usual types of shower valves, or else may be equipped with a single mixing valve for the entire group, this valve being controlled by an automatic thermostat to maintain a suitable water temperature. Each shower head then is fitted with a valve which may be opened by a chain or lever, and which is self-closing by a spring.

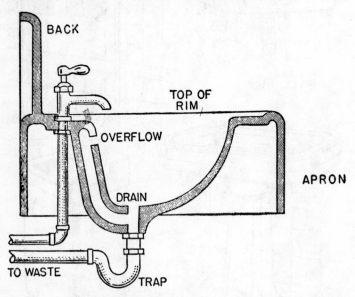

FIG. 7.—Water Passages in a Lavatory.

All shower drains are required to have a strainer. Under the shower compartments is usually installed a sheet lead pan turned up at least eight inches on all sides except the front, which is turned up five inches. This pan is connected to the drain pipe.

Lavatories.—The four general styles of lavatories in most common use are illustrated in Fig. 6. The wall-hung type is supported entirely from its back on brackets fastened to the wall. The leg type is attached to the wall, and has the extra support of one or two legs. The pedestal type is supported entirely by its floor pedestal. The cabinet type may be supported from the wall, with the cabinet acting merely as an enclosure. Fig. 7 shows a section through a wall-hung lavatory. The passage from the overflow to the drain is formed in the bowl. Overflows always must connect to the fixture side of the trap, not to the sewer side. The wall is protected by the back of this fixture, and the bottom of the bowl is concealed by the apron.

Sinks and Laundry Trays.—Kitchen and pantry sinks may be either wall-hung, similarly to one style of lavatory, or may be of the self-supporting style which rests upon a cabinet. Some sinks have no extension on either side. Others have an extension, called a drainboard, on one side, while still others have drainboards on both sides. The sink itself may be divided into two compartments by a partition running from front to back. Many sinks have an apron like that of the lavatory in Fig. 7, while others have a roll rim, which is a rim turned over for only a short ways and leaving the bottom of the sink in view. Sinks may be had with flat rims for building into counters and similar places.

Laundry trays or tubs usually are made or mounted in units of two or three trays having one or more sets of faucets, and all draining together into one trap. A *combination fixture* is one consisting of a sink with either one or two laundry trays in the one unit. Combination fixtures usually drain through a single trap.

Backflow Through Fixtures.—Fig. 8 shows a tub or sink with a faucet whose opening is below the top of the rim. Were the drain opening closed, or were the drain clogged with obstructions in the trap or waste pipe, water might fill this fixture to the top of its rim, or to the flood level, which is above the faucet opening. Under such conditions, were the shut-off closed in the supply line and the fixture faucet allowed to remain partly open, as might occur in case of trouble, dirty water might be siphoned out of the fixture through the water supply pipe. Such siphon action would be almost certain

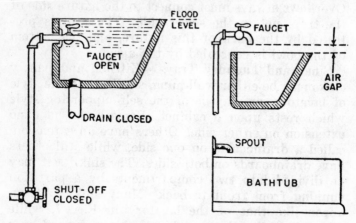

Fig. 8.—How Backflow May Take Place.
Fig. 9.—Over-rim Faucets and Spouts with Air Gaps
Preventing Backflow.

were the shut-off valve fitted with a drain opening providing an air passage into the vertical pipe while the valve is shut against the main supply.

The action illustrated by Fig. 8 is called a back-flow, and the arrangement which permits it is one kind of cross-connection or interconnection between the water supply and drainage systems. Such entrance of water from a fixture, quite likely containing waste matter, into the supply system must be positively guarded against.

Fig. 9 shows how over-rim supplies used with all modern plumbing fixtures prevent backflow. Between the extreme top of the fixture rim, which here is the flood level, and the opening in the faucet or spout is an air gap across which water cannot be siphoned even though the fixture is full to overflowing. The air gap is the vertical distance between the outlet of an over-rim supply fitting and the flood level of the receptacle over which the fitting is mounted. An air gap is shown in the lavatory of Fig. 7.

Artificial ponds, fountain basins, aquariums, and similar receptacles for water may not have a water inlet below the highest level to which water may rise, or an inlet which may be submerged under any conditions. A submerged inlet would form a cross-connection between dirty water and the supply pipes, through which a backflow might take place.

Installation of Fixtures.—Whenever it is practicable the water supply pipes for a fixture should run to the wall rather than to the floor.

If an old copper-lined or "tin lined" wooden bathtub is taken out of service at one place it may not be reconnected and used again. The same thing applies to stationary sinks or washtrays built of wood. In fact, wooden fixtures always are prohibited in all places intended for human occupancy.

It is a general rule that no fixture requiring a trap may be installed in a room having no window in an outside wall unless the room is well ventilated otherwise. A local ventilating pipe, through which foul air is removed from a room or fixture, must be run separately to the outdoors, and may have no connection whatever with other ventilating pipes or ducts within the building.

CHAPTER 3

WATER CLOSETS

So far as their method of action is concerned, there are three principal varieties of water closet bowls in general use at the present time. All employ the siphon principle shown in Fig. 10. The siphon type closet with a *reverse trap* is shown in Fig. 11, the *siphon washdown* type in Fig. 12, and the

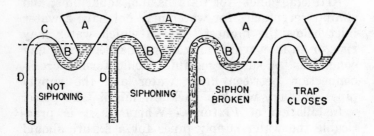

FIG. 10.—How a Siphon Acts.

siphon jet type in Fig. 13. All are siphon types because, during the flushing operation, water is drawn out of the bowls by means of siphon action.

The operating principle of the siphon is illustrated in Fig. 10. If water is poured into *A* at such a rate that it is carried away through pipes *B* and *D* without completely filling space *C* above the broken line, and without filling pipe *D*, the water will remain at approximately the level in the sketch marked *not siphoning*. But if water be added to *A* faster than it can be carried away through pipes *B* and *D*, then the level will rise in *A* and at the end of pipe *B* until it closes the space *C* and completely fills pipe D. Then conditions are as shown in the sketch marked *siphoning*.

With both B and D filled with water there is a greater weight of water in D than in B. Now, if water be no longer added to A, or be added at a reduced rate, the greater weight of water in D will pull the water out of receptacle A until the level falls just below the broken line in the sketch marked *siphon broken*. Now air from A is drawn into pipes

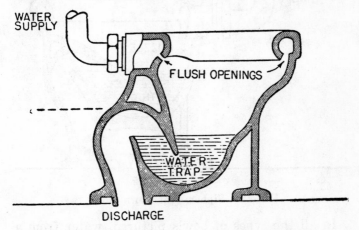

FIG. 11.—Siphon Closet Bowl with Reverse Trap.

B and D. Pipe D empties, no longer contains sufficient weight of water to continue the siphon action, and the water remaining in B partially fills the trap, as shown in the sketch marked *trap closes*. If only a small amount of water now is added to A, the trap will re-fill to the level shown in the first sketch.

Examination of the bowls in Figs. 11, 12 and 13 shows that all of them have water traps between the main part of the bowl and the discharge opening. When the closet is flushed, water flows into the bowl faster than it can be carried away by the discharge. Water rises until it fills the upward bend between the trap and the discharge opening, and then the siphon action commences. The decreasing rate at which flush water finally enters the bowl allows the level to fall until the siphon breaks. The remaining flow of flush water refills the trap to the levels shown in the diagrams of closet bowls.

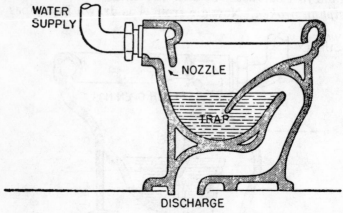

WATER SUPPLY

NOZZLE

TRAP

DISCHARGE

FIG. 12.—Siphon Washdown Bowl.

In all the types of bowls pictured, water from a flush tank or valve enters a hollow rim extending all the way around the bowl. Openings in this flush rim allow water to flow down over the entire inner surface of the bowl. Some low-priced bowls are made with plain rims having no washing feature. Many washdown bowls are provided with the extra nozzle shown in the design of Fig. 12. When the closet is flushed, the relatively large flow from this nozzle assists in thoroughly cleaning out the excreta and also establishes a siphon action without delay.

Prompt and vigorous siphon action is caused in the siphon jet bowl of Fig. 13 by a jet of water expelled from a suitable small opening and directed upward into the siphon chamber. Water for this jet comes through the passage indicated by broken lines in the drawing.

An obsolete style of bowl called the washout type is shown in Fig. 14. Water and waste matter are washed off the upper part of the bowl and into the trap opening by a stream of water from a nozzle at

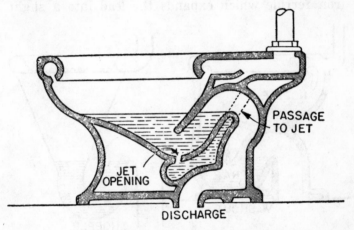

FIG. 13.—Siphon Jet Closet Bowl.

the rear and usually also by water from the hollow rim. This washout style of bowl, and the still older hopper type shown by Fig. 14, are prohibited in nearly all localities. No closet is permitted in which there is an invisible water seal, nor in which the walls are not thoroughly washed during each flushing.

The style of urinal consisting of a trough flushed with a perforated pipe connected to a tank or water line with automatic valve generally is prohibited, as is also the flat-back type made of slate slabs.

Closet Floor Connections.—Fig. 15 shows all the details of one typical method of attaching a closet bowl to the floor and at the same time connecting it with the soil stack. A brass floor flange fits around the closet horn and over the opening through the floor. To this flange is soldered the upper end of a lead nipple or piece of lead pipe of any length required to extend down through the floor of the room. Into the lower end of the lead pipe is driven a cast iron ferrule which expands the lead into a slight

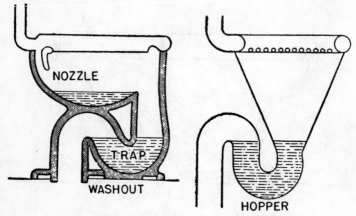

NOZZLE

T.R.A.P.

WASHOUT

HOPPER

FIG. 14.—Obsolete Types of Water Closets.

taper. This expanded end fits into the bell end or hub end of a cast iron *closet bend*. The space between the lead and the bell or hub of the closet bend is calked to make the joint water-tight. Calked joints are described in another portion of this book. The other end of the closet bend connects into a soil stack fitting with another calked joint.

Bolts which have been placed through holes in the brass floor flange have their threaded ends upward. The upper edge of the lead pipe and the inner part of the flange are covered with a one-piece gasket made of lead or asbestos. The closet bowl is set down so that the flange bolts come through openings in the bowl base. Washers are placed over the bolts and cap nuts are screwed down to lock the bowl securely to the piping assembly.

Fig. 16 shows a cast iron elbow with an integral cast iron floor flange which may be used similarly to the flange, the lead pipe, and the closet bend of

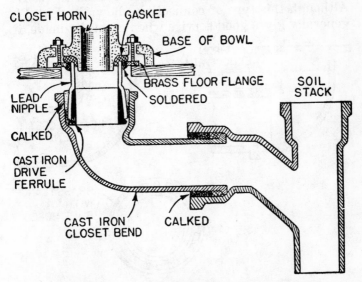

FIG. 15.—Details of a Closet Bowl Connection.

Fig. 15. This elbow is threaded at its lower end to receive the threaded end of a drainage pipe which may be of wrought iron.

Fig. 16 shows also the method of soldering a brass floor flange to the upper edge of a closet bend made of lead. The construction of one style of brass floor flange is shown in this illustration. Instead of the gasket, we find in some cases a metal-to-earthenware type of union or else a metal-to-metal union. With these unions the lead or asbestos gasket of Fig. 15 is not needed. Brass floor connections are available with extensions suitable for making a wiped joint between the brass and a lead pipe or a lead closet bend. The wiped joint is another style that will be described later on.

Closet bowls sometimes are mounted over the end of a lead pipe (closet bend) and bedded in putty. Although this type of connection, shown by Fig. 17, generally gives good service when carefully made, it

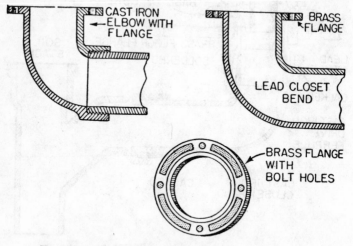

FIG. 16.—Flanges for Closet Bowl Connections.

is prohibited in many localities. The upper end of the lead bend is beaten out with a hammer to form a flat circular flange on the floor. This flange and the entire bottom of the bowl base then are coated with red lead. Enough putty is put around the horn opening on the bottom of the bowl to more than fill this space. The bowl then is placed in position and pressed down firmly, first on one side and then on the other, to force the putty out under the base. After the bowl is well worked down into the putty it is screwed to the floor.

There is great variety in devices for making closet bowl connections. For instance, one arrangement employs a cast iron floor flange with an integral downward extension in the form of a long ring. This extension receives the end of a special type of closet bend of such shape that the joint between the ring and the bend may be calked. All these devices must

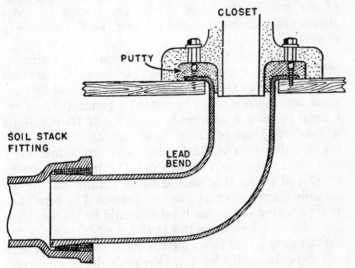

FIG. 17.—Putty Joint for a Closet Bowl.

serve the same purposes of fastening the bowl and connecting it with a soil pipe extension. The same connections used with water closets may be used for floor-mounted urinals and slop sinks.

Closet Tanks and Their Flush Valves.—All modern water closets have low tanks placed back of and just above the bowl. Older styles have tanks near the ceiling and long flush pipes. Most tank flush valves are operated by a hand lever or button. Types used in public and semi-public places often are flushed automatically at certain time intervals.

Some closets are flushed by movement of the seat as it is pressed down by the user and later allowed to rise a short ways, this arrangement being used more often with pressure flush valves connected directly to the water line rather than those with a tank.

Pressure flushing may be accomplished by a closed tank in which the entering water compresses a body of air within the tank. This compressed air then forces the water out rapidly when the flush valve is opened.

The average flushing rate from the ordinary closet tank is about 30 gallons per minute, although the maximum rate, lasting for only a second or two, runs much greater. Flush tanks generally are required to have a minimum capacity of four gallons of water. Most of them have capacities of six to eight gallons. The flush pipe between a low tank and the bowl should be at least $1\frac{1}{4}$ inches in diameter, and preferably should be of tubing having an outside diameter of $1\frac{1}{2}$ to two inches. The pipe supplying water to the flush tank should be no less than $\frac{3}{8}$ inch size, but since the tank may fill slowly after flushing, this size is ample for most needs. The supply pipe to each closet tank should have an accessible shut-off valve.

Tanks for flushing urinals should have a capacity of at least two gallons, or a pressure valve connected directly to supply pipes should furnish this minimum quantity of water for each flushing.

A style of valve mechanism commonly used in flush tanks is shown in Fig. 18. The opening into the bowl pipe is closed by the rubber ball stopper which fits a seat and is held in place by pressure of the water above it. The operating handle pulls down on one end of the flush lever arm and raises the ball to allow flushing. A slip joint on the lift wire allows the hollow ball to float after being released, so that flushing continues until the tank empties. When the tank is empty, the ball drops back to close the outlet.

As the water level drops in the tank, the float drops with it. Movement of the inlet lever arm opens the ball cock and admits water from the supply pipe. The ball cock has a rubber or composition disc held down onto the valve seat by a plunger operated from the float mechanism.

As soon as water commences to flow into the tank from the supply pipe, the weight of water holds the

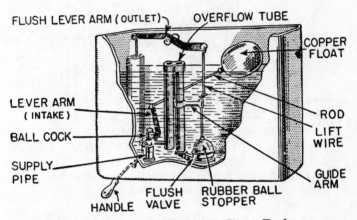

FIG. 18.—Valves in a Water Closet Tank.

ball stopper on the outlet opening while the tank fills. When the water level rises to the correct height, carrying the float with it, movement of the float arm closes the ball cock. An overflow tube allows water to flow into the closet bowl should the ball cock fail to close and the level rise too high in the tank. There are variations in the design of tank valves, but the operation and results are generally similar to those described.

Pressure Flush Valves.—A type of flush valve connected directly to the water supply and closet bowl, and used without a tank, is shown closed and open by Figs. 19 and 20. A rubber diaphragm separates the pressure chamber above from the flush chamber below. Pressure in the pressure chamber is maintained equal to that in the supply pipe at the right by the small bypass opening connecting these two chambers together. When the handle is moved in any direction its plunger is pushed in against the

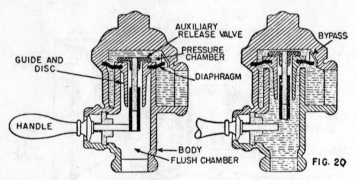

FIG. 19.—Diaphragm Valve in Closed Position.
FIG. 20.—Diaphragm Valve Open.

lower end of the auxiliary release valve. Pressure reaching the under side then raises the auxiliary valve, the guide and disc member, and the diaphragm. Water for flushing now goes down through the valve body and from the lower opening to the closet bowl. While flushing continues there is a small flow of water through the bypass into the pressure chamber. When this flow fills the chamber, the valve is closed by pressure from the supply pipe.

The sudden rush of water through a valve of the pressure flush type may reduce the pressure in the supply lines so much as to interfere with operation

of other parts in a plumbing system. All pipes leading from the street main to the valve should be at
least one inch in diameter in order to provide a sufficient volume of water. Even then, these pressure
valves probably would interfere with operation of
the 5/8-inch water meters generally used in dwellings. Plain pressure valves are undesirable in small
houses, but such valves may be used in connection
with a pressure tank wherein air is compressed by
water pressure, then released by opening of the
valve.

CHAPTER 4

TRAPS

A trap is a device which allows flow of waste water and sewage through a pipe while preventing passage of air or other gases in a reverse direction. Sewer air contains gases resulting from decomposition of fats, soap, solid wastes, and excreta. Gases result also from commercial and industrial refuse discharged into the sewers. Disease-producing bacteria seldom are present in sewer air, but such air should be kept out of buildings because of its offensive odor. In addition to preventing passage of sewer air, traps help keep insects such as water bugs and cockroaches from getting into buildings from the sewers.

The style of trap in most general use consists of nothing more than a downward loop in the piping. Traps such as connected to sinks and lavatories are shown in Fig. 21. The *P-trap* is so called because its shape resembles that of the capital letter **P**, while the *S-trap* is named for its resemblance to the letter S. The P-trap sometimes is called a *half-S trap*.

Trap Seals.—The manner in which a trap permits flow of liquids and prevents flow of gases may be seen in Fig. 22, which illustrates a P-trap of the drainage type. Water from the fixture outlet flows into the upper opening, through the loop, and into the waste pipe. When the fixture has emptied, enough water should remain in the trap to fill it to the level shown in Fig. 22. The weight of this water is too great to be displaced by air pressures on the sewer side of the trap, consequently no air or gas from the sewer side may pass back into the fixture.

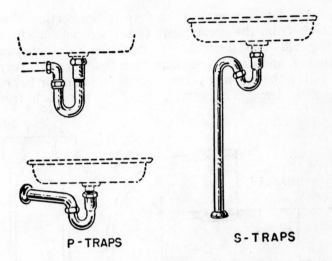

P-TRAPS   S-TRAPS

FIG. 21.—Traps for Sinks and Lavatories.

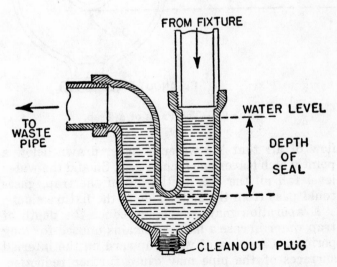

FIG. 22.—A Cast Iron Threaded P-trap.

The depth of seal in the trap is the vertical distance from the *crown weir* to the *dip*, as shown in Fig. 23. This depth never should be less than two inches, and need be no more than four inches in any trap, although many traps have seals six or seven inches deep. The venting must permit such free

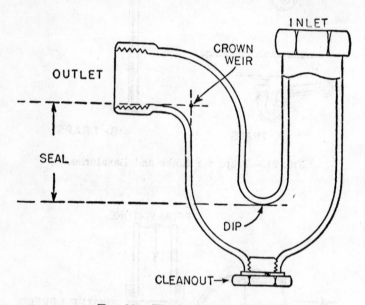

FIG. 23.—The Parts of a Trap.

flow of air that the water is never drawn below a point which leaves one inch of seal. Should the water level fall all the way to the dip of the trap, gases could pass from the sewer side to the fixture side.

Evaporation may gradually reduce the depth of trap water in case a fixture remains unused for long periods. Creeping of water upward on the internal surfaces of the pipe may cause further reduction. If the upper end of the soil stack or vent is subjected to strong upward or downward air currents, the suction or pressure thus created in the stack and vents may cause trap water to rise and fall. This will reduce the level as part of the water spills into the drain piping.

The ability of a trap to maintain an effective seal depends not only on the trap itself, but also on the type of fixture used with it, on the length and slope of the waste pipe, and on the number and location of bends or elbows in the waste pipe.

When water runs out of flat-bottomed fixtures such as sinks, laundry trays and bathtubs, the final discharge forms a sort of delayed trickle which re-fills the trap in case it has been nearly emptied by siphon effect of water flowing away through the waste pipe. In the case of round-bottomed fixtures, such as most lavatories, there is a sudden end of the flow as the fixture empties, and there is no slow trickle to re-fill the trap. For this reason the traps on round-bottomed fixtures are more likely to empty than are traps on flat-bottomed fixtures.

Trap Construction.—Traps in drain lines generally are made of cast iron or of galvanized malleable iron, sometimes porcelain enameled inside. Fixture traps are made of the same materials, also of brass, and occasionally of lead. The diameter of the trap should be the same as the diameter of the waste pipe from the fixture, or the diameter of a waste pipe suitable for the fixture.

The drainage trap of Fig. 22 is a threaded type designed for connection to other threaded fittings or threaded pipes. The style of trap shown in Fig. 21, commonly used with lavatories and sinks, is connected to the waste pipe with a union and to the fixture with a slip joint. These two connections are shown in Fig. 24. In the union end the pipe or tubing leading to the waste line is flanged. The union nut fits over this flange and screws onto one end of the threaded trap bend. A washer of fibre or composition material is shown between the bend and the upper pipe. Instead of having a washer, the butting ends of the two pipes may be faced smooth or ground, and one provided with a brass insert. This style is called a *ground face union*.

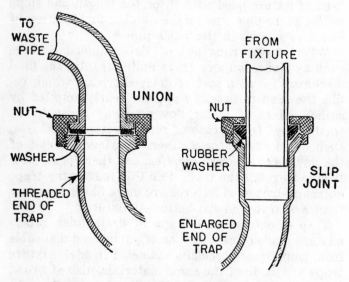

FIG. 24.—Union and Slip Joint for a Trap.

The slip joint also uses a union nut, but this nut squeezes a rubber washer into a space between the tubing from the fixture, the enlarged end of the trap bend, and the flange of the nut. The fixture pipe and bend are pushed together far enough to bring the bend into correct position for the union connection, then the nut of the slip joint is tightened.

Traps having slip joints may have a cleanout plug at the bottom of the bend, as in Figs. 22 and 23, or may be plain as in Fig. 21. Except when a trap is made in combination with a fixture having the water seal plainly visible, and the trap easily accessible, every trap should have a cleanout plug.

A slip joint is permitted only on the fixture end or the inlet end of a trap. A union is required at the sewer end, and in many localities this union must be of the ground face type. The union should not be concealed or made inaccessible. The only places in a plumbing system where combinations of slip joints and unions may be used are in trap seals or on the inlet side of a trap, except that in some cases special approval may be given for expansion joints. An expansion joint is a type of slip joint that allows movement of pipe lines as they expand and contract with heating and cooling.

Drum Trap.—The construction of one style of drum trap is shown in Fig. 25. This trap consists of a cylindrical metal shell, closed at the bottom and fitted at the top with a screw-on cover which may be removed for cleaning the trap. The connection from the fixture enters near the bottom of the trap. The space below this connection forms a settling chamber. The outlet to the waste pipe is higher up. The depth of seal is the vertical distance from the top of the inlet to the bottom of the outlet.

Drum traps frequently are used with bathtubs, lavatories and sinks. The screw cover is set flush with the floor surface so that it is easily accessible for cleaning. This style of trap holds more water than the P- or S-traps.

Trap Vents.—In all the traps examined it is necessary that a back vent connection be made to the waste or drain pipe on the sewer side of the trap. Were a back vent not provided, the trap might be emptied by siphon action. Such siphon action might occur whenever the waste or dra n line filled with water to a height greater than t he trap seal, for then the excess weight of water on the waste side would be sufficient to empty the trap. The back vent prevents such action by admitting air to the waste line. Then the excess weight of water simply draws air through the vent rather than drawing water out of the trap.

In places where the cost of running a vent might be prohibitive, or where a vent might seriously de-

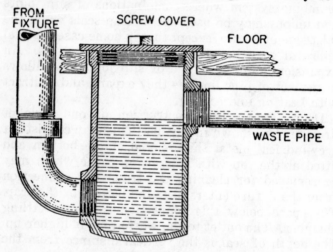

FROM FIXTURE SCREW COVER FLOOR

WASTE PIPE

FIG. 25.—A Drum Trap.

tract from appearances, as in passing through a room above the fixture, permission may be given to use a trap that requires no venting. Such special types are called nonsiphon traps, antisiphon traps, resealing traps, and similar names. These special traps are somewhat more costly than plain ones, and many of the designs are patented. In addition to lessening the number of vents required, these special traps allow using greater lengths of unvented horizontal waste pipes than would be permissible with plain traps. In general, these ventless traps oppose the effects of pressure on the sewer side and, when clean, oppose siphon action better than plain traps.

Traps having partitions or obstructions in their inside passageways, and traps which depend on movement of mechanical parts in maintaining a seal generally are prohibited, or else their use is governed by special local regulations.

Where Traps Are Required.—Between each fixture and the drain pipe or stack there must be a trap, except that one trap may be used for not more than three laundry trays, not more than three lavatories, or not more than two laundry trays and one sink. A single trap used for two or three fixtures is more likely to be emptied of its water by siphon action than are individual traps. The common trap permits waste water flowing out of one fixture to rise in another fixture connected to the trap. The distance from each fixture to a common trap is greater than with individual traps, consequently more fouled internal surface is exposed to the room air.

No fixture may be double trapped so that its discharge has to flow through first one trap and then another before reaching the stack or house drain. The discharge from no other fixture may be connected to flow into the trap of a water closet, urinal or slop sink. In general it is desirable to place the trap for each fixture as near as possible to the fixture outlet.

Grease Traps.—The principle of a grease trap is shown by Fig. 26. This is a device for separating grease from other kitchen wastes. It is connected between the sink and the soil stack or building drain. This grease trap does not provide a water seal, so does not prevent passage of sewer air back to the fixture, and would be used following a sealing type of trap. To avoid violating the rule against double trapping, it may be necessary to connect a vent pipe between the sealing trap or fixture trap and a grease trap.

Greasy water comes through the inlet into the upper part of the grease trap. The capacity of the trap should be at least twice the maximum discharge from the fixture, so that waste water will remain in

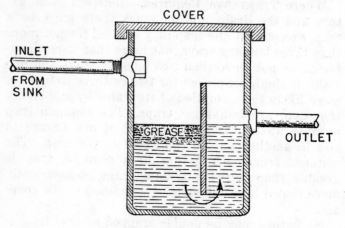

FIG. 26.—A Grease Trap.

the trap until the grease cools, hardens, and floats to the top of the trap contents. The remaining waste water goes into a space partitioned off as shown in Fig. 26, then through the outlet connection. The small clearance under the partition insures sufficient velocity to carry solids such as coffee grounds out of the trap.

A grease trap should be as close as possible to its fixture, but preferably in a location where the offensive odor will not get into a kitchen or other occupied room when the trap is opened for cleaning. Because of odors from the grease, these traps must have a tightly fitting cover. Grease traps often have

connections to the cold water or hot water supply so
that the trap may be flushed after a charge of grease
is removed.

Grease traps are used chiefly for large kitchens
such as in restaurants and hotels, and frequently
with sewage disposal systems using septic tanks
rather than draining into a public sewer. The fact
that grease traps in dwellings seldom are cleaned
when cleaning becomes necessary makes them undesirable for this class of service.

CHAPTER 5

DRAIN AND WASTE PIPES

Drainage pipes and their names are shown in Fig. 27. Although these pipes and their functions have been briefly mentioned in preceding pages, it will be well to note a few further points about some of them before discussing their design and installation.

The building drain or house drain is the lowest horizontal drain pipe in the building drainage system. It receives the discharge from all other drainage pipes within the building and carries the discharge into the building sewer or house sewer.

Waste pipes and stacks may discharge into a soil stack or directly into the building drain. Waste stacks in small installations often are of the same diameter as the largest drain coming into them, although the stack diameter should be not less than two inches, and for larger jobs will be sized according to the total discharge from all connected fixtures.

A horizontal branch or a lateral extends horizontally at a slight pitch or slope from a soil stack or waste stack, and takes the discharge from fixtures which do not connect directly into the stacks. A horizontal branch may consist of only a single straight horizontal pipe, or it may contain also such vertical portions as needed for connecting with fixture drains.

Drain pipes usually are of galvanized wrought iron or galvanized steel in sizes to and including two-inch diameter, and of cast iron in larger sizes. Underground drain piping must be of cast iron, not of wrought iron or steel.

Drain Pipe Size and Diameter.—The required sizes for drain pipes depend not only on the kind of fixtures drained, but also on the class of building in which installed. Private classification includes all

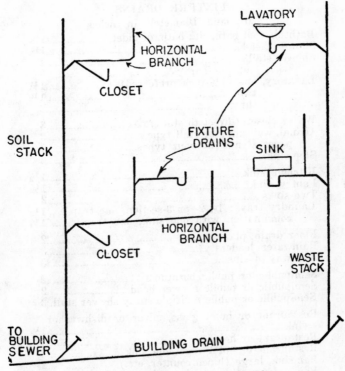

FIG. 27.—Drainage Pipes in a Building.

residences and apartment buildings, also private rooms used by only one person or one family in hotels and similar places. The semipublic classification includes buildings where toilet facilities are intended for use only by occupants of the building, such as in office buildings, dormitories, and factories. The public classification includes places where the facilities are for the unrestricted use of the public, such as in public rooms of hotels, gymnasiums, schools, railroad stations, and comfort stations. This public class includes pay-toilets.

FIXTURE DRAINS
Minimum Diameters in Inches

Bathtub, foot bath, sitz bath, or bidet	1½
Shower head	1½
Shower stall	2
with multiple sprays	3
Lavatory, one (1½-inch preferred)	1¼
two	1½
three	2
Water closet (direct to stack)	3
Urinal, wall hung or stall type	2
pedestal and blowout types	3
Slop sink	2
Kitchen sink	1½
Pantry sink	1½
Two sinks	2
Laundry trays: 1-, 2- or 3-section, one trap	1½
combination with one sink, one trap	1½
Floor drain, plain	2
Rainwater leaders	3
Areaway drains	3
Semipublic or public bathtub	2
Semipublic or public shower head	2
Semipublic or public multiple spray shower stall	3
Restaurant or hotel glass, silver or dishwasher sink	1½
Restaurant or hotel pot sink	3
Restaurant or hotel vegetable sink	2
Bar sink, large (lunch counter, etc.)	2
Bar sink, small (soda fountain, etc.)	1¼
Service sink, plain	2
Slop sink with jet or flushing rim	3
Drinking fountain	1¼

The table of *fixture drains* shows usual minimum sizes in the private classification, and applies also to other classifications except where differences are shown in the lower section of the table. These sizes apply also to the traps used with the fixtures listed.

It is necessary that the drain pipe be of diameter large enough to carry away the maximum normal discharge without so retarding the flow from fixtures as to make it sluggish, and without filling the pipe so full as to cause self-siphonage. On the other hand, it would be desirable to have the pipe no larger than will cause the waste to flow throughout its length with good velocity in the horizontal sections. This helps keep the interior of the pipe clean, free from deposits of solid matter, and unclogged. The smaller the pipe the greater the velocity for any given discharge. Pipes which take the discharge from several fixtures have to be so large that the velocity is low when only one fixture is discharging into them.

When a drain pipe of rather small size discharges into another pipe which is considerably larger, the velocity in the large pipe is much less than in the smaller one. The increased size also causes a rapid drop in temperature of waste liquids, and in combination with the reduced velocity this makes a sort of grease trap where clogging may commence.

Pitch or Slope of Drain Pipes.—Troubles resulting from low velocity of liquids flowing through horizontal drain pipes are greatly lessened by giving these pipes a downward pitch toward the soil or waste stacks, so that drainage flows rapidly through the outlets. Pitches may be from $\frac{1}{16}$ inch to $\frac{1}{2}$ inch per foot of horizontal length. A pitch of $\frac{1}{4}$ inch to the foot is commonly used.

The pitch must not be so great that the outlet from an unvented part of the pipe is lower than the dip of the trap on the fixture, otherwise water will be siphoned out of the trap following a discharge.

Fixture drains which are of considerable length often have too little downward pitch, which allows an accumulation of grease and solid matter in the pipe. When such a pipe becomes partially closed it is in effect a smaller pipe. The smaller inside space fills completely with water during a discharge, and there is danger of siphoning the trap unless there is effective venting. Should the pipe be of such small diameter and little pitch as to allow excessively low velocity, it will fill up during heavy discharges, even though clean, and will tend to siphon the traps.

A rule for determining the slope of horizontal fixture drains is as follows: The total drop from the trap weir to the fitting at which attaches the vent pipe should be no more than one pipe diameter. That is, for a $1\frac{1}{4}$-inch drain pipe the fall should be no more than $1\frac{1}{4}$ inches, for a 2-inch pipe no more than 2 inches, and so on. The developed length (length along center lines) from the trap weir to the vent fitting must be at least two pipe diameters, but not more than 48 pipe diameters. Thus, taking a $1\frac{1}{2}$-inch pipe for an example, the length must be at least $2 \times 1\frac{1}{2}$, or 3 inches, but may be no more than $48 \times 1\frac{1}{2}$, or 72 inches, which equals six feet.

The slope of a horizontal drain pipe should be no less than $\frac{1}{4}$ inch per foot for pipe up to and including 2-inch diameter, no less than $\frac{1}{8}$ inch per foot for pipes $2\frac{1}{2}$ to 4 inches in diameter, and no less than $\frac{1}{16}$ inch per foot for sizes of 5 to 8 inches. The table of *horizontal drain pipe length and slope* is based on these rules. The lengths shown in this table represent common practice. They may be exceeded for flat-bottomed fixtures with which the total horizontal length may run to 72 pipe diameters, or fifty per cent more than shown in the table. These lengths and falls apply to drains from fixtures whose water seals are solely for preventing siphoning and back pressure, but not to fixtures such as water closets which depend on siphon action for their correct operation.

HORIZONTAL DRAIN PIPE LENGTH AND SLOPE

| PIPE SIZE | LENGTH | | FALL IN INCHES | |
Inches	Minimum (inches)	Maximum (feet)	Minimum	Maximum
1¼	2½	5	1¼	1¼
1½	3	6	1½	1½
2	4	8	2	2
2½	5	10	1¼	2½
3	6	12	1½	3
3½	7	14	1¾	3½
4	8	16	2	4
5	10	20	1¼	5
6	12	24	1½	6
8	16	32	2	8

Drainage Fittings for Waste Lines.—A rule applying to joints between pipes in drainage lines is that there should be no enlargement or recess which forms a shoulder or which reduces the area of the piping in the direction of water flow on the outlet side or sewer side of a fixture trap. To meet this requirement, the threaded ends of drainage fittings are of different form than the threaded ends of pipe fittings used for water supply lines. The form for a drainage fitting is shown by Fig. 28.

The inside diameter of the drainage fitting matches the inside diameter of the pipe which screws into it, so that the bore of the drain pipe continues through practically without change when pipes are screwed tightly into the fittings. The inside diameter of a water supply fitting is considerably larger than that of the pipe, the difference being about one-third inch in the 1½-inch pipe size. There is less length of thread in a drainage fitting than in a water fitting, but back of the thread in the drainage fitting is a recess which receives the end of the pipe. The end around the threads which is shown as having a slight bevel in Fig. 28 may be straight in some styles.

As shown in Fig. 28, the inlets of drainage fittings which have horizontal openings are threaded in such direction that pipe screwed into them will be pitched. The outlets of drainage traps are similarly pitched, as shown in Fig. 28.

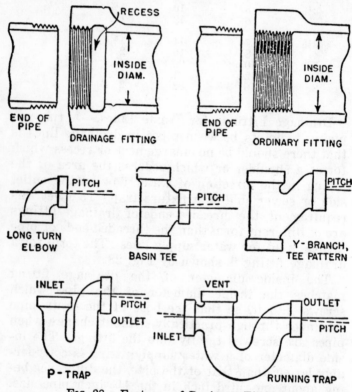

FIG. 28.—Features of Drainage Fittings.

Continuous Wastes.—Waste connections from two or three fixtures connected to a single trap form what is called a continuous waste. As shown in Fig. 29, the continuous waste pipes for two fixtures may be connected to a trap located under one of the fixtures or to a trap located centrally between them. For three fixtures the single trap should be centrally located as shown.

Common Waste Pipes.—The two sets of bathroom fixtures shown by Fig. 30 are on opposite sides of a wall or partition, so that their drain connections are opposite one another. In a case of this kind the pairs of like fixtures may drain into the same waste

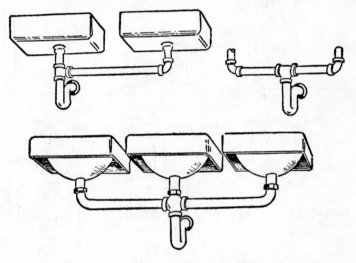

FIG. 29.—Continuous Wastes.

as indicated, and also may have dual vents. Here the two water closets discharge into the soil stack, while the two lavatories and two bathtubs discharge into the same waste line. Fixtures which are arranged directly adjacent to each other in any other positions may similarly have common wastes and dual vents. Of course, the rule still holds that the waste from no other fixture may discharge into a water closet trap.

Indirect Wastes.—A waste pipe that does not connect through closed piping with a soil stack, waste stack, or building drain is called an *indirect waste* or sometimes a special waste. When any food storage space, such as a refrigerator or ice box, requires a drain, the waste pipe may not connect directly with the stack or building drain. The waste should empty above the flood level into an open sink

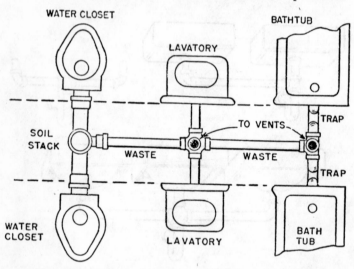

Fig. 30.—Common Wastes and Vents for Fixtures.

or other open fixture that is supplied with water and is trapped and vented the same way as other fixtures. Such connections are shown in Fig. 31. Indirect wastes sometimes discharge into a rain leader trap located inside the building, or into a floor drain. In any case the end of the indirect waste must be exposed, and not in an inaccessible or unventilated space.

Refrigerator wastes for one drain opening should be at least 1¼ inches in diameter, those for two or three openings should be 1½ inches, and for four to twelve openings at least 2 inches in diameter. Each opening must have a trap and the connections are to have suitable cleanouts.

Indirect wastes are required on any appliance used in preparing or processing food or drink where drainage is needed also on any device using water

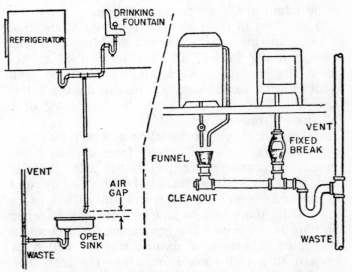

FIG. 31.—An Indirect Waste Draining into a Sink.
FIG. 32.—Indirect Wastes of the Funnel and Fixed Air Break Types.

for cooling or heating, or for treating water, such as sterilizers. Fig. 32 shows in the connection at the left a funnel type of air break or gap for an indirect waste, and shows at the right a type of breaker with a fixed air gap which cannot be altered. Air breaks of these general types avoid the need for discharging the waste into open plumbing fixtures such as sinks.

Cleanouts in Drain Piping.—Were a drainage system fitted with a cleanout plug at every 90° turn it would thereafter be a simple matter to open any section of the piping which might become clogged. So many cleanouts seldom are installed, partly because of extra cost, and in some cases because certain of these cleanouts would be prohibited by local regulations, on the theory that if left open they would admit sewer air to the building.

In addition to the cleanouts required at the foot of each soil and waste stack, a building or house drain running horizontally for some distance between the base of a stack and the building wall should have a second cleanout just inside the building wall. This cleanout should be in one leg of a full-sized Y-branch.

A cleanout should be installed at every 90° turn in drains carrying the discharge from kitchen sinks, since these pipes clog frequently. If a 90° turn is made with a tee-fitting instead of with an elbow, and the unused opening of the tee closed with a brass screw plug, there will be an effective cleanout when the plug is removed. The equivalent for a cleanout is formed wherever a fixture trap is bolted or screwed to a wall connection, since the trap then may be removed with little trouble in order to reach the pipes in the wall.

CHAPTER 6

VENTS AND VENTING

A vent pipe is any pipe whose purpose is to prevent siphoning water out of the traps, to relieve back pressure acting against the traps from the sewer side, and to ventilate the house drainage system.

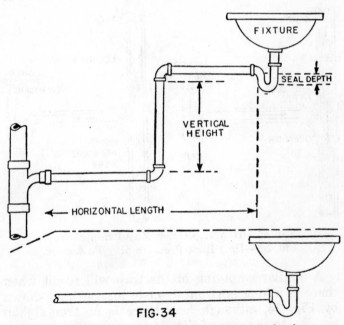

Fig. 33.—Unvented Wastes Which Cause Siphoning.
Fig. 34.—An Unvented Horizontal Waste.

Trap Siphonage.—An arrangement of waste piping practically certain to cause siphoning of trap water is shown by Fig. 33. When a full or nearly full fixture is emptied, water fills the seal, also the horizontal pipe connected to the seal, and the vertical pipe. The vertical height of water in the waste becomes so much greater than in the seal that the excess weight of water in the vertical pipe draws nearly all the water out of the trap. This is a true siphon action, since it depends on the difference between the weights of two columns of water.

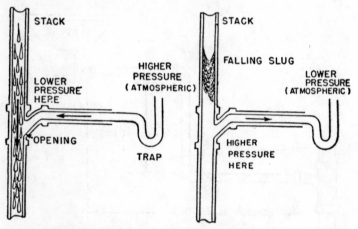

FIG. 35.—How Aspiration May Drain a Trap.
FIG. 36.—How Back Pressure May Be Caused.

A similar emptying of the trap will result when there is a long horizontal waste line such as shown by Fig. 34, although here there is no true siphon action. In the case of Fig. 34 the waste line becomes filled by water from the fixture. Pressure of water from the fixture, plus the downward slope of the waste pipe, causes flow at considerable velocity through the pipe. The momentum of this pipeful of water is sufficient to pull all the water out of the trap at the end of the discharge. This effect of the momentum of moving water is present in all waste pipes, whether they are horizontal, vertical, or at some intermediate angle. It is the chief cause of emptying a trap when the waste is horizontal, since in a horizontal pipe there is practically no siphon action.

Still another action which pulls water out of traps is illustrated in Fig. 35. Here we have water falling through a vertical stack, which may be a waste stack or the soil stack. As this water, and the current of air moving with it, pass the opening from the waste pipe a suction is produced at this end of the waste. Then the excess of pressure (atmospheric) exerted on the trap water through the fixture tends to force some or all the water out of the trap and into the waste pipe. We may say that there is an aspirating effect at the waste outlet. The greatest suction is produced just below the point at which water enters the stack, and this suction decreases at points farther down.

Back Pressure.—The effects of siphoning, momentum, and aspiration tend to draw water out of the trap and into the waste pipe. All these effects result in a pressure on the sewer side of the trap lower than on the fixture side. Water also may be forced out of the trap in the opposite direction, toward the fixture, by back pressure. A back pressure means that there is a higher pressure at the sewer side of the trap than at the fixture side.

Back pressure may be produced as in Fig. 36 when slugs of water extending all the way across from wall to wall fall through the stack, producing a kind of piston effect. Air below the slug is slightly compressed, which means a back pressure. Back pressure may be caused also by gusts of wind blowing downward onto the upper open end of the stack, although there seldom is any effect of this nature in dwelling installations.

Effect of Venting.—The harmful results of both suction and back pressure may be prevented by correct venting. As an example of how venting operates, Fig. 37 shows the same general arrangement as Fig. 33 except that in Fig. 37 a vent pipe extends upward from the vertical waste pipe. When siphoning tends to occur, the weight of water in the vertical waste pulls air through the vent rather than water through the trap. It is easier to draw a large volume of air through the vent rather than even a moderate weight of water out of the trap seal.

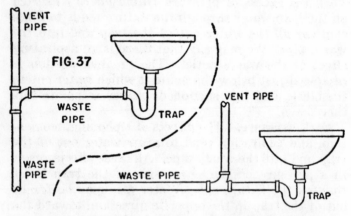

FIG. 37.—Vent Connection for Vertical Waste Pipe.
FIG. 38.—Vent Connection for Horizontal Waste Pipe.

Fig. 38 shows a long horizontal waste, like that of Fig. 34, but now there is a vent pipe connected near the trap. The momentum of water flowing through the waste will pull air down through this vent and into the waste pipe, rather than lifting water out of the trap seal, as when no vent is used. It may be noted that in Fig. 37 there still is an unvented horizontal section of waste pipe from the trap to the vertical pipes. In this unvented horizontal section there will be produced a suction because of the momentum of water flowing in it. Such unvented lengths of waste pipes should be kept short. There is a general objection to long unvented wastes in that the danger of internal corrosion increases rapidly with the length when there is no circulation of air in the pipe.

The suction produced by aspiration is relieved by venting, since here again it is easier for air to be drawn down through the vent, through the waste pipe, and into the stack, than for water to be pulled out of the water seal of the trap.

A vent not only relieves suction which tends to pull water out of the trap into the waste pipe, but also relieves back pressure which tends to force trap water the other direction. When a vent is installed, back pressure simply forces compressed air from the stack through the waste pipe and up the vent, rather than forcing air and water through the trap and into the fixture.

Stack Venting.—Fig. 39 shows an elevation and also a plan view of drainage connections to a soil stack for a lavatory, a bathtub, a water closet, and a sink such as might be used in a kitchen. Here the connections to the stack not only provide for wastes, but also form effective vents so long as none of the fixtures are too far from the stack. This is called *stack venting*. The arrangement shown by Fig. 39 is suitable for the only group of fixtures connected to a stack, as in a one-story house, or where the fixtures form the highest group connected to the stack, as when they are on the top floor of a building. It may be seen that siphonage, aspiration, the effect of momentum, and back pressure all are relieved by air which may enter the system through the stack. Of course, the upper end of the stack itself forms a vent pipe.

A *stack vent* is an extension of the soil stack or waste stack above the highest horizontal branch or highest fixture branch connected to the stack. The

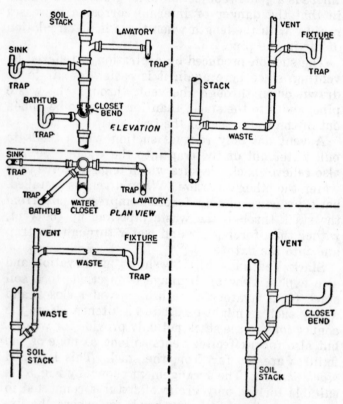

FIG. 39.—Stack Venting for a Group of Fixtures.
FIG. 40.—Connection To Vent Remote from Soil Stack.
FIG. 41.—Connection To Vent Near the Soil Stack.
FIG. 42.—Vent for a Water Closet.

stack vent should be of the same diameter as the soil stack or waste stack if these stacks carry one-half or more of the maximum load which would be allowed for them, or if the stack has horizontal branches on two floor levels or in any two stack sections which are eight feet long. Otherwise the diameter of the vent portion of the stack need be no greater than that required for a separate vent stack. Vent stacks and their sizes will be considered a little later on, as will also the matter of allowable loads on soil stacks.

Fixture Vents.—Fig. 40 shows the connection of a vent pipe for a single fixture other than a water closet when the vertical vent line is at a distance from the soil stack and when the fixture may be placed close to the vent line. This is practically the same connection described in connection with Fig. 37.

Fig. 41 shows the vent connection for a single fixture when the vertical vent line is close to the soil stack and when the fixture may be placed close to the vertical vent.

Fig. 42 shows the vent connection for a single water closet. The vent pipe leads upward from the fitting attached to the closet bend. The vent connections illustrated in Figs. 40 to 42 are those used when other fixtures drain into the same soil stack at points higher up in the system. Under such conditions the highest group of fixtures may be stack vented, as in Fig. 39, but those lower down should have independent venting of the types shown in Figs. 40 to 42 or of types to be shown later. The closer the fixtures are to the soil stack the simpler are the venting connections in any case.

Venting for Several Fixtures in a Group.—Fig. 43 shows a method of venting which may be used for a water closet and a lavatory in a group either on a lower floor with other fixtures connected to the soil stack above, or where there are no other fixtures. Such combinations of closet and lavatory are com-

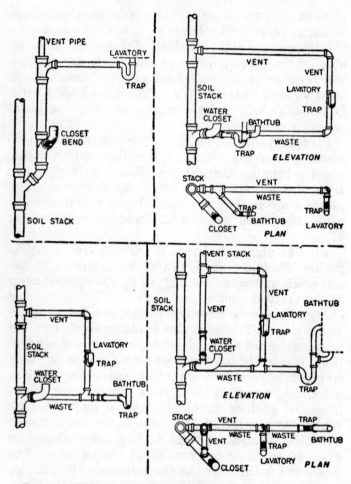

FIG. 43.—Venting for Water Closet and Lavatory in a Group.

FIG. 44.—Venting for Bathroom Group with No Fixtures on Higher Levels.

FIG. 45.—Venting with Lavatory Between Closet and Tub.

FIG. 46.—Venting Used When There Are Fixtures on Higher Levels.

monly used on the lower floors of houses where there are complete bathrooms on a higher floor.

Fig. 44 shows an elevation and a plan view for vent and waste connections which are satisfactory for a complete bathroom with bathtub, lavatory and water closet when located on the highest floor, or at least where no other fixtures are connected at higher levels. On the level shown by Fig. 44 might be connected also an independent waste pipe for a kitchen sink, draining into the soil stack above the water-closet connection much as shown in Fig. 39. This would allow complete connections for bathroom and kitchen as used in an apartment on an upper floor.

Fig. 44 shows a bathtub located between the water closet and the lavatory. Fig. 45 shows the same group of fixtures, but with the lavatory between the water closet and the bathtub. These arrangements might be used where no other fixtures connect in at higher levels, also on a lower floor when fixtures connected at higher levels include no more than a water closet, bathtub, lavatory and sink.

Elevation and plan views are shown by Fig. 46 for a connection which may be used on a lower floor when fixtures connected at higher levels include more than a bathroom group and kitchen sink. Here the vent stack connects not only to the wastes for lavatory and bathtub, but also to the water closet.

Duplex Venting.—Fig. 47 shows the elevation for common wastes and vents used with fixtures arranged in duplex as shown by the plan view of Fig. 32. Here there are two water closets, two bathtubs, and two lavatories directly opposite one another or closely adjacent. This arrangement is suitable for use where no other fixtures are connected into the same stack at a higher level.

Yoke Venting.—The method called *yoke venting* is illustrated by Fig. 48. Here the soil stack and the main vent stack rise parallel and close to each other. At each floor or level where fixtures are to be connected a yoke is run from an elevated point on the vent stack to a lower point on the soil stack, and the

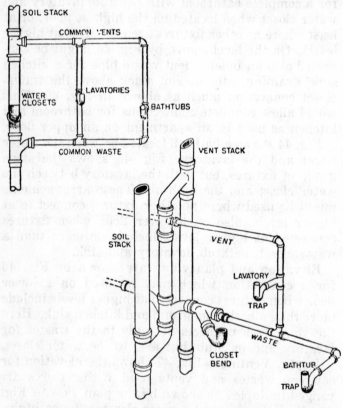

FIG. 47.—Dual Vents and Wastes for Duplex Fixture Groups.
FIG. 48.—Yoke Venting for One Level.

fixture wastes and vents, including the water closet outlet, are connected to this yoke. Yoke venting may be used regardless of what other fixtures are connected to the same system at higher or lower levels, so long as the soil stack and vent stack are large enough to carry the maximum probable discharges from all fixtures. The fixtures at each level are connected to a yoke placed between the two stacks at that level.

Circuit Venting.—Fig. 49 shows one style of *circuit vent* for three fixtures. A vent of this type may be used when the circuit carries the drainage of from two to eight water closets, pedestal urinals, shower stalls, or slop sinks.

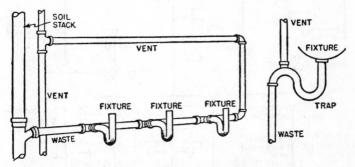

FIG. 49.—Circuit Venting.
FIG. 50.—A Crown Vent.

Crown Venting.—A vent connection not permitted in modern installations is shown by Fig. 50. This is called a *crown vent*. The vent pipe is connected at the crown or top of the curve which forms the trap.

Classification and Names of Vents.—Since the names given to vent pipes in accordance with their location, connections and purpose may be somewhat confusing because of their number, it will be well to go over the principal classifications.

The simplest of all venting arrangements is the *stack vent* illustrated in Fig. 39.

A *branch vent* is any vent that connects from a branch of the drainage system to the stacks. Branch vents are parts of the systems shown in Figs. 44 to 49 inclusive.

A *back vent* is any branch vent installed primarily for the purpose of protecting the fixture traps against siphoning. Consequently, back vents include most of the vents not installed especially to allow circulation between vent stacks and soil or waste stacks.

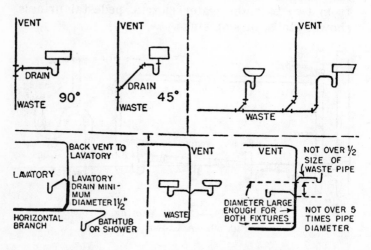

Fig. 51.—Continuous Waste-and-vent.
Fig. 52.—A Side Vent.
Fig. 53.—Group Venting.
Fig. 54.—Dual Vents.

A *continuous waste-and-vent* is a vent pipe that lies in a straight line with the waste pipe to which it is connected, and which forms a continuation of the waste pipe. Continuous waste-and-vents are illustrated in Figs. 37, 40, 41, and 44 to 48 inclusive. Fig. 51 shows two arrangements of continuous waste-and-vents.

A *side vent* is a vent that connects to the drain

pipe through a 45° Y-fitting as shown in Fig. 38 and also in Fig. 52. Here the vent pipe and waste pipe are at 90° to each other rather than being in line.

A *wet vent* is a pipe acting as a drain or waste and also as a vent when not carrying liquids. Wet vents are included in the systems of Figs. 44, 45, 46 and 48. The wet vent usually serves as a waste pipe for the fixture to which most closely connected. When this fixture is not discharging, but when others farther down the line are discharging, the wet vent acts as a vent pipe for those other fixtures.

A *dry vent* is any vent that does not carry liquids, but acts solely as a vent and carries only air at all times. A dry vent is included in Fig. 47.

A *group vent* is a branch vent that provides vent air for two or more fixture traps. Group vents are illustrated in Figs. 44, 45 and 46, also 48 and 49. Fig. 53 shows the general principle of group venting with a lavatory or sink and a bathtub or shower stall. To act as an effective vent for the bathtub or shower, the lavatory drain pipe should be at least 1½ inches in diameter.

A *dual vent* is a form of group vent that connects to the point where two fixture drains come together and which acts as a back vent for both fixture traps. Dual vents frequently are continuous waste-and-vents. Fig. 54 shows dual vents for fixture drains connecting together at the same level, also for drains at different levels. In the latter case the separation between connections should be not over five times the drain pipe diameter, the waste pipe should be large enough for both fixtures all the way up to the top connection, and the drain from the upper fixture should be no more than half the size of the vertical waste pipe. In Fig. 47 there are two dual vents, one for the two lavatories and another for the two bathtubs.

A *circuit vent* is a form of group vent that connects from the vent stack to a point on a horizontal branch in front of the last fixture connection on the branch. Circuit vents are shown in Figs. 46 and 47, also in Fig. 55.

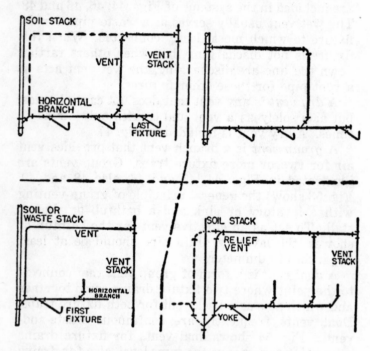

FIG. 55.—Circuit Venting.
FIG. 56.—A Loop Vent.
FIG. 57.—A Relief Vent.
FIG. 58.—Yoke Venting.

A *loop vent* is similar to a circuit vent except that the loop vent is brought back to the soil stack or waste stack instead of being connected to the waste stack. A loop vent is shown by Fig. 56, and a simple arrangement corresponding to the definition is illustrated in Fig. 45.

A *relief vent* is a vent pipe coming from a vent stack and connecting to a horizontal branch or lateral at a point between the first fixture connection on that branch and the soil stack or waste stack. The principle of the relief vent may be seen in Fig. 57. The chief function of the relief vent is to allow circulation of air between the vent stack and the soil or waste stack. Under certain conditions other than on the top floor of a building, circuit vents must be provided with relief vents as shown by the broken line connection in Fig. 55. Offsets at an angle of more than 45° may require relief vents. Connections such as often used for relief vents are illustrated in Figs. 42 and 43.

The *yoke vent* illustrated by Fig. 48, and shown in principle by Fig. 58 is a form of relief vent. The yoke vent is carried from a Y-fitting in the soil stack leading to the relief connection and the horizontal branch. When an extra horizontal branch is handled by yoke venting as shown by broken lines in Fig. 58, we have a dual yoke vent with both parts vented by the same relief.

Connections for Vent Pipes.—Every vent pipe should be run so that liquid collecting in it will drain into either the soil stack, a waste or a drain under the effect of gravity. This means that a horizontal vent pipe should be pitched toward either the soil stack, a waste pipe, or a drain, and that horizontal vents should not have intermediate dips at any point so that water, as from condensation, would remain at that point.

For vents on fixtures except water closets and others having similar outlets, the opening from the vent into the soil stack or waste pipe should be no lower than the dip of the trap protected by the vent.

When a vent pipe is connected to a horizontal waste pipe as in Fig. 38, or is connected to a horizontal soil pipe, the vent must be taken off the other pipe at a point above the center line of that pipe. From its point of connection to the horizontal pipe, the vent must run straight upward, or at an angle of not more than 45° from the vertical, to a point at least six inches higher than the fixture being vented before the vent may turn to a horizontal run, or before it may connect into the main vent or soil stack.

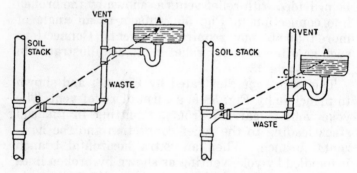

Fig. 59.—Why Vent Pipes May Clog.

In order that vent pipes may not clog at or near their point of connection to the waste pipe it is important that waste water never rise into the vent, for should it do so solid matter eventually will be deposited and more or less completely close the opening. The reason may be seen in the diagrams of Fig. 59, where the connection from the waste pipe into the soil stack or other discharge point is much lower in one diagram than in the other. With the fixture full of water and commencing to drain, it may be considered that the water falls along the broken line from *A* to *B*. Where the point of discharge from the waste is lower down, this line *A-B* is below the connection of the vent to the waste pipe. Consequently, waste water will not rise into the vent pipe connection.

In the diagram having the waste pipe discharge not far enough below the surface, the line *A-B* crosses the vent pipe above its connection to the waste. Consequently, waste water will rise, or may rise, to the level marked *C* on the waste pipe. It will be realized that with the fixture and the waste pipe outlet even more nearly in line, as in Fig. 38, the waste water is practically certain to rise into the vent pipe and sooner or later cause clogging. The same thing will happen with a crown vent, which is the chief reason that such a vent should not be used.

Vent Pipe Diameters.—No vent should be smaller than 1¼ inches in diameter. This minimum size is satisfactory for vents connecting to waste pipes which are no larger than 1¼ inches in diameter. A vent connecting to a waste pipe 1½ inches in diameter should also be of 1½-inch diameter. The 1½-inch vents often are used for traps and wastes up to two inches in diameter, but for larger pipes the vent should be at least two inches in diameter. A bathtub and lavatory ordinarily may be vented with a pipe 1½ or two inches in diameter. A vent of 1½-inch diameter usually will serve for connection to two or three small fixtures, while a vent of 2-inch diameter will do for as many as six small fixtures. Vents never should be of diameter less than half the diameter of the waste or drain pipe that they serve.

Equivalent Lengths of Vent Pipe.—If a vent pipe is of 3-inch diameter for part of its length, say for 20 feet, and is of 2-inch diameter for another 10 feet, the resistance to air flow through the two sections is the same as through 107 feet of 3-inch pipe. This comes about because the air resistance in each foot of the 2-inch pipe is as great as the resistance in 8.7 feet of 3-inch pipe. Consequently, the 10 feet of 2-inch pipe has resistance equivalent to 87 feet of the 3-inch pipe, which, added to the actual 20 feet of 3-inch pipe, makes the equivalent of 107 feet of 3-inch pipe.

The table of *equivalent lengths of vent pipe* lists in the left-hand column the diameter of the smaller of two connected pipes. Following columns are headed with the diameters of the larger pipe. Each foot of length of a pipe listed in the left-hand column is equivalent in air friction to the number of feet shown opposite in the column for the diameter of the larger pipe.

To find the equivalent length of any vent line, multiply the actual length in feet of the smaller pipe or pipes by the equivalent length shown for the larger pipe. Add this product to the actual length of larger pipe. The result is the equivalent length in the larger pipe size. To find the equivalent length in feet of the smaller pipe, divide the actual length of the larger pipe by the factor shown on the line for the smaller pipe diameter, and add this result to the actual length of small pipe.

Each elbow or tee in a vent line has an air resistance equivalent to several feet of straight pipe of the same diameter. Therefore, to find the effective length of a vent pipe containing elbows or tees, or to find the equivalent length in straight pipe of the same diameter, we must add to the actual length of pipe an allowance found by multiplying the number of elbows and tees by the equivalent for the diameter being used. The table of *elbow and tee equivalents* shows the lengths to be added for each such fitting.

For example, assume an actual length of 15 feet of 2-inch vent pipe containing two elbows and one tee. Each elbow and each tee is equivalent to five feet of straight pipe, so the three fittings are equiva-

EQUIVALENT LENGTHS OF VENT PIPE

Number of Feet for Equal Resistances

SMALLER PIPE DIAMETER	LARGER PIPE DIAMETER								
	1½	2	2½	3	3½	4	5	6	8
1¼	2.3	10	26	87	192	375			
1½		4.1	11	36	80	170	529		
2			2.6	8.7	19	36	130	242	
2½				3.3	7.3	14	46	128	530
3					2.2	4.4	14.5	38	160
3½						2.0	6.6	17.5	72
4							3.3	8.7	36
5								2.6	13
6									4.1

ELBOW AND TEE EQUIVALENTS IN FEET
OF STRAIGHT VENT PIPE

ELBOW OR TEE Diameter	PIPE LENGTH	ELBOW OR TEE Diameter	PIPE LENGTH
1¼	2½	3½	11
1½	3	4	13
2	5	5	19
2½	7	6	24
3	9	8	35

lent to 15 feet. Adding this 15-foot allowance to the actual length of 15 feet gives an equivalent length of 30 feet for the line.

The length of a branch vent of any given diameter should be no more than the maximum allowable length given later on in the table of *diameters and maximum lengths of vent stacks* connected to the same diameter soil stack or vent stack.

Replacing Vent Pipes.—When new fixtures are installed to replace old ones, or when a different style of fixture is installed, or the location of a fixture is changed, it may be necessary to install new vent pipes which conform to present standards. A new vent is required when the old one does not go through the roof without reduction in size or does not connect to a vent stack or soil stack underneath the roof in an approved manner. It also is true that old style vent pipes made of sheet metal rather than standard pipes should be replaced.

CHAPTER 7

THE SOIL STACK AND VENT STACK

Any pipe which carries the discharge from one or more water closets to the house drain is called a soil pipe, and when it is vertical is called a soil stack. The soil pipe or stack may or may not carry the discharge from fixtures other than water closets. A soil stack must be installed in every building in which there are closets or similar fixtures. A waste stack may be installed when there are no water closets but when there are other plumbing fixtures.

The lower end of the soil stack connects with the building drain or house drain as shown in Fig. 60. If the stack and the drain are of the same diameter, the connection may be made with a long, easy bend. If the house or building drain is of larger diameter than the stack, the bend which joins the two should be at least one size larger than the stack. The base of the soil stack must be well supported to carry the weight of the pipe.

In some installations the soil stack goes below the surface of the basement floor before turning into the house drain. Under such conditions there should be a cleanout plug in a box sunk into the floor, or in an extension that comes above the floor level. Underground portions of the soil pipe should be made of cast iron, not of wrought iron or of steel.

If there is any likelihood that storm water may back up through the house drain, as may happen when the sewer system is of too small size or from other causes, the inlet from the lowest fixture in the building to the soil stack must be at least three feet above the house drain.

The soil stack or a waste stack should run as directly as possible from its connection with the house drain up to and through the roof. There should be no sharp bends or turns anywhere in the stack, or at least not in the part that carries liquids.

Sometimes it is thought that the height of a soil stack should be limited because of excessive velocity which might be gained by water falling through the stack and turning into the house drain. No such

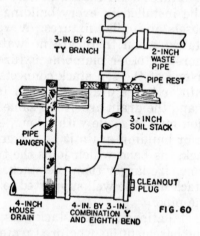

FIG. 60.—The Lower End of a Soil Stack.

limit is necessary, because, after falling water attains a certain speed, the velocity increases no further, since friction between the water and the pipe surfaces provides ample retarding effect.

A soil stack or waste stack should not be placed in an outside wall unless no other location is possible. When the stack is in such a wall it must be well protected against frost by suitable heat insulation. If the stack is placed on the outside of the building it must be similarly protected from frost.

Size and Capacity of Soil and Waste Stacks.—A soil stack which receives the discharge from water closets must be at least three inches in diameter. In many localities the minimum diameter is four inches. Waste stacks which do not receive the discharge from water closets may be from $1\frac{1}{4}$ to $2\frac{1}{2}$ inches in diameter, or, of course, may be of any greater diameter as required for the fixtures they serve.

The diameter required in a soil stack or waste stack depends first on the quantity of drainage the stack must carry. This drainage is measured in *fixture units*, whose values for each type of fixture are given in the table of *fixture unit ratings*. Having determined the number of fixture units according to the fixtures discharging into one soil or waste stack, the diameter may be found from the table of stack capacities in total fixture units.

Fixture Unit.—A fixture unit is a volume of water used as a measuring unit for the rate at which fixtures of average design are assumed to discharge. One fixture unit is equal to a discharge rate of one cubic foot per minute, which is approximately $7\frac{1}{2}$ gallons per minute. As an example of the use of this unit, one bathtub in a residence or apartment or other place of private use is counted as equal to three fixture units, meaning that its discharge rate is assumed to be three cubic feet or about $22\frac{1}{2}$ gallons per minute. Ratings in fixture units as taken from the Recommended Plumbing Code are given in the table. The ratings are given for three classes of service. Class 1 applies to residences and apartments and to fixtures in private bathrooms of hotels and to similar installations where intended for use of a family or an individual. Class 2 applies to office buildings, factories, dormitories, and similar installations where the fixtures are intended for the use of occupants of the building. Class 3 applies to general toilet rooms of schools, gymnasiums, hotels, railroad stations, public comfort stations, and other installations (whether pay or

FIXTURE UNIT RATINGS

KIND OF FIXTURE	CLASSIFICATION		
	1	2	3
Bathtub or bidet	2-3	4	4
Foot bath or sitz bath	2	2	2
Shower head	2	3	3-4
in gang shower		5	5
Shower stall	2	3	3
with multiple sprays	4	6	6
Lavatory	1	2	2
Water closet, tank flush	3	5	6
Water closet, valve flush	6	10	10
Urinal, wall hung or stall type	4	4	4-5
Urinal, pedestal and blowout types	5	5	5-10
Slop sink or service sink, plain	3	3	3
with jet or flushing rim	6	6	
Bathroom groups			
Lavatory, water closet and bathtub, with or without overhead shower head	6-8		
Lavatory, water closet and shower stall	6-8		
Lavatory, water closet, bathtub and shower stall in same bathroom	7-10		
Sink, kitchen, dishwasher or pantry	2-3		
glass or silver		3	
vegetable		6	
pot		8	
bar type, lunch counter		6	
bar type, soda fountain		1½	
Drinking fountain		½	½
Laundry trays, 1, 2 or 3	3		
Combination tray-sink fixture	3		
Floor drain, plain	1	1	1
with flush rim	3	3	3
Any tank or unrated fixture; per gallon per minute of estimated maximum discharge	2	2	2

free) where a number of fixtures are installed so that their use is unrestricted.

The second factor in determining stack size is the type of fittings used. The capacity of a given diameter stack is much greater when the only types of fittings are of Y types. Fig. 61 shows a single combination Y-and-eighth-bend, also a single 45° Y-branch. Double-Y fittings have an additional inlet

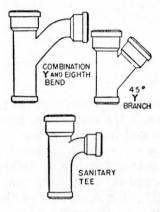

FIG. 61.—Fittings Used in Soil Stacks.

similar to the one shown. The stack capacity for a given diameter is greatly reduced when the fittings are of the sanitary tee type. A single sanitary tee with a side inlet is shown in Fig. 61. In earlier diagrams showing connections for water closets and waste pipes to soil or waste stacks, this connection is made with Y-pattern fittings rather than with tee-patterns. Double sanitary tees, double tees, and double hub fittings generally are prohibited in soil stacks.

The table of *stack capacities in total fixture units* shows also the maximum length for stacks of each diameter. This limitation has an effect only in tall buildings, as may be realized from the fact that the smallest soil stack, 3-inch diameter, may be 212 feet long.

STACK CAPACITIES—TOTAL FIXTURE UNITS

STACK DIAM. Inches	TOTAL LENGTH FEET (Max.)	MAXIMUM FIXTURE UNITS With Only Y-fittings	With Sanitary Tees
1¼	50	1	1
1½	65	12	8
2	85	36	16
3	212	72	48
4	300	384	256
5	390	1020	680
6	510	2070	1380
8	750	5400	3600

The final factor in determining the required diameter for a stack is the number of fixture units that may be discharged into any given length of stack. The table of *stack capacities per branch interval* shows the maximum number of fixture units which may be discharged into any eight-foot length of the stack. A length of stack not less than eight feet high, and generally corresponding to a height of one story, within which horizontal branches from one floor or story are connected to the stack, is called a *branch interval*.

STACK CAPACITY PER BRANCH INTERVAL

STACK DIAM. Inches	MAXIMUM FIXTURE UNITS IN ONE INTERVAL—8 FT. LENGTH With Only Y-fittings	With Sanitary Tees
1¼	1	1
1½	4	2
2	15	9
3	45	24
4	240	144
5	540	324
6	1120	670
8	3480	2088

For an example in using the tables of stack capacities we may assume the following fixtures to be installed in a residential building, for which the fixture unit ratings are taken from the table of such ratings.

Second Story:	4 bathtubs, at 3 units each	12	
	2 shower stalls, 2 units each	4	
	4 lavatories, 1 unit each	4	
	4 water closets, 3 units each	12	
	4 kitchen sinks, 3 units each	12	44
First Story:	2 shower stalls, with multiple sprays, 4 units each	8	
	2 lavatories, 1 unit each	2	
	2 water closets, 3 units each	6	
	2 kitchen sinks, 3 units each	6	22
Basement:	1 lavatory, 1 unit	1	
	1 water closet, 3 units	3	
	2 sets laundry trays, 3 units ea.	6	
	2 floor drains, 1 unit each	2	12

Total for building 78

The first table of stack capacities shows that, even when using all Y-type fittings, the total of 78 units is above the limit for a 3-inch stack, so will call for a 4-inch stack. Checking the number of units discharging into any one branch interval or eight-foot length of the stack, we find that the greatest number is from the second story, with 44 units. This is well within the limit shown by the second table for a 4-inch stack. It also is just within the limit of 45 units for a 3-inch stack had the total requirement not exceeded the 3-inch capacity. Since a 4-inch stack may be 300 feet long, there is no question on this point.

Various other general methods, or different tables, may be used for determining the diameter of soil stacks and waste stacks. With some systems only the major fixtures are counted, omitting kitchen sinks, service sinks, laundry trays, and tray-sink combinations used in private dwellings when figuring stack sizes. Of course, all the fixtures are counted when calculating their waste pipe sizes.

Size of Horizontal Branches.—The number of fixture units which may drain into a horizontal branch is considerably less than handled by a vertical soil stack or waste stack of the same diameter. A horizontal branch is a branch drain extending laterally from the soil or waste stack, with or without vertical sections in the branch. The table of *horizontal branch capacities in fixture units* shows common practice in the maximum number of units on any one branch.

HORIZONTAL BRANCH CAPACITIES— IN FIXTURE UNITS

WASTE PIPE Diameter	MAXIMUM UNITS PER BRANCH	SOIL PIPE Diameter	MAXIMUM UNITS PER BRANCH
1¼	1	3	20
1½	3	4	160
2	6	5	360
3	32	6	640
		8	1200

Vent Stacks.—A vent stack, also called a main vent, is a vertical vent pipe whose primary purpose is to allow circulation of air to and from any other piping in the drainage system of the building. The vent stack may extend up through the roof without reduction in size, or else it may connect with the soil stack or waste stack below the roof, but at least three feet above the highest branch coming from a fixture and at least six inches above the flood level of the fixture highest in the system. The vent stack

DIAMETERS AND MAXIMUM LENGTHS OF VENT STACKS

STACK DIAM. Inches	FIXTURE UNITS	DIAMETER OF VENT IN INCHES								
		1¼	1½	2	2½	3	4	5	6	8
1¼	1 max.	45								
1½	8 max.	35	60							
2	18 max.	30	50	90						
2½	36 max.	25	45	75	105					
3	12		34	120	180	212				
	18		18	70	180	212				
	24		12	50	130	212				
	36		8	35	93	212				
	48		7	32	80	212				
	72		6	25	65	212				
4	24			25	110	200	300	340		
	48			16	65	115	300	340		
	96			12	45	84	300	340		
	144			9	36	72	300	340		
	192			8	30	64	282	340		
	264			7	20	56	245	340		
	384			5	18	47	206	340		
5	72				40	65	250	390	440	
	144				30	47	180	390	440	
	288				20	32	124	390	440	
	432				16	24	94	320	440	
	720				10	16	70	225	440	
	1020				8	13	58	180	440	
6	144					27	108	340	510	
	288					15	70	220	510	630
	576					10	43	150	425	630
	864					7	33	125	320	630
	1296					6	25	92	240	630
	2070					4	21	75	186	630
8	320						42	144	400	750
	640						30	86	260	750
	960						22	60	190	750
	1600						16	40	120	525
	2500						12	28	90	370
	4160						7	22	62	252

or main vent must connect full size at its lower end to the soil stack, waste stack or building drain, either at the connection from the lowest fixture branch or below the lowest fixture branch.

Vent stacks are installed, in addition to a soil stack or waste stack, whenever there are relief vents, back vents, or other branch vents in two or more branch intervals.

The diameter and maximum length of a vent stack should be determined according to the diameter of the soil stack or waste stack to which connected, and according to the maximum volume of water and water-borne waste which may be discharged. The table of *diameters and maximum lengths of vent stacks* is taken from the Recommended Plumbing Code of the U. S. Department of Commerce Building Code Committee. It shows for various diameters of soil or waste stacks the maximum permissible lengths of vents of given diameters for certain rates of discharge to the stack as measured in fixture units.

The length of the vent stack is the total developed length along center lines, starting from the point at which the vent joins the soil stack, waste stack or building drain at the bottom, and continuing to the point at which it ends in open air above the roof. If the vent stack turns into the soil or waste stack below the roof, the distance from this junction to the open air terminal is added to the length of vent pipe proper.

The length of branch vents of any given diameter should be no greater than the maximum allowable length of a vent stack of the same diameter when connected to soil stacks or waste stacks of sizes given in this table.

Offsets in Stacks.—Offsets, as illustrated in Fig. 62, are combinations of elbows, bends, or special fittings which carry one section of a stack to one side of the original line, then allow it to continue on a line parallel to the original direction. A return offset, also called a jumpover, is a double offset which returns the pipe to its original direction after passing around some obstruction such as another pipe. Offsets always are objectionable, and when possible none should be made between horizontal branches to fixtures on two different levels.

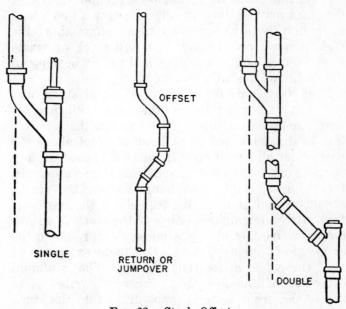

SINGLE   RETURN OR JUMPOVER   DOUBLE   OFFSET

FIG. 62.—Stack Offsets.

Offsets should preferably be made with angles no greater than 45° with the vertical. When a single, double or return offset with no change of direction greater than 45° is installed between two horizontal branches in a stack whose branches are vented according to usual rules, the stack should carry no more than half the maximum number of fixture units specified for a straight stack of the same diameter and height. No horizontal branch should connect to the stack within four stack diameters either above or below a sloping section of any offset. For example, with a 4-inch stack, no branch should connect within 16 inches above or below the offset fittings.

If an offset is installed below the lowest horizontal branch, and made at an angle no greater than 45°, the stack may be the same diameter for a given load as though there were no offset. An offset above the highest horizontal branch in a soil stack or waste stack is, in effect, a vent pipe, and has no bearing on the design of the soil or waste stack.

Roof Terminals for Stacks.—The soil stack, and any vent stack not joined to the soil stack below the roof, should extend through the roof without reduction in diameter and go at least one foot above the roof under all conditions. If the roof is used for any purpose other than protection from the weather, as, for instance, a place to hang clothes, the stacks should extend at least five feet above the roof surface. If the terminal opening of the stack is within ten to twelve feet of any window, door, roof scuttle, or air shaft opening, the stack should extend to at least three feet above that opening. The minimum extension of one foot above the roof surface is to insure that roof water cannot drain into the stack and that articles cannot accidentally be pushed into it. The usual height is from a foot to eighteen inches above the roof surface.

It must be made impossible for the terminal opening of the stack to become closed with frost deposited from the moist air that rises through the stack. Should frost completely close the top of the stack, the traps on some fixtures might be drained, even though those traps were provided with other vents. The danger from closing because of internal frost due to low temperature should not be confused with covering of the terminal by snow. Warm air coming up through the stack will melt openings through snow and provide a vent passage.

The less the top of the stack extends above the roof the less likely it is to become closed with frost, since a short extension remains warmer than does a longer one. Another effective way to reduce danger from frost is to make the terminal section of the stack larger in diameter than the sections lower

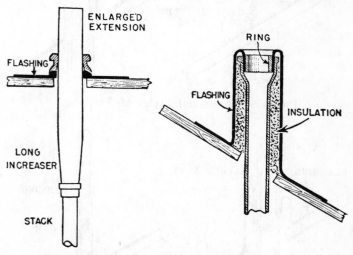

FIG. 63.—An Increaser for the Stack Terminal.
FIG. 64.—An Insulated Stack Terminal.

down. No roof extension of a soil stack should be less than four inches in diameter where there is possibility of frost closing the opening. The extension often is made one or two sizes larger than the lower part of the stack.

An enlargement is made by using a long increaser starting from at least one foot below the roof as shown in Fig. 63. If it is difficult to get out onto the roof to inspect the top of the stack for possible clogging, an opening with a screw plug (like a cleanout) may be provided where the increaser is installed. This opening will allow testing the stack in case of trouble.

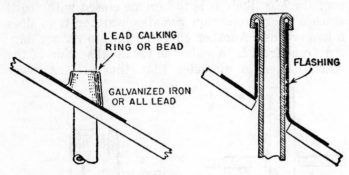

LEAD CALKING RING OR BEAD

GALVANIZED IRON OR ALL LEAD

FLASHING

FIG. 65.—Commercial Styles of Flashing.

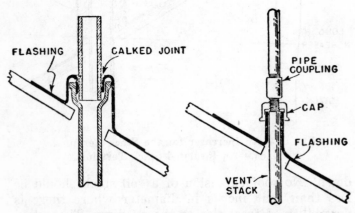

FLASHING

CALKED JOINT

PIPE COUPLING

CAP

FLASHING

VENT STACK

FIG. 66.—Joints for Hub End of Pipe and for Threaded Vent Pipe.

The stack terminal may be protected against frost with insulation as shown by Fig. 64. Here the roof flashing is brought up around the stack, leaving a space of one inch or more between flashing and stack, and the flashing is turned in over the stack top. The turned-in portion is held securely in the stack by a ring that is forced into place. The space between the stack and the flashing is filled with some suitable heat insulation such as rock wool, hair felt or similar materials prepared for such work.

The joint between the roof and the stack must be made weather-tight with flashings of galvanized steel, cast iron plates, copper, or lead. Some such flashings are shown in Figs. 63 and 64. Fig. 65 shows a style of flashing with which the space between the stack and the upper end of the flash plate is closed by calking it with a lead ring or bead. The other flashing shown in this illustration requires a special roof extension having a turned-over top, underneath which fits the flashing brought up the outside.

Fig. 66 shows a roof terminal extension set into the hub or bell at the upper end of a cast iron soil stack. The flashing is turned down into the hub and the joint is calked. Fig. 66 shows also an extension for a vent stack of threaded pipe. Onto the threaded upper end of the stack is screwed a roof cap which goes down around the upward extension of the flashing to make a tight joint.

The flashing plate or flange for stacks up to 4-inch diameter should be 16 inches square, or larger, and flashed into the roofing. The edges of the plates where they rest on the roof surface should be well coated with asphaltum or roofing cement to make the joint watertight. Galvanized steel flashing may be of 24 or 26 gage. Copper flashing may be of 24 gage material weighing a little less than one pound per square foot. Sheet lead for flashing is $\frac{1}{16}$ inch thick, weighing about $3\frac{3}{4}$ pounds per square foot.

When the terminal of a vent stack passes through a wall, it should not come closer than 12 feet horizontally to any adjacent building line. The terminal should be turned to make a horizontal downward opening, it should be fitted with a screen, and where it passes through the wall should be well flashed, calked, or otherwise sealed tight.

Cast Iron Soil Pipe.—The construction of cast iron pipe of the type generally used for soil pipe is shown by Fig. 67. This is called *bell and spigot* pipe or *hub and spigot* pipe. One end is enlarged into the bell or the hub, into which fits loosely the spigot end of the

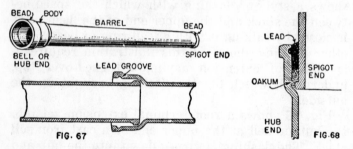

FIG. 67.—Cast Iron Soil Pipe.
FIG. 68.—Parts of a Calked Joint.

next pipe in the line. Around the spigot end runs a raised bead. The space between the spigot and the inside of the hub is filled with oakum or hemp and with lead driven into place to make a calked joint.

Hub and spigot pipe comes in lengths which make up into five-foot sections from joint to joint. The barrel of standard pipe is ⅛ inch thick, and of extra heavy pipe is ¼ inch thick. Because of the danger of breakage, the extra heavy pipe is preferred for all work unless saving in first cost is all-important. The pipe required for most places is the style shown in Fig. 67 with the hub at one end and the spigot at the other. However, it is obtainable also in a double hub style having hubs at both ends of the length. The weight of cast iron soil pipe per five-foot length,

WEIGHT OF CAST IRON SOIL PIPE
Pounds Per 5-foot Length

DIAMETER Inches	STANDARD	EXTRA HEAVY Single Hub	EXTRA HEAVY Double Hub
2	18	25	26
3	26	45	47
4	35	60	63
5	45	75	78
6	52	95	100
8		150	157

either single or double hub, is given in the accompanying table. The diameter is the inside diameter of the barrel of the pipe. The dimensions of the hubs are approximately the same for both extra heavy and standard weights.

Making Calked Joints.—In making a calked joint between the hub of one length of soil pipe and the spigot end of the following length, the inner part of the space is packed with oakum, which is stranded hemp such as used in ropes, or with twisted jute fibre. The remaining space is filled with lead, poured into place while molten. Such a joint is shown by Fig. 68. About one-third of the joint depth is filled with oakum or jute, but room must be left for at least one full inch of pure lead on top of the oakum. It takes about one ounce of oakum per joint for each inch of pipe diameter. That is, for a four-inch pipe, about four ounces of oakum will be required. The oakum is laid in place and then firmly packed by ramming it down with a yarning iron as in Fig. 69.

The next step is to place a joint runner around the inner pipe at the open end of the joint to close all but a small hole leading into the joint. This is shown by Fig. 70. The runner may be made of asbestos fibre about ¾ inch in diameter, of sufficient length to go around joints in pipe of any usual diameter, held in place with some suitable type of clamp. When no regular joint runner is at hand, the work may be done by taking a strand of jute long enough to go around the pipe and to turn back at the pouring opening, then covering the jute with moistened clay worked into such shape as to make a band about one inch in diameter. This band is packed around the joint. The jute and clay runner must

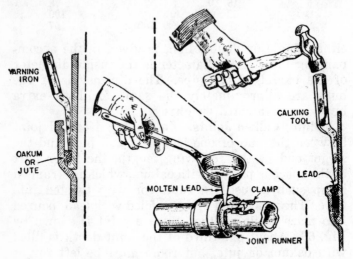

FIG. 69.—Using the Yarning Iron.
FIG. 70.—Pouring the Lead.
FIG. 71.—Using the Calking Tool.

be moistened frequently if pouring several joints. When using any jointer which is moist, great care must be exercised to keep spattered hot lead from the eyes and skin, since the heat will form bursts of steam from the wet clay.

The joint must be filled with molten lead at a single pouring. It takes from a half to a full pound of lead per inch diameter of the pipe, so this quantity should be ready for each joint. Pig lead for calked joints is obtainable in bars, usually weighing about five pounds each.

If local regulations do not require the use of molten lead for calked joints, it is possible to use *lead wool*, which is lead in fibrous or shredded form in the shape of a loose rope. This material may be calked tight without being heated. The same weight is required of the wool as of molten lead for each joint. There also are various prepared jointing compounds which require no calking.

After molten lead has been poured, or lead wool put in place, it is driven tight with a calking tool such as shown in Fig. 71. The end of this tool is flat, about a half-inch wide and three-fourths of an inch long. At first the driving is done lightly around the joint several times. Then, as the lead becomes more compact, the driving is done with more force, possibly changing to a second tool that fills most of the space but does not bind between the pipes.

Soil Pipe Fittings.—Fig. 72 shows one group of hub and spigot soil pipe fittings. The $\frac{1}{4}$-bend turns at 90°, the $\frac{1}{8}$-bend turns at 45° and the $\frac{1}{16}$-bend turns at 22½°. The $\frac{1}{4}$-bend is made also with an inlet for a smaller pipe in the heel. This inlet may be from one to three sizes smaller than the run through the bend. The bends turn on a rather short radius, while sweeps turn on larger radii. A 4-inch bend has a turning radius of 4 inches, while the same diameter of short sweep turns on 6 inches and a long sweep turns on 9 inches.

The $\frac{1}{8}$-bend offset is specified according to the pipe diameter and the offset distance in inches. The offset O of Fig. 72 is the same distance as dimension L. The offset distance may be from 2 to 24 inches with pipe diameters of either 2, 3, 4, 5 or 6 inches in standard types.

The *increaser* shown by Fig. 72 has a hub at the top and a spigot below. The long increaser has a spigot below, but is simply a length of straight pipe

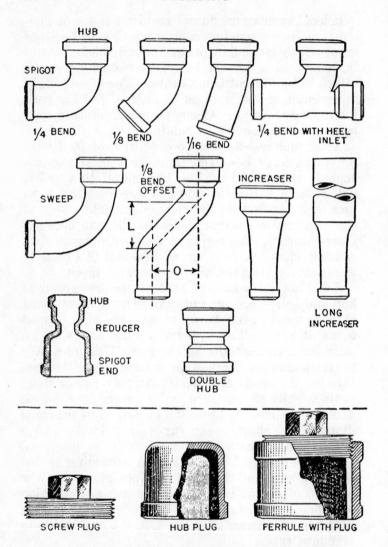

FIG. 72.—Soil Pipe Bends, Increasers and Reducers.
FIG. 73.—Plugs Used in Fittings.

above. The overall length may be from two to four feet. Instead of the spigot, either style of increaser may have pipe threads tapped in the lower end.

The upper end of a *reducer* is a hub and the lower end a spigot. The hub pipe size may be one or more sizes smaller than the spigot pipe size. The double hub has hubs at both ends, and both ends are for the same pipe size.

Plugs for closing openings in fittings are shown by Fig. 73. The screw plug, made of brass, may go into any threaded opening of 1¼ to 6 inch pipe size. The hub plug is shaped like the spigot end of a pipe, and is calked into a hub opening. The ferrule allows putting a brass screw plug into the hub end of a fitting. The body of the ferrule is of cast iron, shaped at one end like the spigot end of a pipe, so that it may be calked in the hub.

Fig. 74 shows several styles of tee-fittings with hubs and spigots for soil pipe connections. The tee-branch has a hub inlet on one side. The side opening may be the same size as the run or one or more sizes smaller. Tee-branches are to be used only for vent connections and for cleanouts, not for waste inlets. Instead of a hub for the side opening of the tee-branch this opening may be tapped with pipe threads, or may be threaded to take a brass screw plug for cleanout purposes, both styles being shown in Fig. 74. The tapped tee-branch may have either one or two side openings, as indicated.

A sanitary tee-branch is shown in Fig. 61, and in Fig. 74 is shown such a branch with an extra inlet one-quarter way around from the main branch. Sanitary tee-branches may have the side inlet, or two opposite inlets, tapped with pipe threads rather than having a hub. The tapped inlets are used for threaded waste pipe or vent pipe.

Fig. 75 illustrates several commonly used Y-fittings for soil pipe connections. The combination Y-and-⅛-bend may be either single or double, as indicated. The side inlets may be of the same size as the run, or may be one or more sizes smaller. The Y-branches, also called 45° Y-branches, have the

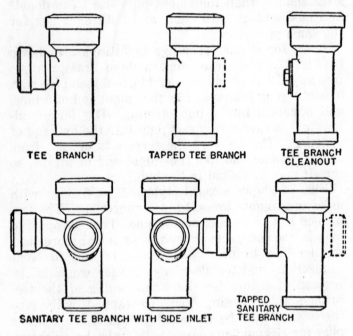

TEE BRANCH   TAPPED TEE BRANCH   TEE BRANCH CLEANOUT

SANITARY TEE BRANCH WITH SIDE INLET   TAPPED SANITARY TEE BRANCH

FIG. 74.—Tee-branches for Soil Pipe.

inlets at 45° rather than at right angles as in the combination Y-and-⅛-bend. The Y-branches may be either single or double, as indicated. Y-branches may be arranged to take cleanout plugs either on the main, as shown, or on the branch. The combination Y-and-⅛-bend may be arranged for a cleanout plug on the main. The plug ends of any of these fittings are threaded instead of being a hub type. The Y-branch, or 45° Y-branch, may have an additional side inlet just like the one used on the sanitary tee.

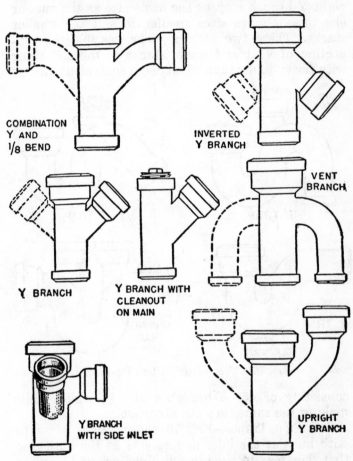

COMBINATION Y AND 1/8 BEND

INVERTED Y BRANCH

Y BRANCH

Y BRANCH WITH CLEANOUT ON MAIN

VENT BRANCH

Y BRANCH WITH SIDE INLET

UPRIGHT Y BRANCH

FIG. 75.—Y-branches for Soil Pipe.

The vent branch shown in Fig. 75 is used where the upper ends of vent stacks join the soil stack below the roof. The upright Y-branch is used where vent stacks and waste stacks join the lower end of

the soil stack or the house drain connection. **The**
side branches of either the vent branch or the **up-**
right Y-branch may be the same size as the run, **or**
else one or more sizes smaller to suit the smaller
stacks. These two fittings make possible the connection of vent and waste stacks to the soil stack
with fewer joints than when using equivalent fittings

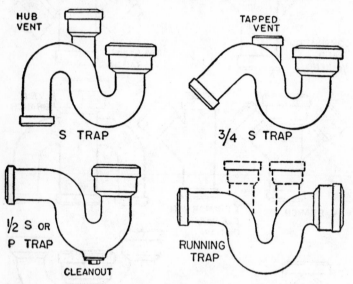

FIG. 76.—Traps Used in Soil Pipe Lines.

consisting of 45° Y-branches and ⅛-bends, while
making the same turns in direction.

Soil Pipe Traps.—Fig. 76 shows styles of traps
with hubs at the inlet and spigots at the outlet, so
that they may be used in soil pipe lines and between
soil pipes and house drains. The S-trap is shown
with a hub type of vent connection, which may or
may not be used on this trap or on any of the others
in Fig. 76. The ¾ S-trap will connect on the outlet
end to any suitable 45° Y-fitting. This trap is shown

with a tapped or threaded vent outlet, which may or may not be used on this or any of the other traps shown.

The ½ S-trap, more commonly called a P-trap, is shown with a cleanout plug. This plug may be used or omitted on any of the traps illustrated. The running trap may be used between the lower end of the soil stack and the entrance to the house drain. This trap either may have no vent connections, or else may have one or both the vent openings shown by broken lines in Fig. 76. These vents may be of either the hub or tapped types.

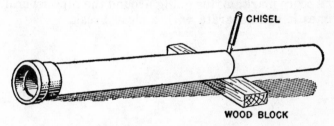

Fig. 77.—Cutting Cast Iron Soil Pipe.

How Fittings Are Described.—The size of a fitting is the nominal inside diameter of the soil pipe to which it connects. For branch fittings, the size of the main run is given first, then the size of the branch. For reducers, increasers and offsets, the size of the run is given first, then the outlet size or the amount of offset, and finally the length if the fitting is available in more than one length.

To determine whether side inlet fittings are right-hand or left-hand types, place the hub toward you with the spigot lower than the hub. For branches, turn the branch toward you with the spigot lower than the hub. For traps with side inlets, hold them in the installed position with the hub toward you.

Specify right-hand or left-hand according to the side on which the inlet then is located.

Cutting Cast Iron Pipe.—Full lengths of soil pipe may be too long to fit into certain sections of a line, in which case they must be cut down. As shown in Fig. 77, the first step is to lightly groove or score the pipe squarely and all the way around. This may be done with light blows of a cold chisel, with a coarse file, or with a wheel-type of pipe cutter.

With the pipe slightly raised on a piece of wood placed underneath the cut, the chisel then is used with increasingly heavy blows around and around the score mark. After going around the pipe several times it will separate with a clean break.

CHAPTER 8

BUILDING DRAINS AND SEWERS

The building drain or house drain is the horizontal pipe which receives the discharge from soil stacks, waste stacks, and any other drainage pipes within the building, and carries the discharges to a point five feet beyond the inside face of the building wall, at which point the building drain runs into the building sewer, called also the house sewer. The house sewer is the portion of the horizontal piping that runs from the building drain out to the street sewer or other point of disposal for sewage, such as a septic tank or cesspool. The building sewer ordinarily carries sewage from only one building site.

Any part of the building drain pipe which is above ground may be of galvanized wrought iron or steel, of cast iron, brass or lead. Parts of the drain which are underground may be of cast iron, brass or lead. Cast iron usually is preferred for underground work. Clay pipe or sewer tile generally is prohibited inside the building walls.

A running trap may or may not be used in the building drain. When such a trap is used it may be vented on one or both sides, or not at all. Running trap connections with drainage fittings are shown in Fig. 78. The purpose of the running trap is to prevent sewer air from entering the drainage pipes within the building. If most of the buildings in a district have running traps, thus preventing circulation of outdoor air through the public sewers from the various soil and waste stacks, then a running trap may be desirable for the reason that in such places the sewer air may have strong odors. Other-

wise a running trap generally is considered unnecessary or even objectionable.

When moist air from the sewers rises through the
soil stacks in very cold climates, the moisture may
produce excessive frost at the tops of the stacks.
Under such conditions the air circulation and frost-
ing may be retarded by a running trap which shuts
off sewer air. A running trap which is underground

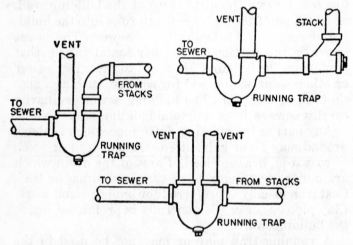

FIG. 78.—Running Traps with Single and Double Vents.

should be accessible through a covered manhole and
be provided with at least one cleanout.

Size of Drains and Sewers.—The minimum diameter of pipe in the building drain and building sewer
depends on several factors. The diameter must be
increased with increase of the discharge as measured in fixture units. The greater the pitch of the
pipe, measured in inches of fall per foot of length,
the smaller may be the diameter for a given discharge. Finally, the capacity of a drain or sewer
of given diameter usually is considered to be greater

SANITARY BUILDING DRAIN AND SEWER CAPACITIES

Maximum Fixture Units Allowed

PIPE DIAM.	FIXTURES ON SAME LEVEL			NOT ON SAME LEVEL		
	⅛-in. Pitch	¼-in. Pitch	½-in. Pitch	⅛-in. Pitch	¼-in. Pitch	½-in. Pitch
1¼	1	1	1	1	1-2	1-2
1½	2	2	3	2	2½-5	3½-7
2	5	6	8	7	9-21	12-26
2½	12	15	18	17	21	27
3 a	24	27	36	33-36	42-45	50-72
3 b	15	18	21	24-27	27-36	36-48
4	82	95	112	114-180	150-215	210-250
5	180	234	280	270-400	370-480	540-560
6	330	440	580	510-660	720-790	940-1050
8	870	1150	1680	1300-1600	1850-1900	2200-2600
10	1740	2500	3600	2500-2700	3250-3600	3750-5250
12	3000	4200	6500	4200-4400	5000-6300	6000-9000

a—No water closets.   b—Not more than 2 water closets.

when fixtures are on floor levels above the drain than when they are on the same level. The table of *sanitary building drain and sewer capacities* shows capacities of pipe of various diameters in numbers of fixture units for various pitches. This table applies only to sanitary drains and sewers which do not receive storm water or similar discharges.

No horizontal branch which receives discharges from water closets on the same floor or level should be less than three inches in diameter, and no building drain or sewer receiving discharges from water closets should be less than four inches in diameter. As shown in the table, the capacity of a three-inch pipe varies according to whether it receives or does not receive discharges from water closets. As a general rule, building drains are no less than four inches in diameter.

Primary Branches of Building Drains. — When there are two or more soil stacks or soil and waste stacks in a building, the horizontal pitched pipes from the bases of the stacks to the main building drain are called primary branches of the building drain. Primary branches are indicated in the line diagram of Fig. 79. Primary branch capacities in fixture units ordinarily are about the same or a little less than the capacities of the main building drain, although special rules apply in many localities. When an offset located between horizontal branches in a soil or waste stack is made with an angle of

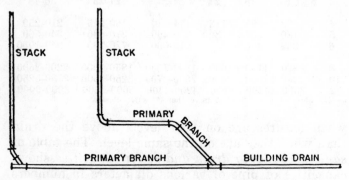

Fig. 79.—Primary Branches of the Building Drain.

more than 45°, the offset and its fittings may be considered as a primary branch in determining the pipe size.

Cleanouts.—Cleanouts should be installed at the base of each soil stack or waste stack, or near the base, also wherever there is a change of direction of more than 45° in the building drain. In the case of long, horizontal soil pipes there should be a cleanout at least every 50 feet of length. Cleanouts usually are required at the base of any rainwater leader run inside the building. Cleanouts are made of the same size as the drain pipe up to and including four inches, and no less than four inches for larger drain pipes.

Building Sewer or House Sewer. — The house sewer, which commences five feet outside the inner face of the building wall, may be made of extra heavy cast iron soil pipe or else of vitrified (glazed) clay pipe called clay sewer pipe. This vitrified pipe comes in straight lengths, of which Fig. 80 shows a section, and also in curves, tees, double tees, Y-branches, double Y-branches, and V-branches. Laying lengths, exclusive of the socket, are 2, 2½ and 3

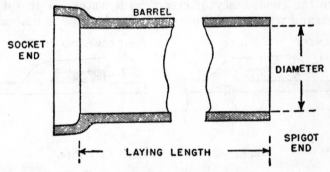

FIG. 80.—Vitrified Clay Sewer Pipe.

feet. Diameters are 4, 6, 8, 10 and 12 inches, then in intervals of 3 inches up to 42 inches in diameter.

It is a general rule that each building should have its own building sewer. An exception may be made when one building is behind another, and when it is impossible to run a separate sewer to the rear building through a driveway, yard, court, or alley. In such cases the house or building drain from the front building may be extended on to the rear building and considered as a single building drain connecting to the building sewer which then will serve both structures.

Old building drains and sewers which have served a building demolished or removed may again be used for another or a new building provided everything is found to be in good condition upon inspection.

Joints in Clay Pipe.—Joints between lengths of clay sewer pipe may be made in either of the ways shown by Fig. 81. The first step is to prepare a strand of jute, oakum or old rope long enough to go around the spigot end of one pipe, and soak this strand in a grout made of half and half Portland cement and clean sand mixed dry and then brought to the consistency of cream with water. With this strand wrapped around the pipe, the pipe is pushed

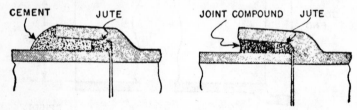

FIG. 81.—Joints in Vitrified Clay Pipe.

into the socket end of the next length and jute or oakum is packed in evenly and tightly to a depth of about a half inch.

The joint then may be filled with freshly mixed mortar made of equal volumes of Portland cement and clean sand thoroughly mixed, or of one part cement and two parts sand. This mortar should be forced into the joint and tamped home to fill all the space, then beveled off around the outer face of the joint. Earth should be packed around the joint and allowed to remain until the mortar sets.

The cement joint also may be poured with a thin. grout of the cement and sand mixture by using a sheet metal form which is left in place for at least 24 hours after the pouring. The pipe should not be moved before the mortar has thoroughly set.

Instead of using cement, the joint in sewer tile may be filled outside the jute or oakum with a prepared jointing compound poured in place while hot. This method requires that a joint runner of asbestos or rubber be clamped around the opening to leave a small pouring hole, much as the joint runner is used when pouring lead into a joint to be calked. Openings between the jointer and socket edges may be filled with wet clay to prevent the hot compound from escaping. The joint must be filled completely at one pouring. The jointer may be taken off as soon as the compound sets. The compound makes a semi-flexible joint, while cement makes a joint that is rigid.

When pouring a joint with hot compound, the packing and the space between the pipes must be thoroughly dry. Just enough jute or oakum should be used to keep the hot compound from flowing inside the pipe. Compounds for hot pouring flow freely at their pouring temperature and adhere tightly to the pipe surfaces. Instructions that come with these compounds should be followed exactly.

Sometimes one or more lengths of sewer pipe are held in a vertical position before laying, and the joints are poured without the use of a runner or jointer. After the compound sets, these lengths of pipe are carefully lowered into the trench and the remaining joints are poured with the jointer in the usual manner.

Storm Drainage.—As has been explained earlier, a sanitary sewer or drain is one to be used only for carrying liquids and water-borne wastes coming from plumbing fixtures or from the interior drainage system of the building. A *storm drain or sewer* is one used for carrying rainwater, cooling water, water from condensation and similar processes, and water collected from seepage through the soil.

A *combined storm and sanitary drain or sewer* is one designed and used for carrying both sanitary waste and storm drainage. The combined storm and sanitary drain or sewer receives the discharge from a sanitary branch and also from a storm branch, which unite in the combination line. Rainwater drainage consists of water coming from roofs and from paved areas such as courts and courtyards.

Leaders or downspouts from gutters which drain a roof should not be connected into a sanitary drain or sewer, but may be connected into a storm or combined storm and sanitary drain or sewer. This rule applies also to other kinds of so-called storm water drainage.

Drain connections to a storm sewer need not be trapped, nor are traps required for roof drains into a combined storm and sanitary sewer when the gutter opening is 12 feet or more from any window, air shaft, scuttle or doorway, and at least three feet above any such opening. If the gutter openings are closer to windows and other openings mentioned, and drainage is into a combined storm and sanitary sewer, a trap or traps must be provided. One trap, generally in the building storm drain, often is all that is required. This trap must be set below the frost line if in the ground, or else inside the building where it will not freeze.

Rainwater conductors which are inside a building, or in a courtyard or a ventilating shaft, are made from cast iron pipe, galvanized wrought iron or steel pipe, brass, copper or lead pipe, or copper tubing. When outdoor sheet metal down spouts connect into the building storm drain, the connection is made at a cast iron pipe which extends upward from the building drain to at least one foot above the grade line.

No soil pipe, waste pipe or vent pipe should be

used as a rainwater conductor, nor should any rainwater conductor be used also as a soil, waste or vent pipe.

It is preferable to carry rainwater discharge directly to the building storm sewer or combined storm and sanitary sewer instead of into the building drain if such a connection may be made conveniently. When led into the house drain it is preferable to make the rainwater connection between the sewer and the soil stack, and at least 10 feet downstream from any primary branch of the sanitary system, rather than to make the rainwater connection back of the stack. Such practices help lessen back pressures during exceptionally heavy rainfalls.

The size of a horizontal drain pipe for rainwater depends only on the area of the roof or other space being drained. The table for *storm drains and leaders* gives usual minimum pipe diameters in inches for various horizontal areas when the drain

STORM DRAINS AND LEADERS
Maximum Drained Area, Sq. Ft.

PIPE DIAMETER	DRAINS	LEADERS
1¼	130	
1½	210	
2	350-440	500
2½	670-790	960
3	1050-1250	1500
4	2150-2650	3100
5	3600-4700	5400
6	6000-7500	8400
8	12000-16000	17400

pipe is pitched ¼ inch per foot of run. If the slope is only ⅛ inch per foot, the drained area may be only 70% to 75% of that shown, while if the slope is ½ inch per foot the drained area may be 40% to 50% greater than listed. This table also gives sizes for leaders.

The areas considered are horizontal projected areas. For a flat roof this is the same as the area of the roof itself. For pitched roofs it is the area of the horizontal surface that would be covered by the roof. The projected area of a pitched roof is less than its actual surface area.

Combined Storm and Sanitary Drains.—The size of pipe to be used in a combined storm and sanitary building drain or sewer depends on the area to be drained into the storm drain branch, and on the number of fixture units discharging into the sanitary branch.

The table for *combined storm and sanitary drainage* shows typical limits for combined drains and sewers of diameters from three to eight inches when the pitch is $\frac{1}{4}$ inch per foot of run. The left-hand column lists drained areas in square feet. The other columns list numbers of fixture units which may be discharged into the sanitary branch along with the storm drainage for each area. To use the table, follow down the column of areas to the number of square feet to be drained, or to the next larger number. From this point follow to the right until reaching the number of fixture units or the next number which is larger than the actual number of units. At the top of this column is the minimum diameter for the combined storm and sanitary drain or sewer.

For an example in using this table, assume a building with a rainwater drainage area measuring 40 by 50 feet, making 2000 square feet, and with a total of 126 fixture units. Following down the left-hand column we come to 2100 as the number of square feet next greater than the actual area of 2000 square feet. Then, following to the right on this line, we find 180 as the number of fixture units next greater than the actual 126 units in the building.

At the top of this column is shown the minimum diameter of 5 inches when the slope is ¼ inch per foot.

COMBINED STORM AND SANITARY DRAINAGE
House or Building Drain and Sewer Minimum Diameters

DRAINED AREA Sq. Ft.	MAXIMUM NUMBER OF FIXTURE UNITS ON PIPES OF FOLLOWING DIAMETERS				
	3-inch	4-inch	5-inch	6-inch	8-inch
0	45	150	370	720	1860
330	24	95	310	640	1860
500	18	95	310	640	1860
610	13	75	310	640	1860
700	9	75	260	640	1860
790	7	75	260	640	1860
880	5	60	260	640	1560
980	3	60	260	640	1560
1080	2	60	260	640	1560
1180	1	45	260	640	1560
1250	0	39	220	640	1560
1500		33	220	640	1560
1800		18	220	560	1560
2100		11	180	560	1560
2500		2	150	560	1560
2650		0	150	490	1560
3000			120	490	1560
3500			75	430	1260
4000			13	370	1260
4500			1	310	1260
4700			0	310	1260
5200				260	1260
5800				180	1260
6400				45	1020

Combined storm and sanitary drains usually are at least four inches in diameter, and at least as large as the largest branch discharging into the combined drain. If each branch carries more than half its normal maximum load, the combined drain should be made larger than either the storm branch or the sanitary branch.

Floor Drains.—Floor drains are commonly installed in basements, and always in garages, pump rooms, and other places where water will be spilled. The drain body is made of cast iron, and has an iron or brass perforated or slotted strainer or grate as shown in Fig. 82. One of the floor drains illustrated is designed to be connected into a trap, while the other one has a trap as part of its construction. Other styles with bottom outlets instead of side outlets are used when the drain pipe is far enough below the floor. All floor drains must discharge through a trap. The grate or strainer must be located where it is in full view.

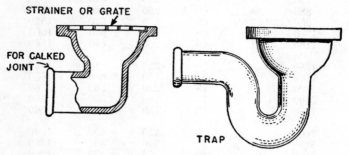

FIG. 82.—Floor Drains.

The trap for a floor drain requires no venting when the trap discharges into the building drain on the sewer side of the soil stack and at least five feet from the base of the stack. Since water may flow into these drains only at infrequent intervals, it is a good idea to occasionally fill the trap to make up for evaporation.

Back-water Traps and Valves.—In districts which have undergone rapid growth, and have more buildings or higher buildings than for which the sewers originally were designed, the public sewers may become so heavily overloaded that sewage occasionally backs up into building drains. If the sewerage system is such that there is danger of back pressure or of water coming from the sewer through a trap, a back-water trap or valve should be installed. A back-water valve makes a mechanical seal which remains closed at all times except when waste water is discharging through the valve, or else closes automatically upon any reverse flow from the drain into the room. Floor drains are available which have in one unit both a back-water valve and a trap.

CHAPTER 9

WATER SUPPLY AND DISTRIBUTION

Water is delivered to the building under pressure from a street main of a public or private water works. The pipe coming into the building is called the *service pipe*. *Distributing pipes* carry water from the service pipe to the plumbing fixtures. Any pipe which extends vertically one full story or more, and carries water to fixtures or branch pipes, is called a *riser*. The supply pipe between a water distributing pipe such as a riser and the fixture is called a *fixture branch*.

Water pipes are made of steel and of wrought iron, either of which must be galvanized. Large pipes may be of cast iron. Brass pipe, also copper pipe and copper tubing are used for water lines, especially on the hot water side or anywhere that it is necessary to avoid corrosion. Lead pipe may be used for water supply lines only when it has been definitely determined that no poisonous lead salts are produced by contact of lead with the particular water supply; at least this is the rule in most places.

Water supplies for individual installations often are taken from wells by means of windmills, power pumps, or hand operated pumps. The water may be pumped into a tank which usually is at an elevated position in or near the building, from which it flows to the fixtures under pressure supplied by the force of gravity. Pressure may be supplied also by compressing air in the water storage tank.

Water tanks are provided with overflow pipes which will carry away surplus water in case the pumping system is not correctly operated, or in case the pump control should fail. This overflow pipe must either discharge onto the roof, or else be led through a trap into some open fixture such as a sink. The overflow must not be connected directly to a waste pipe, the soil stack, or the building drain.

Some installations are served by two different supplies, one furnishing water for drinking and cooking, and the second furnishing water for all other purposes. Because there always is danger that the two supplies may be confused or mixed, this is a rather dangerous practice and should be avoided if possible.

Shut-off valves or cocks are required in certain water lines, as illustrated in Fig. 1. First, there must be an accessible shut-off just inside the foundation wall of the building, also a separate shut-off for each flat or apartment in the building. A separate shut-off should be provided also for each water heater or hot water tank, for each water closet flush tank or each water closet pressure valve, and for each pipe leading to a hose bibb or lawn sprinkler in localities where freezing may occur.

Life of Piping.—Aside from accidental breakage the life of water piping usually is limited only by its ability to resist corrosion. The matter of corrosion is a highly technical problem, so only a few general notes will be given here.

Hard water, as a general rule, is less corrosive than soft water. There are two kinds of hardness; carbonate hardness which actually protects the metal in pipes, and sulphate hardness which gives no protection. Water which is alkaline is less corrosive than water which is acid. Some public water supplies carry much oxygen, and if acid is present these waters will cause rusting.

Galvanized iron or steel pipes are suitable for both service and distribution lines with soft water containing much carbonic acid. Service pipes sometimes are lined with cement, which gives excellent protection. Hot water pipes of copper, or of brass containing at least 67% copper, give good service.

Soft water from wells, especially if tinged with color, may energetically attack pipes of iron or lead. Artificial softening of water may not greatly increase the corrosiveness, since softening processes are applied only when the water originally is excessively hard.

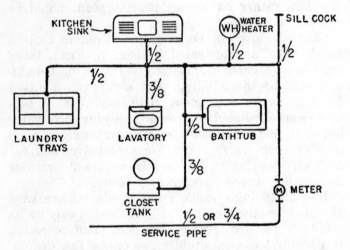

Fig. 83.—Minimum Sizes for Water Supply Pipes.

Chlorine, which often is added to water as a disinfectant, causes no noticeable increase in corrosion. Whiting or lime added to water that is acid will reduce the acidity and will lessen corrosion. Alum, which is used in some methods of filtering, will increase the corrosion unless completely removed from the water.

Coal tar, asphaltum and similar substances used for coating iron pipe give fair protection against corrosion. Some special grades of steel pipe resist corrosion slightly better than genuine wrought iron pipe. Corrosion increases with rise of temperature, so hot water pipes ordinarily are affected more than those carrying cold water. The velocity of water through pipes also affects corrosion, the more rapid the flow the greater the corrosion. For this reason, small pipes corrode more quickly than large ones when carrying the same quantity of water.

For underground work, cast iron and lead pipes generally have longer life than those made of other metals. Next comes galvanized wrought iron pipe, then ordinary grades of galvanized steel pipe. Uncoated (black) wrought iron pipe has relatively short life when used underground.

WATER SUPPLY PIPE SIZES

PURPOSE OF PIPE	MINIMUM SIZE	SIZE USUALLY INSTALLED		
		High Pressure	Medium Pressure	Low Pressure
Service pipe	½	¾	¾-1	1-1¼
Bathtub or shower stall....	½	½	½	½
Lavatory supply	⅜	½	½	½
from wall or floor..........	⅜	⅜	⅜	⅜
Closet tank supply..............	⅜	½	½	½
from wall or floor..........	⅜	⅜	⅜	⅜
Closet flush valve..............	1	1	1	1¼
Urinal, pedestal	1	1	1	1¼
wall or stall type............	½	½	½	¾
Kitchen sink	½	½	½-¾	¾
Laundry trays, set..............	½	½	½-¾	¾
Sill cock, hose bibb............	½	½	¾	¾
Water heater, domestic......	½	½	½	¾

Required Size of Water Pipes. — The table of *water supply pipe sizes,* also Fig. 83, show minimum permissible sizes and the sizes generally used in dwellings, in accordance with the available supply pressure. Although the minimum size for service pipe is given as ½-inch, this size is not large enough in case two or more fixtures are used at the same time, and especially when a garden hose is being used.

When it is desired to guard against the clogging effects of corrosion or rust in water pipes it is advisable to use pipe one size larger for soft water than for hard water, and possibly two sizes larger if the water is definitely corrosive. That is, where a ½-inch pipe would be used for hard water, a ¾-inch size might be used for soft water, and a 1-inch size for definitely corrosive water.

WATER DEMANDS FOR FIXTURES
Gallons Per Minute

FIXTURE	PRIVATE Dwellings	PUBLIC AND SEMI-PUBLIC
Lavatory or wash stand	3	6
Bathtub	5	10
Separate shower head or stall	5	10
Bathroom group, flush tank	10	14
Water closet, flush tank	3	5
pressure valve flush	10	16
Urinal, pedestal		10
wall or stall, with tank		3
with pressure valve		5
Slop sink, plain	3	6
Kitchen sink	4	8
Laundry tray set	4	
Sill cock, hose bibb	5	

Water Demands.—The maximum rate of water flow required for any fixture depends on the size of the pipe feeding fixture and on the kind of valve or faucet which admits water. The table of *water demand for fixtures* gives average rates in gallons per minute which may be used for calculating water demands in fixture branches and other distribution pipes.

The rate of flow in service pipes and main distribution pipes which feed several fixtures seldom, if ever, will equal the sum of the rates for all the connected fixtures, as listed in the table of fixture demands. The reason is that there is little likelihood that all the fixtures ever will be taking water at the same time. The greater the number of fixtures in the installation the smaller becomes the actual maximum demand in relation to the sum of all the connected loads.

The table of *water demands for small buildings* shows usual maximum rates for the entire building. These figures include allowances for laundry trays, but the requirements for sill cocks should be added, according to the number of such outlets. Failure to allow for the large quantities of water used for sprinkling is a common cause for unsatisfactory pressure at fixtures.

WATER DEMANDS FOR SMALL BUILDINGS
Gallons Per Minute

SINGLE FAMILY DWELLINGS
    With 1 bathroom 12
    With 2 bathrooms 16
    With 3 bathrooms and 2 sinks...20

SMALL APARTMENT HOUSES
    With 4 bathrooms and 4 kitchens.......................................25
    With 8 bathrooms and 8 kitchens.......................................35
    With 16 bathrooms and 16 kitchens...........................50 to 55

SILL COCKS OR HOSE BIBBS
    1 5
    2 9
    3 12
    4 14
    For each one when 5 or more... 3

Demand rates for single fixtures and for small groups such as the lavatory, bathtub and water closet in a bathroom, may be used when calculating pipe sizes for lines to these units or groups. The demand rates for the entire building should be used for service pipes and for main distribution pipes within the building. Before going into the matter of pipe sizes it will be advisable to discuss pressures acting on water.

Pressure in Pipes Carrying Water or Air.—Open air at sea level exerts a pressure of approximately 14.7 pounds per square inch in all directions on everything in contact with the air. This pressure is called *atmospheric pressure*. It decreases very slowly as the elevation above sea level increases.

A pressure greater than atmospheric pressure is called *gage pressure*. It is the pressure indicated by an ordinary pressure gage. Gage pressure is equal to the total pressure (*absolute pressure*) minus 14.7 pounds per square inch.

Pressures less than atmospheric are called *vacuums*. Vacuums cause suction effects. If there is a vacuum at one end of a pipe whose other end is open to the air within a building or out of doors, the atmospheric pressure at the building end or out-door end is greater than the pressure on the vacuum end, and the higher atmospheric pressure will force air or water toward the end of the pipe subjected to the vacuum.

Differences between the pressures at two points in a water system often are measured in a unit called *one foot of water*, rather than in pounds per square inch. One pound of water in a vertical pipe having a cross sectional area of one square inch will be about 2.3 feet high. Since the downward pressure of the 2.3 feet of water will be one pound on the one square inch of area, we may say that a pressure of one pound per square inch is equal to a pressure of 2.3 feet of water, and that pressures measured in pounds per square inch may be multiplied by 2.3 to find the equivalent pressures in feet of water. Also, a pressure measured in feet of water may be divided by 2.3, or multiplied by 0.433, to find the equivalent gage pressure in pounds per square inch. Pressure differences measured in feet of water are spoken of as the *head* of water.

The head of water or the pressure which must be available to send water through piping depends on the height to which the water must be delivered above the source of pressure, and on the resistance of the pipe to flow of water through it, since pressure is consumed in overcoming the resistance. Pipe resistance depends on the diameter of the pipe, on its length, on the number and kind of valves, elbows, and other fittings included in the length, and on the roughness of the inside of the pipe. Because water delivered to a faucet should issue with reasonable force, it is necessary to provide some additional pressure to insure satisfactory flow.

Calculating Water Pipe Sizes.—The head or pressure available from the water supply seldom can be varied, so the practical problem usually is that of determining the pipe size required for a given length of pipe and rate of flow at the total available head. To solve such a problem we may proceed as follows:

1. If the total available pressure is given in pounds per square inch, multiply it by 2.3 to find the equivalent head in feet of water.

2. Subtract from this head the following:

    a. The number of feet in a vertical line that the outlet is above the source.

    b. An additional 3 to 10 feet to provide for satisfactory flow from the outlet. This also allows for the extra resistance of two or three fittings in fairly straight pipe lines.

3. The result found in step 2 is the net head remaining to overcome pipe resistance.

4. Multiply this net head by 100.

5. Divide the product found in step 3 by the total

length of pipe, in feet, from the point where pressure is measured, such as the service pipe, through to the faucet or other outlet. Call the result of this division the *conductance factor*.

6. In the left-hand column of the table for *maximum water flow* find this conductance factor, or the one of next *lower* value.

7. In the table follow to the right until reaching the number of gallons per minute of required water flow, or the number next *higher* than the actual flow. At the head of this column read the minimum diameter of pipe which should be used.

For an example in using these rules, assume the following conditions:

MAXIMUM WATER FLOW
Gallons Per Minute in Pipes of Given Size

CON-DUCTANCE FACTOR	NOMINAL DIAMETER OF PIPE—INCHES							
	⅜	½	¾	1	1¼	1½	2	2½
10	1	2	5	9	19	29	50	90
15	1½	3	6	11	23	35	60	112
20	1½	3	7	13	28	40	72	130
25	2	4	8	15	30	47	80	150
30	2	4	9	16	33	50	90	160
40	2½	5	10	20	40	60	105	190
50	3	5	12	22	44	68	125	220
65	3½	6	13	25	50	80	140	255
80	4	7	15	29	59	88	150	290
100	4½	8	17	31	65	100	180	315
125	5	9	19	35	73	110	200	370
150	5½	10	20	40	80	125	220	405
200	6	12	25	46	98	150	270	470
300	8	15	30	60	120	180	315	
400	9	17	36	68	140	210	380	
500	10	19	40	78	155	240	410	
600	11	21	45	84	175	275	470	
800	13	25	52	100	200	310	500	
1000	15	29	60	110	230	365		

Pressure: 20 pounds per square inch at the service pipe.

Load: one bathroom requiring a total flow of 10 gallons per minute, in which the average height of outlets above the service pipe is 20 feet.

Length of Pipe: 30 feet from the end of the service pipe to the farthest faucet.

The numbered rules may be applied thus:

1. 20 lbs. per sq. in. $\times$ 2.3 = 46 feet, total head.

2. Total head..46 ft.
   a. Minus 20 feet vertical height.......20
   b. Minus 10 feet for flow at faucets..10   30

3. Net head remaining...............................16 ft.

4. 16 ft. net head $\times$ 100 = 1600.
5. 1600 $\div$ 38 ft. length = 42, approximately.
6. The next lower conductance factor in the table is 40.
7. One column shows a maximum water flow of 10 gallons per minute, which is the actual flow in this problem. At the head of this column we find that the pipe should be $\frac{3}{4}$-inch diameter.

Diameters for service pipes may be found in a similar manner, using the pressure at the street main or other supply. If the end of the service pipe at the building is higher than the end at the street main, deduct the vertical distance in feet from the total available head. If the building end is lower than at the main, add the vertical difference in feet to the available head. In this case no deduction need be made for forcing flow through a faucet.

Allowances for Pressure Loss in Fittings.—In the problem of pipe sizing just handled we ignored the loss of pressure in the few fittings between the service pipe and bathroom faucets, or considered it cared for in the faucet allowance. A few fittings in pipes no larger than 1½-inch diameter may be safely ignored, but when there are many turns and fittings it is good practice to make allowances for their effects by adding a certain number of feet to the actual length of piping. The table of *equivalent lengths of pipe for fittings* shows what length in

EQUIVALENT LENGTHS OF PIPE FOR FITTINGS —IN FEET

KIND OF FITTING	SIZE OF FITTING								
	⅜	½	¾	1	1¼	1½	2	2½	3
Coupling, or straight run through a tee	0.3	0.6	0.8	0.9	1.2	1.5	2.0	2.5	3.0
Elbow, 90°	1.0	2.0	2.5	3.0	4.0	5	7	8	10
45°	0.6	1.2	1.5	1.8	2.4	3	4	5	6
Tee, turning 90°	1.5	3	4	5	6	7	10	12	15
Valve, globe	8	15	20	25	35	45	55	65	80
angle	4	8	12	15	18	22	28	34	40
gate	0.2	0.4	0.5	0.6	0.8	1.0	1.3	1.6	2.0

feet of pipe has the same resistance as one fitting of the types listed. For example, if we are considering a 1-inch 90° elbow we look in the column for 1-inch fittings and on the line for 90° elbows, and there find that the resistance of this elbow is equal to the resistance of three feet of 1-inch pipe.

As an example in using this table we may assume an 80-foot length of ¾-inch pipe containing the following fittings, which are listed with their equivalent lengths of pipe. The factors are taken from the table in the column for ¾-inch fittings.

4 couplings ....4 × 0.8 ft. = 3.2 ft.
2 90° elbows........................2 × 2.5 ft. = 5
1 tee turning 90°................1 × 4   ft. = 4
1 angle valve......................1 × 12 ft. = 12

$$\overline{}$$

24.2 ft.

Thus we find that all the fittings have a combined resistance equal to that of 24.2 feet, or about 24 feet of pipe. Adding this 24 feet to the actual length of 80 feet gives 104 feet, which should be used in figuring the required size of pipe.

The actual loss in fittings is reduced when the ends of pipe lengths are well reamed and when pipes are screwed up tightly into the fittings. If threaded fittings are of the drainage type, and when streamlined fittings are used with copper tubing, the allowances may be reduced to half those given in the table.

CHAPTER 10

VALVES AND FAUCETS

Compression Faucet.—The kind of faucet which is by far the most generally used for all types of fixtures is the *compression type,* of which the constructional principles are shown by Fig. 84. The style illustrated is such as might be found with lavatories, sinks, and some bathtubs. By rearranging the positions of the inlet, the outlet, and the handle, the same general construction may be used anywhere that a faucet is needed. The drawing which shows a complete faucet has the inlet and outlet at right angles to each other, and has a female thread at the inlet. One rearrangement of the body is shown in the other drawing. Here the inlet and outlet are in line, and the inlet has a male thread. This type might be turned a quarter way around on the axis of the inlet pipe, so that the handle would be on one side rather than at the top.

The moving part of the compression faucet, to which is attached the handle, consists of a shaft or spindle of which an enlarged portion carries screw threads. These threads fit others in the body so that the spindle moves up or down as the handle is turned. At the lower end of the spindle is a disc washer made of fibre, rubber, or some composition material. When the handle is turned to shut off the flow of water, this disc washer is forced down against the ground seat which is faced off flat and true.

The spindle threads are a loose fit. Consequently, with the faucet opened to allow flow of water, water might come up around the threads and out near the handle. To prevent such leakage there is a packing washer fitting snugly around the shaft, and held on the outer edge by the cap nut which screws down onto the body of the faucet.

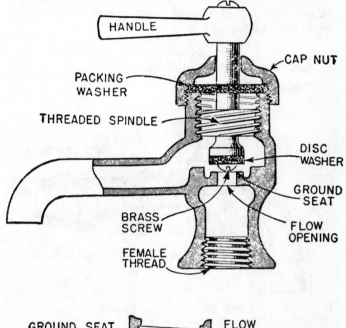

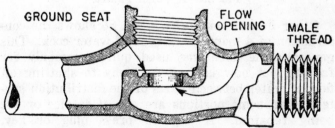

FIG. 84.—A Compression Faucet.

Fuller Faucet.—The construction of a Fuller faucet is shown by Fig. 85. Attached to the handle is a spindle having at its lower end an offset or eccentric extension. On this eccentric is a shaft carrying a rubber ball. When the eccentric is moved by turning the handle one way or the other, the ball is pressed against a beveled seat to shut off the water flow, or is moved away from this seat to allow flow of water.

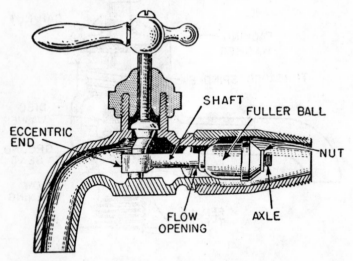

SHAFT

FULLER BALL

ECCENTRIC END

NUT

FLOW OPENING

AXLE

FIG. 85.—A Fuller Faucet.

Other Faucets or Cocks.—Fig. 86 shows the construction of a *ground key* type of water cock. This general style once was used quite commonly for faucets, but now is limited chiefly to shutting off flow of water between parts of the distribution system when some portions are out of service or are being repaired. A tapered brass plug or key, through which is an opening or waterway, fits into a tapered opening in the brass body. The plug is held in place, and is adjusted for tightness, by a nut screwed onto the threaded lower end of the plug.

The cock is open when the handle is in line with the piping. With the handle crosswise of the piping the cock is closed.

Ground key cocks often have a small extra hole in the plug and a corresponding opening through one side of the body. When the cock is closed to the main flow, water from piping on one side may issue through these small openings. The purpose is to allow draining distribution piping when shut off from the service supply.

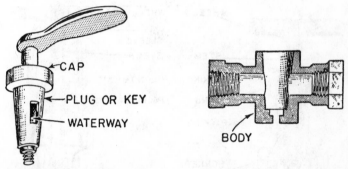

FIG. 86.—Ground Key Shut-off Cock.

A *combination faucet* consists of two valves, one for cold water and the other for hot, connected to a single nozzle. A *mixing faucet* consists of a single valve with one handle by means of which various proportions of cold and hot water may be admitted to one nozzle or one pipe. *Self-closing faucets* have a spring that tends to shut off flow of water, or that will close the faucet when the handle is released. Self-closing faucets may be operated from a hand lever, a foot pedal, or a lever moved by the knee or elbow.

The size of a faucet is specified as the size of the pipe to which it will attach. That is, a faucet having its body threaded for half-inch pipe is a half-inch faucet. It is necessary to specify also whether the faucet has male or female threads, as shown in Fig. 84. If a faucet is of larger size than its supply pipe the flow from the faucet will be sluggish.

Faucets for bathtubs should be of the over-rim type rather than of the style which projects through holes in the tub. The latter style may produce a cross connection and backflow in the same manner as when the outlet of a lavatory faucet is below the top of the lavatory rim.

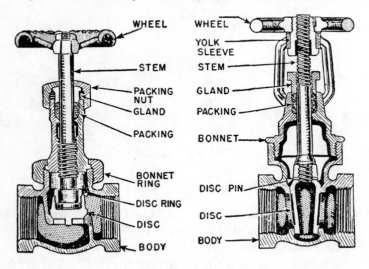

Fig. 87.—A Globe Valve.
Fig. 88.—A Gate Valve.

Globe Valves.—The construction of a globe valve is shown by Fig. 87. The operating principle is much like that of the compression faucet. The disc which is pressed down upon the seat to close the valve may be of composition material or of metal, the latter giving metal-to-metal contact between disc and seat. Leakage around the stem is prevented by valve packing which is compressed by a packing nut. This packing may be replaced by closing the valve, then unscrewing the packing nut and lifting the packing gland if such a gland is used. To replace the seat it is necessary to shut off water from pipes leading to the valve, then unscrew the bonnet ring to allow lifting out the stem and seat.

Globe valves must be connected so that water or other liquid flows upward through the seat and against the bottom of the disc. An arrow on the valve body may show the correct direction of flow.

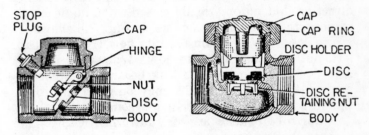

FIG. 89.—Swing Check Valve.
FIG. 90.—Horizontal Check Valve.

Globe valves are used for practically any kind of work. The size of the valve is the size of the pipe to which it attaches.

Angle Valves.—An angle valve has a disc and seat similar to those of a globe valve, but the inlet and outlet are at right angles rather than in line as with the globe valve.

Gate Valves.—The principle of one style of gate valve is shown by Fig. 88. In this valve the flow is controlled by a tapered member drawn upward to open the valve and moved downward to shut off the flow. An open gate valve opposes flow of water

much less than an open globe valve or angle valve.
With the screw and yoke construction shown by
Fig. 88, the operating wheel does not rise and fall,
but remains at the same elevation while moving the
stem. Other valves, of the rising stem type, have
the stem and threads arranged as in Fig. 87, which
means that the wheel will rise and fall with movement of the gate. To replace the disc or to renew the
stem packing, the gate valve is handled in the same
way as a globe valve.

Check Valves.—A check valve is a device which
permits free flow of liquids through the valve in one
direction, but automatically closes when liquid commences to flow the other way. Fig. 89 shows a
swing check valve which permits flow from right to
left, but prevents opposite flow. When this particular design commences to leak because of wear or
pitting, the face of the disc may be reground to fit
the seat by using valve grinding compound.

A *horizontal check valve* is shown in Fig. 90. The
design shown has a renewable composition disc
which is replaced when leakage develops. Other
styles have renewable metal discs, and also seat
rings which may be screwed out of the body and
replaced when the disc is renewed. Still other styles
of check valves have a metal ball which rises and
falls upon a metal seat, the ball taking the place of
the disc used in other styles.

CHAPTER 11

STEEL AND IRON PIPE AND PIPE FITTINGS

Water supply pipes, waste pipes, and vent pipes usually are of steel or wrought iron which is galvanized, meaning that it is coated with zinc. The size of the pipe is specified as its nominal or approximate inside diameter. The table for *steel pipe and wrought iron pipe* shows the nominal sizes in general use, also the actual outside and inside diameters, the number of threads per inch, and the weights in pounds per foot of length.

This table lists pipe of three weights; standard weight, extra strong, and double extra strong. The standard weight is used in most plumbing jobs, since it has ample strength for the pressures encountered. Pipe of the heavier weights has the same outside diameter as the standard weight, but has thicker walls and hence smaller inside diameter.

Standard weight pipe comes in random lengths of 16 to 22 feet. As a rule, up to 5% of the total number of lengths may consist of two pieces coupled together, which are called "jointers." The extra strong and double extra strong pipe come in random lengths of 12 to 22 feet, although as many as 5% of the total number of lengths may be six to 12 feet long. These heavier grades of pipe come regularly with plain unthreaded ends.

Standard weight welded steel pipe usually has both ends threaded and has a pipe coupling screwed onto one end of each length. All other pipe comes with unthreaded ends unless ordered otherwise. The couplings which come with threaded pipe are of

STEEL PIPE AND WROUGHT IRON PIPE

SIZE	Outside Diam. Inches	STANDARD WEIGHT		EXTRA STRONG		DOUBLE EXTRA STRONG		Threads Per Inch
		Inside Diam.	Pounds Per Ft.	Inside Diam.	Pounds Per Ft.	Inside Diam.	Pounds Per Ft.	
⅜	.675	.493	.57	.423	.74	......	......	18
½	.840	.622	.85	.546	1.09	.252	1.71	14
¾	1.050	.824	1.13	.742	1.47	.434	2.44	14
1	1.315	1.049	1.68	.957	2.17	.599	3.66	11½
1¼	1.660	1.380	2.28	1.278	3.00	.896	5.21	11½
1½	1.900	1.610	2.73	1.500	3.63	1.100	6.41	11½
2	2.375	2.067	3.68	1.939	5.02	1.503	9.03	11½
2½	2.875	2.469	5.82	2.323	7.66	1.771	13.70	8
3	3.500	3.068	7.62	2.900	10.25	2.300	18.58	8
3½	4.000	3.548	9.20	3.374	12.51	2.728	22.85	8
4	4.500	4.026	10.89	3.826	14.98	3.152	27.54	8
5	5.563	5.047	14.81	4.813	20.78	4.063	38.55	8
6	6.625	6.065	19.19	5.761	28.57	4.897	53.16	8
8	8.625	7.981	28.81	7.625	43.39	6.875	72.42	8
10	10.75	10.02	41.13	9.75	54.74	......	......	8
12	12.75	12.00	50.71	11.75	65.42	......	......	8

wrought iron for wrought iron pipe, and of either wrought iron or steel for steel pipe.

Pipe Fittings.—Fittings include all the pieces which are used to connect lengths of pipe together. The joint between a fitting and a pipe, or other fitting, may be made by calking, as with hub and spigot joints in soil pipe, or with flanges which are bolted together, or with screw threads. Most joints, other than in soil pipe, building drains and building sewers are of the threaded type using threaded fittings. Threaded fittings are made of malleable iron, cast iron, brass, and for some work of cast steel or of forged steel.

Fittings for ordinary indoor low-pressure wrought iron or steel pipe in the water supply system and also in vent pipes are of galvanized malleable iron or of galvanized cast iron. Cast iron fittings are used for cast iron pipe when such pipe is installed. Brass fittings are used with brass or copper pipe.

Fig. 91 shows many of the most generally used malleable iron fittings. Nipples are short pieces of pipe threaded on both ends. A close nipple is just long enough to take full threads on each end with the threads meeting at the center. Close nipples allow fittings on opposite ends to be screwed up until they almost meet. On short nipples the threads do not meet, there being an unthreaded space of a half to three-quarters of an inch in the middle of the nipple. Long nipples come in several different overall lengths, those most commonly used being three, four, five or six inches long.

Couplings have internal threads so that they may connect together two lengths of pipe end-to-end, or connect together any two parts which have male threads. A straight coupling is of the same size at both ends. A reducing coupling, called also a reducer, is larger at one end than at the other so that

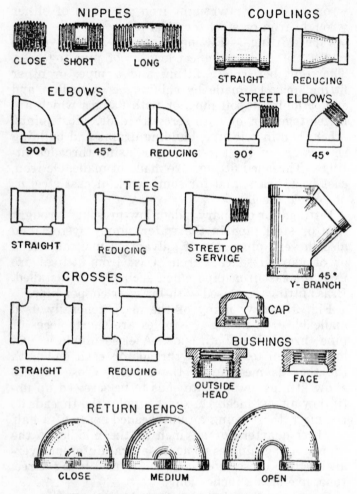

FIG. 91.—Malleable Iron Pipe Fittings.

it will connect two pipes of unequal size. In addition
to the malleable iron couplings shown by Fig. 91,
which have bands around the ends, steel couplings

without the end bands are in common use, and are
the kind most often supplied with lengths of threaded pipe.

Elbows have female threads at both ends. They
are specified according to the angle in degrees between the two lengths of connected pipe. A reducing
elbow has a smaller thread at one end than at the
other, and connects two pipes of unequal size. Street
elbows have a female thread on one end and a male
thread on the other end. They will connect a length
of pipe, or a fitting having a male thread, with any
fitting or with a faucet or valve having a female
thread.

Tees are used for connecting a branch pipe at
right angles to the through pipe or to the run. A
straight tee has threads of the same size at all three
openings. A reducing tee has one opening larger
or smaller than the other two, or may have three
different sizes for the three openings. The two openings which are in line are called the run openings,
and the one at right angles is called the outlet. The
following list illustrates some of the combinations
of thread sizes found in reducing tees having one
run opening of 1-inch size:

1st Run Opening	2nd Run Opening	Outlet Opening
1	1	1½
1	1	1¼
1	1	¾
1	1	½
1	1	⅜
1	¾	1
1	¾	¾
1	¾	½
1	½	1
1	½	¾
1	½	½

Street tees, called also service tees, have one run opening with a female thread, the other run opening with a male thread, and the outlet opening with a female thread. They allow making connection to faucets, valves and other fittings which have a female thread, when the supply pipe is to turn at right angles where the connection is made. A 45° Y-branch serves somewhat the same purpose as a tee, but allows the connecting pipe to enter the run at 45° rather than at right angles.

Crosses are used chiefly in vent piping and sometimes in water supply lines. A straight cross is of the same size at all four openings. A reducing cross ordinarily has each pair of opposite openings of the same size, but the two pairs are of different sizes. That is, the outlet openings are of different size than the run openings. Reducing crosses may be had also with outlets of two different sizes, both of which are different from the run openings.

A cap is used to close the end of a pipe when the pipe opening is no longer to be used or when an air chamber is to be formed for the purpose of taking up the shock of stopping a column of water which has been flowing. Bushings are used when a pipe end, a fitting, a faucet or a valve is to be connected to a threaded opening of larger size than the pipe or other piece being used. Bushings have female threads on the inside and male threads on the outside as shown in Fig. 91. The smaller female thread may be from one to four sizes smaller than the outer male thread. For example, by using a suitable bushing it is possible to connect into a one-inch threaded opening a piece whose thread size is $\frac{3}{8}$, $\frac{1}{2}$ or $\frac{3}{4}$ inch. The bushing head is of hexagonal or octagonal shape so that it may be tightened with a wrench. Other bushings have recesses to take a hexagonal or octagonal wrench.

Return bends are used where a pipe line is to be turned back upon itself, chiefly for assembling banks of pipe. Spacing between adjacent pipes may be varied by using the different styles of bends. For example, with one-inch return bends, the close pattern allows the two pipes to be separated by $1\frac{1}{2}$ inches center to center, the medium pattern allows $1\frac{7}{8}$ inch separation, and the open pattern allows $2\frac{1}{2}$ inch separation center-to-center.

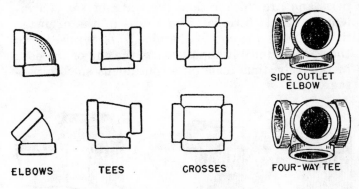

SIDE OUTLET ELBOW

ELBOWS   TEES   CROSSES   FOUR-WAY TEE

FIG. 92.—Cast Iron Pipe Fittings.

Drainage Fittings.—Fig. 92 illustrates a few types of cast iron fittings, chiefly to show the difference in appearance between cast iron and malleable iron fittings. The cast iron types have bands about twice as wide as the malleables, and the metal of the body is thicker in the cast iron types. In this illustration are shown also an elbow and a tee having additional outlets on the side. The side outlet elbow and the four-way tee usually are available also in malleable iron.

The differences between the ends of the same nominal size of threaded fittings in malleable iron, ordinary styles of cast iron, and cast iron drainage types are shown by Fig. 93. The diameter of the threaded opening and the number of threads per inch are the same for fittings of any given nominal size. The internal diameter of the body is the same for malleable and cast iron fittings, but is smaller in the drainage type. The smaller bore of the drainage fitting matches the internal diameter of the pipe so that there is neither enlargement nor restriction to form pockets. The walls of the bodies of cast iron fittings and drainage fittings are of the same thickness, and are thicker than the walls of the equivalent malleable fittings. The recess of the drainage fitting allows the end of the pipe to be screwed into the opening until it almost meets the end of the bore in the body, thus forming a continuous smooth passage.

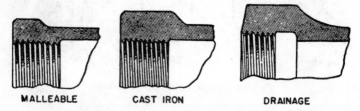

MALLEABLE   CAST IRON   DRAINAGE

FIG. 93.—Differences Between Types of Fittings.

Fig. 94 shows some of the more common drainage fittings. The broken lines indicate the pitch of the threaded opening, which allows for the slope required in waste and vent pipes. Elbows are available for making turns at various angles. Such turns will allow running waste lines quite directly from fixtures to soil stacks or waste stacks between floors and ceilings without the necessity for sharp bends. The $5\frac{5}{8}°$ elbow used where fittings have no pitch in themselves will allow a pitch or slope of about $1\frac{1}{8}$

inches per foot of pipe. The three-way elbow allows
a tee connection in waste lines so that two horizontal
pipes may enter a single vertical pipe.

The basin tee of Fig. 94 has the side outlet pitched
upward, thus allowing one horizontal connection

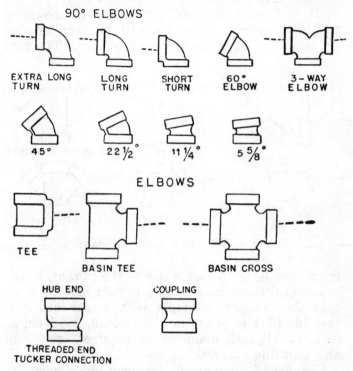

FIG. 94.—Cast Iron Drainage Fittings.

from a wash basin or similar fixture to connect with
a vertical pipe whose upward extension is the vent
and whose downward extension is the waste line.
The basin cross allows two horizontal pipes from
opposite directions to enter a vertical waste and dual
vent line. The Tucker connection has its lower open-

ing threaded like any drainage fitting, and has the upper end in the form of a hub which takes a calked joint. The hub end will fit wrought iron pipe, or may have a loose ring that slips over the wrought iron pipe.

Other drainage fittings are shown by Fig. 95. All of these types have a single side inlet as shown by full lines, or may be double, with two similar side inlets as indicated by the broken lines. The side

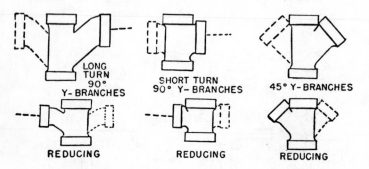

Fig. 95.—Cast Iron Drainage Y-branches.

inlets may be of the same size as the run, or, in the reducing fittings, may be one to four sizes smaller than the run. For example, with a four-inch run, the side inlet or inlets may be 3-inch, 2½-inch, 2-inch, or 1½-inch diameter as required for waste and vent line connections.

Changes of direction in drainage pipes generally are made by using, singly or in combination, 45° Y-branches, and long sweep quarter bends or sixth, eighth or sixteenth bends (elbows). Single sanitary tees may be used in vertical drains or stacks. When the direction of a soil or waste pipe changes from horizontal to vertical, short quarter-bends may be used. Double sanitary tees, double tee fittings, and double hub fittings generally are prohibited in drainage lines. A double hub fitting is like a hub and spigot fitting, but has hubs on both ends rather than a hub on one and a spigot on the other end. No

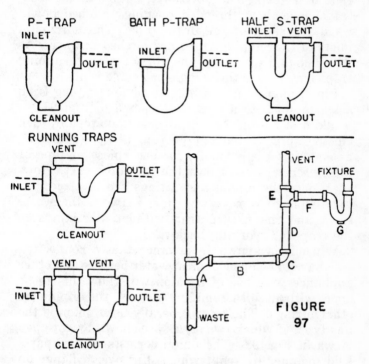

Fig. 96.—Cast Iron Drainage Traps.
Fig. 97.—Order In Which Piping Is Assembled.

change of direction of more than 90° should be made at any one turn in a drainage line. Plain tees, also crosses, may be used in vent lines and in water distributing lines, but not in drainage lines.

Drainage Traps.—Cast iron drainage traps are illustrated in Fig. 96. The ordinary P-trap may be used for most fixtures such as sinks and laundry trays, but the limited space underneath bathtubs may require the lower inlet provided by the bath type of P-trap. The horizontal outlets of all these traps have their threaded openings pitched downward for slope of the drain pipe. The horizontal inlets of the running traps are pitched upward. As with hub and spigot designs, these threaded running traps may have either single or double vents.

Pipe Unions.—In assembling a line of piping from a waste stack to a fixture as shown in Fig. 97 we would first put on the Y-branch A, then pipe B, then elbow C, pipe D, tee E, pipe F, and trap G. Such an assembly is easily made, for each piece of pipe or fitting screws into or onto the preceding part. However, once the piping and fittings are in place it is impossible to remove any part between the waste stack and the fixture trap without starting from the trap and working backward.

When it is known in advance that a connection may have to be opened, as at water heaters and other appliances, the use of a union will allow this to be done without disassembling any of the piping or other fittings. The most generally used union is the nut type, of which two styles are shown by cut-open views in Fig. 98. The union consists of two parts held together by a nut which slips over a flange on one part and screws onto threads cut on the other part. The two parts of the union are screwed onto the ends of threaded pipes, the union is brought together, and its nut tightened to make a secure joint. Tightening or loosening the nut on the union does not require turning either of the parts which are screwed onto the lengths of pipe.

The lip type union of Fig. 98 has smoothly finished iron surfaces between which is a gasket compressed by the nut. The union having a brass-to-iron seat has an insert made of brass, which makes a tight joint without a gasket. The two unions shown in section by Fig. 98 have female threads on both ends. Unions are available also with a female thread on one end and a male thread on the other end. Unions with two female threads are used between two pieces of pipe. The union with male and female threads may have one end screwed over the end of a

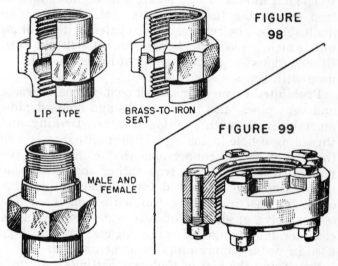

FIGURE 98

LIP TYPE

BRASS-TO-IRON SEAT

FIGURE 99

MALE AND FEMALE

Fig. 98.—Nut Unions.
Fig. 99.—A Flange Union.

pipe, and the other end screwed into a fitting. For example, the male and female union might be used in Fig. 97 between pipe *F* and either the tee *E* or the trap *G*. Pipe *F* might also be cut near its center, and both cut ends threaded and screwed into a union having two female threads.

A flange union is illustrated by Fig. 99. Each half of the union has a female thread so that it may be screwed onto the end of a pipe. The two halves of the union then are held securely together by from three to twelve bolts, depending on the size of the pipe and union. Flange unions are employed more commonly in steam lines and for high pressure work than for ordinary plumbing. Although this type of union is made in sizes as small as one-half inch, it usually is used only on pipe two inches or larger in diameter.

The nut unions of Fig. 98 are entirely of malleable iron except the inserted brass seat. Unions with malleable bodies sometimes are fitted with a brass nut, which is easier to loosen since it will not rust. Other unions are made entirely of brass, these being used with brass and copper pipe.

Prohibited Connections.—All connections to waste and vent pipes, also to soil stacks and house drains, must be made with suitable fittings. Drilling and threading a hole in the pipe is prohibited, as is also the use of saddle connections that clamp over the pipe with a band. Cast iron rather than malleable iron fittings are preferred for drainage piping because the cast iron will better withstand the action of corrosive gases and of soft water containing a considerable amount of acid. All cast iron fittings used in water supply pipes must be galvanized.

Specifying the Size of Reducing Fittings.—In specifying the size of reducing fittings, the order in which the sizes are given follows a certain convention according to the locations of the openings.

For reducing elbows and couplings the larger size is given first. For bushings the male thread is given first, then the female thread.

For tees and Y-branches the larger run size is given first, then the smaller run, and the outlet last. Examples are shown in Fig. 100. A tee having the outlet larger than the run may be called a bullhead tee.

For crosses on which the two run openings are the same size and the two outlets the same size it is sufficient to give the run size first and the outlet last. When the two runs or two outlets are not of the same size, the rule is to first give the larger run, then the smaller run, then the larger outlet, and finally the smaller outlet. This is shown in Fig. 100.

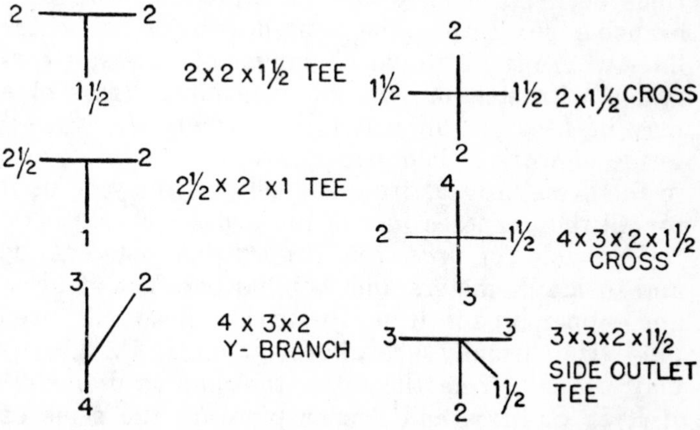

FIG. 100.—How Reducing Fittings Are Specified.

For side outlet elbows, tees and crosses, the outlet size is given last, with the other sizes given in the orders previously explained.

Cement Lined Pipe.—Galvanized steel, black iron, and cast iron piping sometimes is lined with cement to resist the action of water which is acid or otherwise productive of considerable corrosion. The cement lined pipe is of the same outside diameter as unlined pipe, and, of course, is of somewhat smaller inside diameter due to the lining. In order to maintain an acid proof lining throughout a run, it is necessary to use special fittings which usually are internally coated with lead.

CHAPTER 12

BRASS AND COPPER PIPE AND TUBING

Brass pipe of the same outside dimensions as steel or wrought iron pipe frequently is used for connections between fixtures and the wall, the floor, or a branch pipe. Brass pipe is used also for hot water lines where there would be danger of excessive corrosion with steel or wrought iron pipe. Brass pipe may be used for all water lines where the highest grade of work is being installed. Copper pipe, also in the same sizes as iron or steel pipe, may be used for all the purposes just mentioned.

The table for *brass and copper pipe* lists outside and inside diameters and weights per foot of brass and copper pipe in iron pipe sizes. The words "iron pipe size" usually are abbreviated "I. P. S." As may be seen from the table, the outside diameters of I. P. S. brass and copper pipe are the same as for corresponding nominal sizes of steel or wrought iron pipe. The wall thicknesses and inside diameters vary in some of the sizes, but not by enough to be of much importance. Brass and copper pipes are threaded with the same tapered threads and the same number of threads per inch as are iron and steel pipe.

Brass pipe is available in various compositions. The weights in the table are for brass containing 65% to 68% of copper; most of the remainder being zinc. Muntz metal is brass containing less copper. Admiralty brass and red brass contain more copper. The type of brass may require selection according to the kind of water when there is danger of corrosion. A greater percentage of copper increases the resistance to corrosion. Copper pipe is made of copper in which is not more than 1/8 of one per cent of other metals.

BRASS AND COPPER PIPE
Iron Pipe Sizes (IPS)

SIZE	OUTSIDE DIAMETER Inches	INSIDE DIAMETER Standard	Extra Strong	WEIGHT—POUNDS PER FOOT Standard Brass	Copper	Extra Strong Brass	Copper
3/8	.675	.494	.421	.61	.64	.81	.85
1/2	.840	.625	.542	.91	.96	1.19	1.25
3/4	1.050	.822	.736	1.24	1.30	1.62	1.71
1	1.315	1.062	.951	1.74	1.83	2.39	2.51
1 1/4	1.660	1.368	1.272	2.56	2.69	3.30	3.46
1 1/2	1.900	1.600	1.494	3.04	3.20	3.99	4.19
2	2.375	2.062	1.933	4.02	4.23	5.51	5.79
2 1/2	2.875	2.500	2.315	5.83	6.14	8.41	8.84
3	3.500	3.062	2.892	8.31	8.75	11.24	11.82
3 1/2	4.000	3.500	3.358	10.85	11.41	13.67	14.37
4	4.500	4.000	3.818	12.29	12.94	16.41	17.25
5	5.563	5.062	4.813	15.40	16.21	22.52	23.67
6	6.625	6.125	5.751	18.44	19.41	31.32	32.93
8	8.625	8.000	7.625	30.05	31.63	47.02	49.42
10	10.750	10.019	9.750	43.91	46.22	59.32	62.40

Fixture waste and drain connections made of brass or copper should have walls not less than 36/1000 inch thick, which corresponds to number 19 American or Browne & Sharpe gage. Sheet brass and sheet copper used in plumbing work should be not less than 40/1000 inch thick, which corresponds to number 18 gage.

Only brass fittings should be used with brass or copper pipe. These fittings are of the same size and style as malleable iron fittings. Iron or steel fittings would cause an electrical action where the two kinds of metal come together, with the result that the iron or steel would rust rapidly.

Brass and copper are softer than iron or steel and are more easily damaged. Consequently, toothed pipe wrenches should not be used for turning the pipe, nor should the pipe be held in a vise having toothed jaws such as ordinarily are used for iron and steel pipe. The vise should have smooth-faced jaws which hold by means of friction, and wrenches should be of the friction type with a metal strap for gripping the pipe. Even with correct tools, excessive force applied during assembly may bend or crush brass

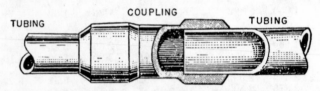

SOLDERED OR SWEATED FITTING

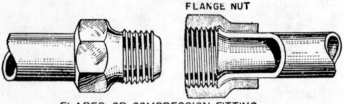

FLARED OR COMPRESSION FITTING

FIG. 101.—Connections for Copper Tubing.

or copper pipe. Threaded joints may be made up tight by applying a pipe dope to the male thread. This dope may be of boiled linseed oil and red lead, or of oil and graphite.

Copper Tubing.—Copper tubing may be used for interior plumbing in cold water and hot water distribution lines, also for underground water service lines. Connections are not made with threaded fittings, but by means of soldered joints or else with joints which require flaring the ends of the tubing so that it may be held by compression nuts somewhat in the manner of a nut union. Both kinds of connections are illustrated in Fig. 101, where one end of the tubing and part of the fitting have been cut away to show the construction.

To assemble the soldered fitting the end of the tubing is cut smoothly, reamed to remove any inside burr from the end, then cleaned on the outside with steel wool until bright. The opening in the fitting is similarly cleaned. Soldering flux is applied to the end of the tubing and to the hole in the fitting. Then the end of the tube is pushed into the fitting as far as possible and the two parts are heated by means of a blow torch until at a temperature which causes solder to melt when touched to the fitting.

The flame now is taken away and wire solder is touched to the fitting so that the solder runs in between the fitting and tubing to make a solid metal joint when the solder cools. With some types of fittings the solder is applied between the fitting and the tubing. Other types have a small hole in the fitting through which solder is allowed to flow into the joint while the parts are hot. The clearances in the joints are small enough so that the molten solder is drawn in by capillary action.

To make up a compression joint the end of the tubing is passed through the flange nut and then is spread outward into cone shape by means of a special flanging tool that is driven into the end of the tubing. The flange on the tubing is enlarged to an outside diameter which just enters the threaded opening in the nut. Then the nut, carrying the flared end of the tubing, is screwed onto the other part of the fitting, which has a rounded end or tapered end that fits snugly into the flared end of the tubing as the nut is drawn tight.

By means of special fittings it is possible to connect copper tubing to steel or wrought iron pipe having threaded ends. Several such fittings are shown in Fig. 102. The threaded ends of the fitting for steel or iron pipe are shown toward the top, with the tubing connections toward the bottom. The tee shown here is designed to take tubing in both the run openings, and threaded pipe in the outlet. These fittings usually are made of cast brass, but sometimes of wrought copper.

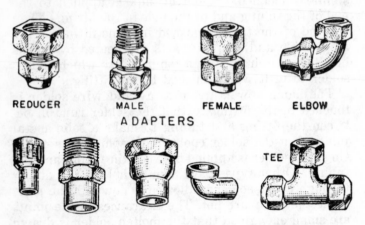

REDUCER   MALE   FEMALE   ELBOW

A D A P T E R S

TEE

FIG. 102.—Connectors for Tubing To Threaded Pipe.

Kinds of Copper Tubing.—The table for *copper tubing* shows dimensions and weights for the three wall thicknesses in which copper tubing is available. The tubing with the heaviest or thickest wall is *type K*, the one with a wall of intermediate thickness is *type L*, and that with the thinnest wall is *type M*. Types K and L are available in either soft temper or hard temper, while type M is used only in the hard temper variety. Tubing with soft temper may be bent or offset in moderate degrees while cold, either by hand in small sizes or by means of bending tools in large sizes or where first class appearance is essential. The hard temper tubing may be bent only after it is annealed or softened by heating.

COPPER TUBING

SIZE	OUTSIDE DIAMETER Inches	INSIDE DIAMETER			POUNDS PER FOOT		
		K	L	M	K	L	M
⅜	.500	.402	.430	.450	.27	.20	.14
½	.625	.527	.545	.569	.34	.28	.20
¾	.875	.745	.785	.811	.64	.45	.33
1	1.125	.995	1.025	1.055	.84	.65	.46
1¼	1.375	1.245	1.265	1.291	1.04	.88	.68
1½	1.625	1.481	1.505	1.527	1.36	1.14	.94
2	2.125	1.959	1.985	2.009	2.06	1.75	1.46
2½	2.625	2.435	2.465	2.495	2.92	2.48	2.03
3	3.125	2.907	2.945	2.981	4.00	3.33	2.68
3½	3.625	3.385	3.425	3.459	5.12	4.29	3.58
4	4.125	3.857	3.905	3.935	6.51	5.38	4.66
5	5.125	4.805	4.875	4.907	9.67	7.61	6.66
6	6.125	5.741	5.845	5.881	13.87	10.20	8.91

Since the soft temper tubing may be easily bent, nearly any required run may be made up with only 90° elbows, tees, and unions. Bends of less than 90°, also any needed offsets, are easily made in the tubing itself.

Although the type L tubing, of medium wall thickness, may be used for exposed horizontal runs and for vertical runs which are either exposed or concealed, the type K is preferred because of its longer life and greater margin of strength. Soft temper tubing may be used for water supply pipes where the flow results from positive pressure, but for drainage lines this tubing is likely to sag and fail to maintain a uniform pitch. Consequently, drainage pipes which run horizontally should be made of straight lengths of hard temper tubing. Soft temper type K tubing should be used for underground water supply lines, and preferably should have flared rather than soldered fittings. For indoor work the flared or compression fittings are used with soft temper tubing, and the soldered or sweated fittings with hard temper tubing.

Tubing Compared with Pipe.—As may be seen from the copper tubing table, the actual outside diameter of this tubing always is 0.125 or ⅛ inch greater than its nominal size. For example, the outside diameter of the 1-inch tubing is 1.125 or 1⅛ inches. Comparing the inside diameters of copper tubing with the inside diameters of the same nominal sizes of steel or wrought iron pipe will show that the bore of the tubing is smaller than the bore of standard weight steel or iron pipe. However, since the tubing does not tend to scale or corrode so much as the steel or iron, the same nominal size generally will be satisfactory.

For the same loss of pressure, new steel or iron pipe in sizes smaller than ¾-inch carries more water than the same nominal sizes of type L copper tubing. The ¾-inch sizes carry about the same flow, while in larger sizes the iron or steel pipe carries about the same or a little less water than the type L tubing. When the inside of the steel or iron pipe has become fairly rough, due to corrosion, it carries considerably less water for a given pressure loss than does the copper tubing.

CHAPTER 13

PIPE CUTTING AND THREADING

Steel, wrought iron, brass and copper pipe are threaded with the standard tapered pipe thread shown by Fig. 103. The taper is ¾ inch per foot, cr 1 in 16. When pipe is correctly threaded it may be screwed into a fitting or other threaded opening to a depth of several threads by hand, then the remaining good threads may be screwed up tight with a pipe wrench. The few imperfect threads at the pipe

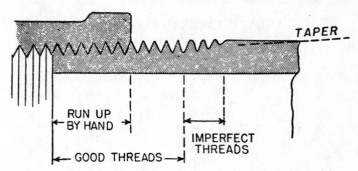

FIG. 103.—Standard Tapered Pipe Thread.

end will not enter the fitting. The number of good threads and the number of threads which normally may be screwed up by hand will vary with the size of the pipe. Average numbers are shown by the table of *standard tapered pipe threads*.

When the threaded end of a pipe is screwed into a fitting for part of the pipe length, the distance between fittings will be less than the overall length

157

of the pipe, or the total length of pipe will be greater than the distance between fittings. The pipe thread table shows the length in inches taken up by threads on one end and on the two ends of the pipe. When distances between fittings are to be precise measurements, the pipe must be cut of enough greater length to allow for thread engagement. For example, assuming that a 2-inch pipe is to extend just 24 inches between the faces of two fittings, we find from the table that the pipe length must be increased by $1^{33}/_{64}$ inches, which is practically $1\frac{1}{2}$ inches. Therefore, the piece of pipe must be cut to a total length of 24 inches plus $1\frac{1}{2}$ inches, or $25\frac{1}{2}$ inches, then screwed up tight, to maintain the correct distance between fittings.

STANDARD TAPERED PIPE THREADS

PIPE SIZE	Threads Per Inch	GOOD THREADS Number	Inches of Length One End	Two Ends	Threads Engaged By Hand
$\frac{3}{8}$	18	7.2	$\frac{13}{32}$	$\frac{13}{16}$	$4\frac{1}{4}$
$\frac{1}{2}$	14	7.5	$\frac{17}{32}$	$1\frac{1}{16}$	$4\frac{1}{2}$
$\frac{3}{4}$	14	7.6	$\frac{35}{64}$	$1\frac{3}{32}$	5
1	$11\frac{1}{2}$	7.8	$\frac{11}{16}$	$1\frac{23}{64}$	$4\frac{1}{2}$
$\frac{1}{4}$	$11\frac{1}{2}$	8.1	$\frac{45}{64}$	$1\frac{27}{64}$	5
$1\frac{1}{2}$	$11\frac{1}{2}$	8.3	$\frac{23}{32}$	$1\frac{22}{64}$	5
2	$11\frac{1}{2}$	8.7	$\frac{3}{4}$	$1\frac{33}{64}$	5
$2\frac{1}{2}$	8	9.1	$1\frac{9}{16}$	$2\frac{9}{32}$	$5\frac{1}{2}$
3	8	9.6	$1\frac{13}{64}$	$2\frac{13}{32}$	6
$3\frac{1}{2}$	8	10	$1\frac{1}{4}$	$2\frac{1}{2}$	$6\frac{1}{2}$
4	8	10.4	$1\frac{13}{64}$	$2\frac{13}{32}$	7
5	8	11.1	$1\frac{13}{32}$	$2\frac{1}{8}$	$7\frac{1}{2}$
6	8	12.1	$1\frac{33}{64}$	$3\frac{3}{32}$	$7\frac{1}{2}$
8	8	13.7	$1\frac{23}{32}$	$3\frac{27}{64}$	$8\frac{1}{2}$
10	8	15.4	$1\frac{57}{64}$	$3\frac{57}{64}$	$9\frac{1}{2}$
12	8	17	$2\frac{1}{8}$	$4\frac{1}{4}$	11

Cutting and Reaming.—While pipe is being cut to length and threaded it is held securely in a pipe vise such as illustrated in Fig. 104. The hinged pipe vise opens on one side to admit the pipe and is provided with toothed jaws for clamping steel or iron pipe and with smooth friction jaws for holding brass or copper pipe. Pipe is held in the chain vise by looping one end of the chain over the pipe, then turning the handle for clamping. This vise, too, should have smooth jaws for brass or iron pipe. Pipe vises may be mounted on a bench, but often

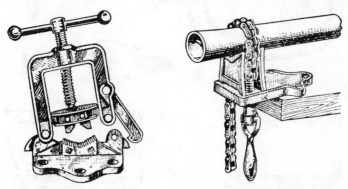

FIG. 104.—Pipe Vises.

are clamped to a post or pillar in a basement or unfinished building where work is being installed.

A hand operated pipe cutter is shown in Fig. 105. In the end of this cutter are two steel rollers, and in the movable part is a tool steel wheel with a knife edge. This cutting wheel may be moved toward or away from the rollers by turning the threaded shaft and handle. To operate the pipe cutter it is opened enough to pass over the pipe, then the wheel is pressed firmly, but not too hard, against the pipe at the point where the cut is to be made. The cutter then is turned around and around the pipe by means of the handle, and while the turning progresses, the handle is screwed in at frequent intervals to force the cutting wheel through the wall of the pipe.

The cutter will leave a burr on the inner edge of the cut end of the pipe, as shown in Fig. 105. This burr materially reduces the inside diameter of the

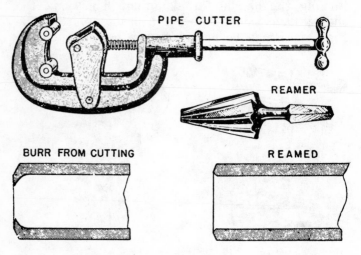

FIG. 105.—Pipe Cutting and Reaming.

pipe at this point, and must be removed by reaming. The burring reamer is held in a hand brace and turned around in the end of the pipe to remove the burr and leave a slightly rounded opening as shown.

Copper tubing will collapse under the ordinary pipe cutter, but may be cut with a special tubing cutter having a thinner wheel. Tubing may be cut also with a hacksaw having 32 teeth to the inch. A coarser saw will catch and its teeth will break out. A hacksaw may be used for cutting iron, steel, brass or copper pipe when a regular cutter is not available. The pipe ends should be reamed after sawing to length.

Thread Cutting.—Threads are cut on the end of the pipe by means of a pipe die, one style of which is shown in Fig. 106. The die has an opening which fits over the pipe. Around the inside of the opening are four hardened and tempered projections having teeth of the size and spacing which will cut one size of tapered pipe thread. The solid die of Fig. 106 is placed in a die stock so that the smaller end of the taper is toward the end of the pipe which is being threaded. Covering the die is a pivoted plate. Underneath the die in the stock is placed a guide which fits around the size pipe for which the die is designed and keeps the stock and die square on the pipe so that a true thread will be cut. When a different size pipe is to be threaded, the die and guide are changed to whatever size is required.

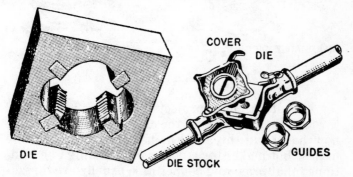

FIG. 106.—Solid Pipe Die and Die Stock.

Instead of the four cutting edges of the die being in one piece there may be two pieces with two cutters on each, or, as shown in Fig. 107, there may be four separate cutters held by the stock. The die stock of Fig. 106 and one of those in Fig. 107, have two long handles by means of which the stock and the die are turned around on the end of the pipe to cut the threads. There also are ratchet stocks, as pictured in Fig. 107, having only one handle which is moved back and forth to rotate the die always in the same direction.

With the pipe held near its end in a vise, the die is placed in position and turned to the right (for a right hand thread) until the teeth of the die just catch on the end of the pipe. Then thread cutting oil or lard oil is applied to the end of the pipe between the cutters of the die. The die now is turned until

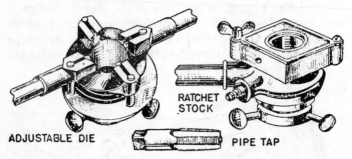

RATCHET STOCK

ADJUSTABLE DIE   PIPE TAP

FIG. 107.—Tools for Pipe Threading and Tapping.

the end of the pipe projects about one-half thread through the front end of the die. The end of the pipe now has a full thread. Further turning is not only useless but makes for a poor joint. It might be mentioned that brass and copper pipe usually are threaded without any oil, or else by using soapy water instead of the thread cutting oil.

When the thread is completed, the stock and die are turned back to the left until they leave the pipe. Excess oil then is wiped off the threaded pipe, and the pipe removed from the vise. In order to dislodge any metal chips that may have gotten inside the pipe it may be held vertically and bounced lightly on a soft wood block to clean it out. The die and stock should be thoroughly cleaned of oil and metal chips after each thread is cut. Grit and chips in the die and stock will result in imperfect threads, which mean leaky joints later on.

So long as dies are sharp and not excessively worn, and so long as the cutters are correctly adjusted, the procedure just outlined will result in the correct number of good threads on the end of the pipe. The pipe then should screw by hand into a good fitting for about the number of threads given in the table of pipe threads.

If the pipe thread is good, but will not screw into the fitting, the threads of the fitting should be examined. If the threads are defective in the fitting they often may be trued up by screwing in a pipe tap of correct size. Such a tap is shown in Fig. 107. Forcing imperfect threads together will not make a tight joint. If threads already cut on lengths of pipe are found to be slightly imperfect, they may be trued up by running the correct size of die onto the pipe just far enough so that the end of the pipe comes through the face of the die. Pipe threads which are badly jammed should be cut off and the end of the pipe rethreaded.

CHAPTER 14

LEAD PIPE AND MISCELLANEOUS PIPE JOINTS

Lead pipe, which once was generally used for both water supply and drainage, now is usually restricted to short bend connections at water closets and slop sinks and to making replacements in existing drainage lines which otherwise are in good condition. Of course, lead pipe may be used for any purpose specifically permitted by local plumbing codes. Lead bends frequently are used between a water closet bowl and the soil pipe fitting. Traps which are made of heavy drawn lead should have brass trap screws and cleanouts. No lead pipe or lead trap should be used nearer than 12 inches to the floor unless protected by a casing of wood or sheet metal.

Although lead does not corrode to the same extent as iron or steel pipe, the lead pipe is not suitable for use with water which is acid, and even with ordinary hard water enough lead may be dissolved to cause some trouble with health. Water which has stood in lead piping should be drawn off and wasted before any is used for cooking or drinking.

The accompanying *lead pipe* table gives for types of lead pipe generally used, the diameters and wall thicknesses in inches and the weights in pounds per foot. The size of lead pipe is specified according to its *caliber,* which is the inside diameter in inches. Various weights or wall thicknesses are available in each caliber. The weights known as extra light, strong, and extra strong are listed in the table.

LEAD PIPE

Dimensions in Inches, and Weights

CALIBER Inches Inside	EXTRA LIGHT			STRONG			EXTRA STRONG			DOUBLE X STRONG		
	Outer Diam.	Wall	Lbs. Per Ft.	Outer Diam.	Wall	Lbs. Per Ft.	Outer Diam.	Wall	Lbs. Per Ft.	Outer Diam.	Wall	Lbs. Per Ft.
⅜	.52	.072	.56	.73	.178	1.5	.75	.188	2.0	1.01	.25	3.0
½	.66	.080	.75	.89	.195	2.0	.94	.220	2.5	1.14	.26	3.5
⅝	.84	.108	1.25	1.02	.193	2.5	1.08	.228	3.0			
¾	.97	.110	1.5	1.16	.205	3.0	1.23	.240	3.5	1.34	.29	4.75
1	1.23	.115	2.0	1.43	.215	4.0	1.49	.245	4.75	1.60	.30	6.0
1¼	1.49	.120	2.5	1.66	.205	4.75	1.77	.260	6.0	1.89	.32	7.75
1½	1.78	.135	3.5	1.93	.215	6.0	2.05	.275	7.5	2.27	.39	11.25
2	2.28	.115	4.75	2.46	.230	8.0	2.52	.260	9.0	3.01	.50	19.5
2				2.41	.205	7.0	2.75	.375	13.75			
3	3.25	.113	6.0									
4	4.25	.113	7.88									
5	5.25	.113	9.88									
6	6.25	.113	11.81									

Weights often are specified by letters as follows: XL or D (extra light), L (light), M (medium), S or A (strong), XS or AA (extra strong), and XXS or AAA (double extra strong). The weights also are specified directly in pounds of weight per foot of length. No pipe thinner than the extra light should be used in soil, waste, vent, or flush pipes, including bends and traps. The extra light grade is generally used for waste pipes. Strong pipe is used in water lines for pressures up to 50 pounds per square inch, extra strong for pressures between 50 and 75 pounds, and double extra strong for pressures between 75 and 100 pounds per square inch.

Wiped Joints.—Connections between two lengths of lead pipe are made with a wiped joint. A wiped joint is used also when lead pipe is connected to brass or copper pipe, or to ferrules, nipples, bushings or traps. Lead joints on the sewer side of a trap must be of the wiped variety, and must be wiped also on the inlet side of the trap if this joint is concealed. A wiped joint is made by applying molten solder in a semi-fluid state while shaping the joint by wiping it with a greased cloth pad or the like.

Making a Wiped Joint.—Fig. 108 shows a cut-open wiped joint as made between two pieces of lead pipe. The end of one piece of pipe is slightly tapered and the end of the other one is flared outward to receive the taper. The two ends are pushed together and the space around them is built up with solder to form an egg-shaped joint.

Fig. 109 shows the steps in preparing the ends of the pipe for the solder. First of all, if the two ends have not been cut truly square, they are squared off with a file. Then any burrs are removed from the inner edges by using a round or half-round file, or else the shave hook illustrated in Fig. 109. Next,

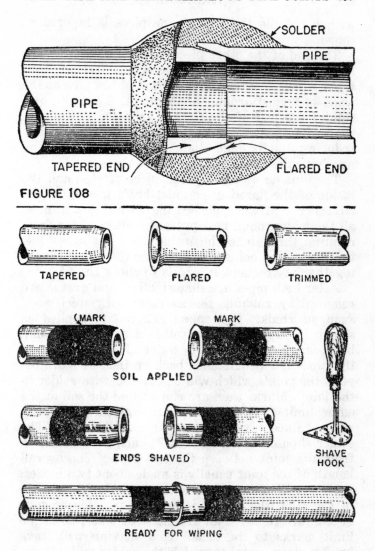

FIGURE 108

FIG. 108.—Details of a Wiped Joint.
FIG. 109.—Steps in Preparing a Wiped Joint.

with a flat file the end of one piece is tapered as
shown.

The end of the other piece is flared outward. The
flaring is done with a cone-shaped piece of hard
wood which is tapped into the end of the pipe as the
wood is turned around and around. Then the outside of the end of the flare is trimmed down with
the file held parallel with the length of the pipe, thus
reducing the outside diameter of the flared end
nearly to the original diameter of the pipe.

The outside of the tapered piece of pipe and the
inside of the flared piece must be formed into true
circles so that when pushed together they will meet
all the way around and prevent molten solder from
running through to the inside of the joint. While
the pieces are being formed they should be placed
together at frequent intervals to check the fit.

After both pipes are shaped, all oil and grease are
removed by rubbing the surfaces with steel wool,
sand, or chalk. Then *plumber's soil* is applied as
shown in Fig. 109. This soil is a mixture of lamp
black and glue dissolved in water. It is painted onto
the pipes from their ends back an inch or more beyond the points which will be covered with solder in
the joint. Marks then are run around the soil at the
outer limits. These marks are conveniently made
with chalked string drawn around the pipe. The
solder should extend at least ¾ inch each direction
from the joint between the two pipes. The overall
length of the joint usually is made about two inches.

Now, with a scraper or shave hook, such as shown
in Fig. 109, the soil and the least possible amount
of lead are removed all around both pipes, from the
limit marks to the ends. This shaving will leave
bright, clean metal to which the solder will adhere.
Only enough lead should be scraped off to leave the
metal bright, since all the metal removed tends to

weaken the joint. As soon as the metal is exposed it should be covered with a coating of tallow to prevent oxidation from the air. Tallow or resin act as fluxes for lead. Oxide will prevent the solder from uniting with the pipe metal.

The two prepared ends then are pushed firmly together and supported so that they cannot move out of line while the wiping is done. The pipes may be held in place with screw clamps, by cords, by blocking, or any device which insures rigidity. A large piece of cloth or cardboard is placed under the joint to catch solder which drops during the wiping process.

The cloth used for wiping is of fustian, sometimes called moleskin, which is a coarse twilled cotton fabric with a close nap. A piece of cloth about nine inches square, or else nine by twelve inches, may be folded twice in each direction to make nine thicknesses with a finished size of three by three or three by four inches, then sewed down to make a pad. The pad is soaked in melted tallow, pressed while hot, and then rubbed over with talc or chalk so that solder will not stick to it.

WEIGHT OF SOLDER FOR WIPED JOINTS

Pipe Caliber	Pounds Solder	Pipe Caliber	Pounds Solder	Pipe Caliber	Pounds Solder
⅜	0.41	¾	0.75	2	1.44
½	.49	1	0.89	3	1.83
⅝	.68	1¼	1.02	4	2.35
		1½	1.16		

The solder is melted in a solder pot over a plumber's furnace, and will be dipped out with a solder ladle having a long handle. The accompanying table shows the weight in pounds of solder required for each joint two inches long and ⅜ inch thick at its center when using solder consisting of two-thirds lead and one-third tin.

The wiping pad is held in the left hand, far enough forward to cover the tips of the fingers. With the ladle in the right hand the molten solder is stirred and dipped up. With the wiper held underneath the joint the solder is poured on top, drop by drop, while moving the ladle to distribute the metal. Some solder is poured onto the soil in order to heat the pipe. The wiper is used to catch excess solder and to press some of it onto the bottom of the joint where it will adhere to the cleaned pipes. Solder which gathers on the wiper is placed back on top of the joint where it will be heated by solder coming from the ladle.

Enough solder is poured to make up the required bulk for the joint. The metal will become semi-fluid or pasty as it is worked into shape. The ladle is laid aside and the wiping continued by working from the soil at the ends in toward the top of the joint which is to be made approximately of the shape illustrated by Fig. 108. Should the solder become too cool to work, it may be reheated with a blow torch or a large soldering copper. After the joint is shaped it is set by spraying with cold water. After the pouring is finished, the wiping may be done by using an extra wiper of smaller size for the right hand. The smaller cloth is used on top of the joint and the larger one below. The finished joint should be kept at least ⅜ inch thick at its thickest part.

Connections Between Lead and Other Pipes.—The end of a lead pipe may be connected to the hub end of cast iron soil pipe or to the hub of a soil pipe fitting in either of the ways illustrated by Fig. 110. With one method a brass ferrule is slipped over the end of the lead pipe and fastened with a wiped joint. Then the bell end of the ferrule is attached to the soil pipe or fitting by means of a regular calked joint. This is the style of connection used between a lead closet bend and the soil pipe fitting. Brass calking ferrules have an inside diameter ¼ inch greater than the nominal pipe size, and usually are 4½ inches long.

When lead pipe is to be wiped onto a fitting of brass, the pipe is soiled and shaved in the usual way for such joints. Both the inside and outside of the

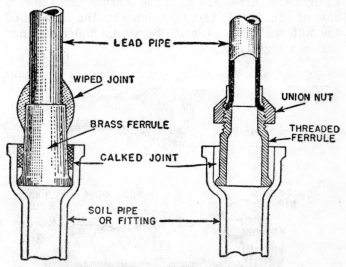

FIG. 110.—Lead Pipe To Soil Pipe Connections.

brass are scraped bright with steel wool, a file, or a scraper. The inside and outside of the brass are coated with soldering flux. The flux may be chloride of zinc made by dissolving a stick of zinc, such as a battery zinc, in muriatic (hydrochloric) acid until the acid will take up no more zinc. The solution should be made in a glass or porcelain dish. This liquid may be diluted with a little water, then applied to the cleaned brass with a brush. The addition of two heaping teaspoonfuls of sal ammoniac to each pint of chloride of zinc may improve the fluxing action.

The other connection shown by Fig. 110 consists of a brass ferrule with a union on one end. The spigot end of the ferrule is calked into the hub of the soil pipe or fitting. The union nut is slipped over the lead pipe, the end of the pipe is flared to fit over the threaded end of the ferrule, and the outside of the flare is trimmed down so the threads of the nut will pass over it. Screwing down the nut makes a tight joint.

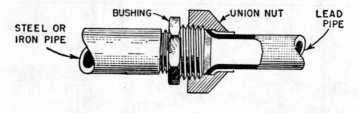

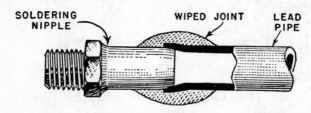

FIG. 111.—Lead Pipe To Threaded Pipe Connections.

Lead pipe may be connected to threaded steel or iron pipe or to threaded pipe fittings as shown in Fig. 111. To connect lead pipe to steel or iron pipe, a bushing, which is part of a union, is screwed onto the end of the threaded pipe. The union nut is slipped over the lead pipe, and the end of this pipe is flared and trimmed so that the nut will screw down over it and onto the bushing.

When lead pipe is to be connected to a threaded

fitting having a female thread, a soldering nipple is wiped onto the lead pipe as shown in Fig. 111. The lead pipe is flared and trimmed to pass over the end of the nipple. The lead is prepared by soiling and scraping as for any wiped joint. The brass nipple is cleaned and fluxed on the outside so that the lead of the joint will adhere to the brass. The joint then is wiped in the usual manner. Connections between lead pipe and I. P. S. brass or copper pipe, or brass or copper threaded fittings, are made

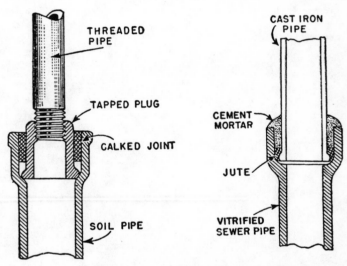

Fig. 112.—Soil Pipe and Sewer Pipe Connections.

in the same way shown by Fig. 111. Soldering nipples are made from brass pipe of iron pipe size or from heavy cast red brass.

Other Pipe Connections.—Threaded pipe, which may be steel, iron, brass or copper, is connected to the hub end of a soil pipe or a soil pipe fitting as shown in Fig. 112. Onto the threaded end of the pipe is screwed a tapped cast iron plug whose lower end is of the spigot type. The joint between the plug and the hub is calked in the usual way.

Fig. 112 shows also a joint between cast iron soil pipe and vitrified sewer pipe. The spigot end of the cast iron pipe is turned into the hub of the tile and the joint is made up with jute and cement mortar as between two lengths of vitrified pipe. When this joint is underground it should be protected with a collar of cement six inches thick and 18 inches long.

CHAPTER 15

PLANS AND LAYOUTS

Before commencing the work of installing and connecting plumbing fixtures it is advisable to draw sketches showing where the fixtures are to be located in the rooms, the directions the piping will run in reaching the fixtures, and the sizes and lengths of all the lines. A plan showing floor dimensions and wall positions often will be enough for simple jobs, but in most cases it is safer to draw an elevation as well. Drawings carefully made to scale are desirable, but even the roughest kind of sketch is better than none at all, for without a drawing of the pipes and connections it is almost certain that lengths will turn out to be incorrect, and that some structural features of the building will not be considered.

Manufacturers of fixtures furnish *roughing-in* dimensions and measurements for each type and kind of fixture. Such measurements for a typical water closet are shown by Fig. 113. Roughing-in sheets give all the information necessary in determining the space required by a fixture, the clearances needed, and the positions for all water supply pipes with reference to the building walls and to one another. There are no standard dimensions for fixtures, consequently it is necessary to obtain them for whatever units are selected.

The first step in laying out an installation is to make a plan of the room, preferably drawn to scale, but in any event showing width and length, position of windows and doors, and any obstructions such as chimneys, beams, and any present piping which may be in or near the walls. Then the fixtures may be roughly pencilled in on the plan. The positions of equipment for bathrooms, kitchens, laundries and basements must be chosen not only for convenience in use, but also with reference to economical installation of the piping.

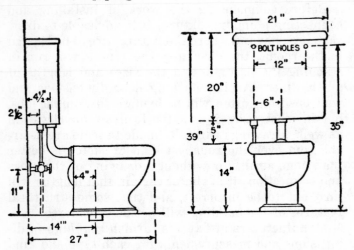

Fig. 113.—Roughing-in Dimensions for a Water Closet.

Since the soil stack is the largest pipe, and since water closets require the largest connections for drainage, the first consideration will be a suitable location for the stack and the water closet or closets. If the stack already is in place, the fixtures should be placed as nearly as possible where connections may be most advantageously made. It is to be remembered that soil pipes and waste pipes must be placed in interior walls, floors and ceilings unless these pipes are covered with heat insulating material to protect them from frost. The same rule applies to water supply pipes which, however, are more easily protected than the larger soil and drain

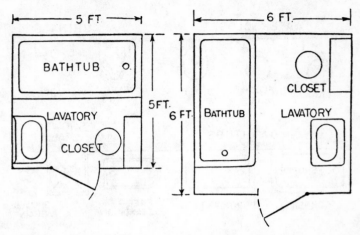

Fig. 114.—Plans for Small Square Bathrooms.

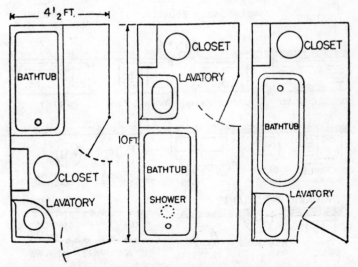

Fig. 115.—Plans for Long Narrow Bathrooms.

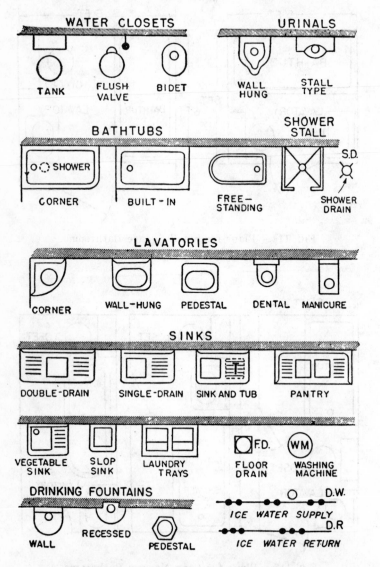

FIG. 116.—Standard Symbols for Fixtures.

pipes. Water pipes and drainage pipes must not be run exposed above unprotected electrical machinery because of drippings from condensation which gathers on the cold surfaces of the pipes.

Much labor and material may be saved by compromising between some arrangement desired for the sake of convenience or appearance, and one that allows the shortest and most direct piping layout. Typical plans for small bathrooms are shown in Fig. 114, while arrangements which may be used with long, narrow bathrooms are shown in Fig. 115. Although the size and shape of a room may limit the possible placing of fixtures, there almost always is a choice between several plans.

Plumbing Symbols.—Fig. 116 shows standard symbols for fixtures as used in plans for plumbing installations. The symbols shown here are not necessarily to be drawn to the same size or even to the same proportions as in the drawing, but should be followed in a general way.

Standard symbols for piping and fittings are shown in Fig. 117. Again it is not necessary to make these symbols exactly as shown here, but they should be made in such manner that no mistakes can occur. Note that the piping lines are shown in one way for views where the pipe extends horizontally, and in another way for views where the pipe runs vertically. In many cases initials are used along with the symbol to more definitely identify the kind of pipe or fittings, or the use to which they are put.

Whether the plan is drawn with standard symbols or otherwise, it will be necessary to indicate and identify by size and type all fittings to be used. The plan will show also the length of all sections of pipe. The developed length, which is given on the drawings, is the length measured along the center-line of the pipe and through the center-lines of the fittings.

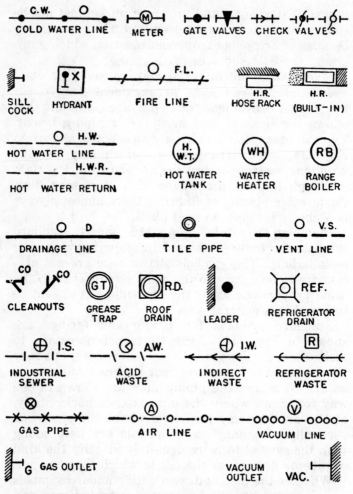

Fig. 117.—Standard Symbols for Lines and Fittings.

The actual length to which pieces of pipe are cut will depend on allowances for threaded ends entering the fittings, which calls for a cut length somewhat greater than the developed length measured on the plans.

The drawings must show exactly how the piping is to be run in order to meet the connections at the various fixtures, and must show the direction in which threaded openings are to be turned.

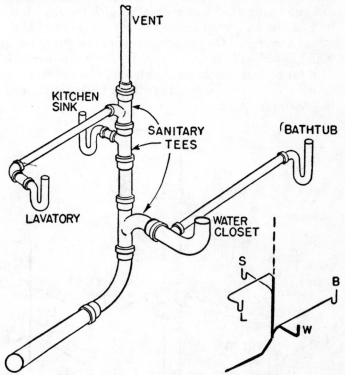

FIG. 118.—Drainage for One-story House.

Venting Arrangements.—Single-story houses designed for occupancy by only one family allow the simplest plumbing installations, chiefly because the fixtures in such places usually may be so arranged as to require little or no extra piping used solely for the purpose of venting. In most other building types more or less vent piping is needed, and in many cases the correct arrangement of vents becomes one of the chief problems.

Fig. 118 shows the drainage piping for a one-family one-story house. The bathroom connections are shown on the near side of the soil stack; lavatory at the left, water closet in the center, and bathtub at the right. On the other side of the partition in which is the soil stack is the drain for a kitchen sink. The large soil stack terminates at the tee for the lavatory drain. Above this point is a vent pipe leading through the roof.

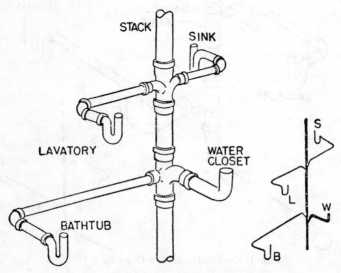

FIG. 119.—Connections for One-story House.

The small line diagram in Fig. 118 shows the same piping circuit as the larger, more complete drawing, and indicates the same locations for the drains and vent pipe. Line diagrams of this kind are employed in many of the following illustrations of piping arrangements.

Fig. 119 shows the drainage piping for another one-family one-story house having the same fixtures as used in Fig. 118, and shows also the corresponding line diagram. In any of these simple layouts the order of the several fixtures around the soil stack may be varied as required by the structural features

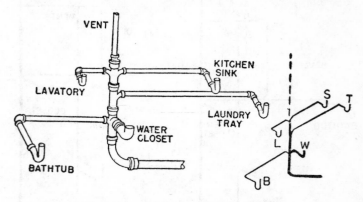

FIG. 120.—Adding a Laundry Tray.

of the building and by the desires of the occupants.

Still another drainage system for a one-family one-story house is shown in Fig. 120, where there is a drain for a laundry tray in addition to those for sink, lavatory, bathtub and water closet as shown in preceding diagrams. In Fig. 120 all the fixtures are on the near side of the stack, but either the laundry tray, the sink, or the bathroom group might be turned around the other direction, if necessary. The simple arrangements illustrated in Figs. 118, 119 and 120 give excellent service, with very little trouble, and are economical to install. Consequently they are favored wherever they may be used.

Single-family Two-story Layouts.—Figs. 121 to

128 inclusive are line diagrams for drainage and vent systems such as may be used in houses of two and three stories occupied by one family. Soil stacks and water closet connections are shown in heavy lines, other drainage piping in lighter solid lines, while vent connections which do not also carry wastes are shown in broken lines. These, in com-

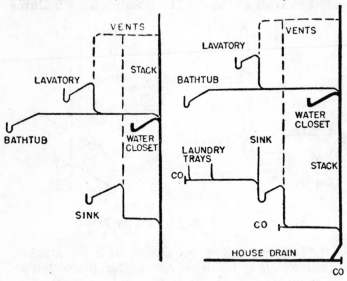

FIG. 121.—Two Stories with Bathroom and Kitchen.
FIG. 122.—Adding Laundry Trays on Main Floor.

mon with other layouts shown, will meet the code requirements in most localities, especially where rules and regulations have undergone rather recent revision.

Fig. 121 shows connections for a kitchen (sink) on the lower floor and a bathroom group on the upper floor. In Fig. 122 laundry trays have been added to the equipment on the lower floor, with the single bathroom group remaining above. Fig. 123 shows a layout for a lower floor washroom having a water closet and lavatory, a kitchen sink on the same floor, and a bathroom on the upper floor.

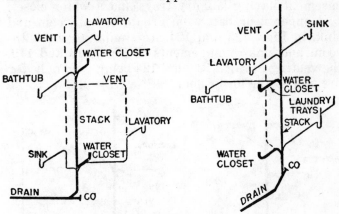

FIG. 123.—First Floor Washroom in Two-story House.
FIG. 124.—Basement Closet and Laundry.

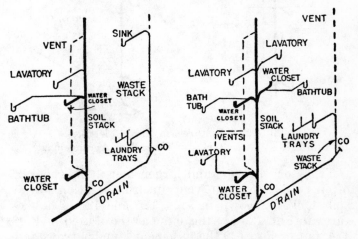

FIG. 125.—A Separate Waste Stack.
FIG. 126.—Two Bathrooms on Second Floor with Washroom in Basement.

Fig. 124 illustrates the drainage system for a one-story house with basement, having a bathroom group and kitchen sink on the main floor, and in the basement having laundry trays and a water closet. The upper floor bathroom group, or bathroom and sink, in Figs. 123 and 124 are similar to the bathroom and sink arrangements of Figs. 118 and 119, the venting in Figs. 123 and 124 being used only for fixtures on the lower floor.

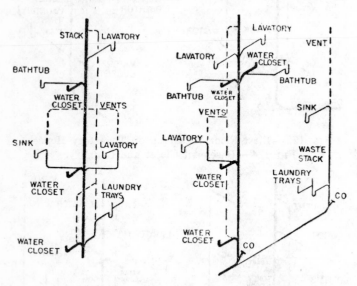

Fig. 127.—Fixtures on Three Floors.
Fig. 128.—Waste Stack for Three-floor Arrangement.

Two-story houses, and larger houses in general, often need a separate vent stack in addition to the soil stack, as shown in Figs. 125 and 126. The fixtures in Fig. 125 are the same as those used in Fig. 124, but in Fig. 125 the basement laundry trays and the main floor sink are connected to a waste stack that leads into the house drain.

Fig. 126 illustrates a system for a two-story house with two bathroom groups on the upper or main floor, and with a basement containing laundry trays, a water closet, and a lavatory. The laundry trays are handled with a separate waste stack. A kitchen sink may be added either on the soil stack or on the waste stack, whichever makes the better connection.

Figs. 127 and 128 show drainage systems for houses having fixtures on three levels, which ordinarily would be the basement and the first and second stories. With fixtures on three floors it becomes necessary to vent the branch wastes. However, it generally is possible to use group vents rather than individual vents for each fixture. In Fig. 127 the basement contains a water closet and laundry trays, the main floor next above contains a kitchen sink, also a washroom with water closet and lavatory, while the upper floor has a bathroom group.

In Fig. 128 the basement and main floor equipment is the same as in Fig. 127, while the upper floor has two bathroom groups. Here the basement laundry trays and the main floor kitchen sink are handled by means of a separate waste stack.

Two-story Apartments.—Figs. 129 to 133 inclusive illustrate drainage connections such as may be used in buildings having one apartment on the lower floor and another on the second floor. Fig. 129 shows the arrangements when each apartment has a bathroom group and a kitchen sink. Here the two sinks are connected to separate waste stacks. Instead of this arrangement, the sinks might be connected at the same point as the lavatories and into the same continuous drain and vent pipe should the arrangement of rooms allow it. The connections of Fig. 129 might be used for the two highest stories of any building.

Fig. 130 shows the drainage piping for a two-apartment building with each floor having a bathroom group and having a combination sink and

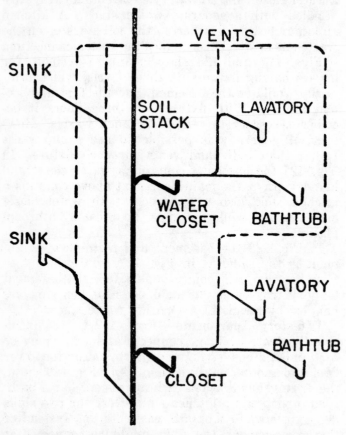

FIG. 129.—Drainage for Two-apartment Building.

laundry trays. Fig. 131 shows exactly the same fixtures, but with the combination sinks and trays connected to a separate vent stack instead of to the soil stack.

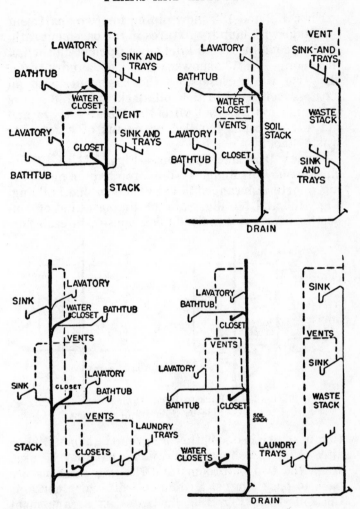

FIG. 130.—Two Apartments with Combination
Laundry-kitchen Equipment.
FIG. 131.—Waste Stack in Two-apartment Building.
FIG. 132.—Fixtures on Three Floor Levels.
FIG. 133.—Waste Stack for Three-floor Installation.

Figs. 132 and 133 show piping for two-apartment buildings with laundry fixtures in the basement rather than combined with kitchen equipment on the living floors. Fig. 132 shows two sets of laundry trays, also two water closets, in the basement, with all fixtures connected to the soil stack. Fig. 133 shows the same fixtures, but with the laundry trays and the kitchen sinks handled by means of a separate waste stack.

Duplex Drainage Systems.—Figs. 134 to 137 inclusive show drainage systems for two or more living quarters arranged side by side in one building. Figs. 134 and 135 illustrate the simplest kind of connections for two-family duplex houses, in each por-

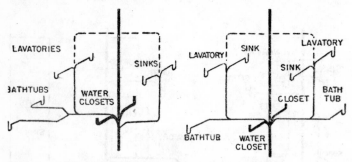

Fig. 134.—Back to Back Duplex Layout.
Fig. 135.—Side by Side Duplex Layout.

tion of which is one bathroom group and one kitchen sink. Fig. 134 shows connections that may be used when the two bathrooms and the two kitchens are back to back against a common wall which contains the soil stack. Fig. 135 illustrates an arrangement that may be used when bathrooms and kitchens are adjacent, but not back to back.

Figs. 136 and 137 show drainage systems that may be used for bathrooms which, on each floor, are on opposite sides of a common wall. If there are more

than two floors, as shown, the top floor connections
remain the same as in these diagrams, while lower
and intermediate floors are connected on additional
yoke-vented circuits. It may be seen in Figs. 136
and 137 that the lower floors in both cases have complete self-contained units connecting at the lower
left into the soil stack and at the upper right to the
vent line.

The connections of Fig. 135 may be used for
lower and intermediate floors with yoke venting as

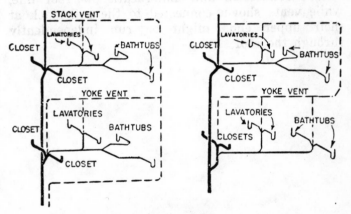

FIG. 136.—Four-apartment Layout.
FIG. 137.—Alternative Arrangement for Four Apartments.

shown in Figs. 136 and 137. Instead of the vent
running into the upper part of the soil stack as in
Fig. 135, it is connected into the yoke arrangement
of Fig. 137. The top floor connections will remain
as in Figs. 136 or 137.

The plans which have been shown for various
buildings and various arrangements of fixtures are
intended to illustrate the principles which should be
followed in laying out the waste and drain pipes, and
especially in laying out the venting system. Many

minor alterations may be made in order to suit the piping circuits to certain buildings. The direction that waste pipes take with reference to one another and to the soil or waste stack may be varied, as may also the lengths of the pipes so long as they conform to rules for slope, for diameter and total length, and for length between traps and vents.

Vent stacks which have been shown in the diagrams as extending independently through the roof might be run into the soil stack above the highest fixture connection and underneath the roof line, while vents shown connected to the soil stack at their upper ends might be run independently through the roof.

CHAPTER 16

ROUGHING-IN

Roughing-in is that portion of the work in a plumbing installation which brings the piping from the building or house sewer through to the floor lines and wall lines where connections are made to the fixtures. It includes the installation of all piping and fittings which will be concealed within the walls, under the floors, or in any unfinished spaces, including basements.

Every part of the roughing-in job must be done with the following in mind: There must be no future leakage of water nor of air from sewers and drains resulting from poorly made connections, from normal settlement of the building and ground, from ordinary vibration, from temperature changes during winter and summer, nor from freezing of unprotected piping. Furthermore, do not cut, notch or otherwise seriously weaken any joists, plates, studs or other structural members of the building unless the members are then suitably strengthened or braced so that they will carry their loads as well as when originally installed.

Roughing-in commences with installation of the house drain, from which the soil stack is carried upward through the building. Soil stack fittings are assembled so that the inlet hubs and threaded connections face in exactly the correct direction to receive the waste and drain pipes. To insure correct positions it is usually necessary to have a working plan or sketch whenever several lines will come to the stack. Water supply piping is assembled in the same general manner, with fittings correctly positioned for their connections.

Roughing-in tools for work in frame buildings include wood saws, chisels, bits and hammers. A 6-foot folding rule is used for measurements over short distances, while a steel tape is handy for longer lines. For running true lines it is advisable to have a carpenter's square, a straight edge, spirit level, and plumb bob with cord. For work on metal supports it is necessary to have a hack saw, cold chisels, twist drills and hand brace, and wire cutting pliers.

Fig. 138 illustrates common practice in running piping through walls of frame construction. The wide horizontal soles and partition caps above and below the joists are notched or cut away to allow passage of vertical pipes passing from floor to floor, while the vertical studs are notched for horizontal pipes running through the wall spaces. Horizontal pipes under the flooring, as for bathroom fixtures, are laid in notches cut in the joists.

In some cases it is possible to run the smaller pipes through holes, rather than notches, in the joists. If the holes can be made near the center of the joist, measuring from top to bottom, and if the diameter of the hole is no greater than one-fourth the depth of the joist, but little weakening results.

When a joist is notched it is weakened proportionately to the depth of the cut. That is, a 2x8 joist notched four inches deep has remaining strength equal only to a 2x4 piece, whereas were the notch only two inches deep the remaining portion of the joist would have as much strength as a 2x6. When a joist is cut deeply enough to materially weaken it, the load should be distributed to other members by inserting headers, adding joists, or reinforcing the ones that are cut.

The farther from its end supports a joist is notched the greater is the weakening effect. The joist is under compression on the upper edge and

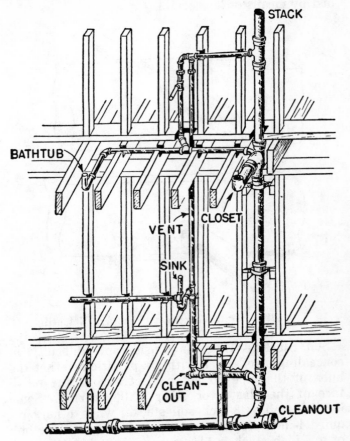

Fig. 138.—Roughing-in for Soil Stack and Drains.

under tension on the lower edge, consequently there is less danger from notches on top than on the bottom. Bottom notching allows the wood to tear apart. A top notch may be reinforced to take the compression strain by tightly fitting a block as shown in Fig. 139, while a bottom notch may be helped by fastening a steel plate or strap under the joist by means of lag screws.

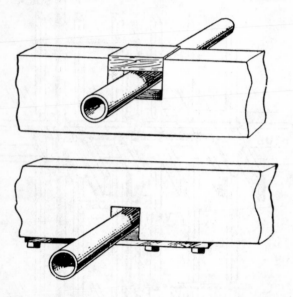

FIG. 139.—Reinforcing Joists That Are Notched.

Soil Stacks.—There is considerable difficulty in concealing a soil stack within a partition so that the hubs of the pipe do not project beyond the finish face of the plaster or other wall covering. Some localities allow 3-inch soil stacks, while others require 4-inch pipe even in small dwellings. The hub of a 3-inch stack is $5\frac{1}{8}$ inches in outside diameter, which is just the thickness of the ordinary partition made with 4-inch studs. To take even the 3-inch soil pipe the partition must be made with 6-inch studs or else the usual 2x4 studs must be furred out with 1x2 furring strips on both sides.

A 4-inch soil pipe has a hub $6\frac{1}{8}$ inches in outside diameter. This will go inside a partition built with 6-inch studs, or in one made with smaller studs which are furred out on both sides. Sometimes the soil stack may be so located that it passes through the wall for a closet or other place where the extension beyond the wall surface will not be objectionable. No matter how the stack is put in, no plaster or other wall finish should be allowed to touch the metal of the pipe, for with the settling that always occurs, the finish will become cracked.

The connection of a closet bend to the hub in the soil stack fitting sometimes causes difficulty in showing at the point where the wall and ceiling come together in a room below. This, and similar situations, must be given careful consideration before choosing the location for plumbing pipes and fixtures.

Pipe Supports.—Soil stacks use the heaviest pipe of any in a building, and in addition carry some of the weight of drains and wastes connected to the stack. Consequently, the stack must be well supported both at the bottom and in the vertical sections. Suitable supports for small buildings are shown in Fig. 138. Here the vertical portion of the stack is carried upon clamps made from steel straps bolted around the pipe just underneath the hubs and carried by strong cleats attached to the studs. Wrought iron clamps are available for the same type of support.

Horizontal piping not supported by structural parts of the building must be supported by steel straps, wrought iron hangers, or, in smaller sizes by wire hooks or by plumber's tape. Plumber's tape is shown toward the left on the horizontal soil pipe of Fig. 138, a position in which this kind of support ordinarily would be too light. Plumber's tape consists of a galvanized steel strip about $\frac{3}{4}$ inch wide, perforated to take $\frac{1}{4}$-inch bolts. Instead of using a strap passing completely around the pipe, as at the right on the horizontal soil pipe in Fig. 138, a galvanized steel ring may be placed around the pipe and bolted to the lower end of a single piece of flat steel whose upper end is fastened to some building member.

When pipes, pipe hangers, or fixtures are supported on masonry or concrete the fastening must be with some form of expansion bolt made entirely of metal rather than with a screw or nail driven into a wooden plug in the masonry or concrete.

Horizontal piping of cast iron should be supported at least every five feet, while wrought iron or steel pipe should be supported about every eight feet, and at least every ten feet of length. Long vertical lines of piping should be fastened to building members by means of wrought iron clamps such as shown on the vent pipe of Fig. 138 just under the tee for the kitchen sink drain pipe. When pipes pass through cinder concrete they should be coated with asphaltum or otherwise protected against corrosion on the outside.

All horizontal drainage piping should be run at a uniform slope of not less than $\frac{1}{4}$ inch per foot for sizes up to and including 2-inch diameter, not less than $\frac{1}{8}$ inch per foot for sizes of $2\frac{1}{2}$- to 4-inch diameter, and not less than $\frac{1}{16}$ inch per foot for sizes of 5- to 8-inch diameter.

Methods of making calked and cemented joints, also joints between pipes of different materials and sizes, have been explained in other parts of this book. Threaded pipe should be inspected to see that burrs have been removed and that the interior of the pipe is free from chips and other foreign matter before assembling. Holding each piece vertically while tapping it lightly will dislodge such particles.

The male thread, but only the male thread, usually is coated with some kind of commercial pipe paste or joint filler, or else with a paste made up with graphite and oil, litharge and glycerine, or red lead mixed with boiled linseed oil. After the joint is made up tight, the threads which remain exposed outside the fittings should be coated with red lead or with asphaltum to prevent the rusting which generally commences at this point.

Tools for assembling threaded pipe and fittings include pipe wrenches large enough to grip the largest pipe being handled, a pipe vise for holding parts pre-assembled before going into the lines, and monkey wrenches for handling unions and various kinds of fittings which provide flat gripping surfaces or projections.

Drainage lines must be made up with drainage fittings which have no internal recesses or ledges providing a lodging place for grease and other obstructions to flow. There must be no obstruction in the direction of flow in any drainage pipe, nor should there be any enlargements which provide a sort of settling chamber. Standard drainage fittings are not subject to any of these faults when made up tight so that the pipe thread enters the fitting to the correct depth.

CHAPTER 17

HOT WATER SUPPLY

All of the rules which apply to the installation of water supply pipes in general apply also to the piping which carries hot water from the service to water heaters, and from heaters to fixtures. Because the demand for hot water represents only part of the total demand, the hot-water branch from the service pipe or main distribution pipe to the heater and hot-water fixture branches ordinarily need have only about two-thirds as much capacity as the service pipe or main distribution line. However, when the service pipe is small, $\frac{1}{2}$ inch or $\frac{3}{4}$ inch, the hot water branch should be of the same size. When the service is 1 inch in diameter the hot-water branch usually may be $\frac{3}{4}$ inch, for a service $1\frac{1}{4}$ inches in diameter the hot-water branch may be 1 inch, for a $1\frac{1}{2}$-inch service the branch may be $1\frac{1}{4}$ inches, and so on. In no case should the supply pipe to a heater be smaller than $\frac{1}{2}$ inch size. The supply pipe running to the water heater or hot-water storage tank must have an accessible shut-off valve, which may be closed for repairs or when replacements are being made, but which must never be closed while heat is being applied, or may be applied, to the water.

In buildings having a water meter there often is a check valve which prevents hot water backing up into the meter in case pressure becomes excessive on the heater side. Then it is essential that the water heater or its piping have a relief valve which will release the pressure before the danger point is reached. A relief valve must be installed where no other valve comes between it and the water heater. Relief valves should be installed also when the sup-

200

ply side contains a pressure regulator or a pressure reducing valve such as often found when the pressure in street mains is greater than desirable in the building.

Pressure relief valves may be normally held closed either by a weight or a spring. Some valves are adjustable and may be set to release at pressures from 30 pounds per square inch up. Others are not adjustable. The usual setting for hot-water heaters is 125 pounds per square inch. Some of these valves have a fusible plug which melts and opens when the temperature reaches the boiling point for water, or a little above, regardless of the accompanying pressure. This plug would melt in case the relief valve should stick while the water is overheated.

When the flow is not impeded, hot water rises and colder water drops down to take its place. This is the force utilized to carry heated water to the tops of heater tanks from where it is drawn off to the hot-water pipes.

Pipes between a hot-water tank and heating coils or other heating devices outside the tank either should be level or else should have the tank end of the hot water side slightly higher than the heater end, and the tank end of the cold water side slightly lower than the heater end, thus assisting rapid circulation.

Coils of the pipe-bank style shown in Fig. 140, as often used in furnaces, must be set perfectly level when their pipes are parallel. Otherwise the circulation will be slow, and if there is much tilting at one end there may be steam pockets formed. Coils sloping steadily upward from the cold side to the hot side are preferable. Water backs, which are cast iron cavities mounted in cooking ranges, must be set perfectly level and set so that the hot water outlet is not below the highest point inside the cavity.

Hot water heaters and tanks should be located as close as possible to hot water risers in order to shorten the length of pipe through which hot water must flow to reach the fixtures. When hot water is drawn, all the cool water in the pipes must first flow out through the faucet. Then all the hot water remaining in the pipe cools off after the faucet is closed.

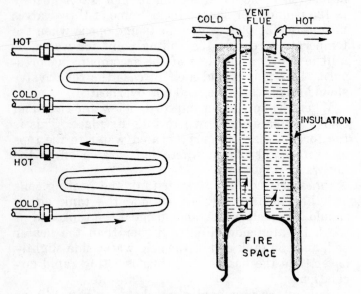

FIG. 140.—Pipe-bank Heating Coils.
FIG. 141.—Self-contained Heater and Tank.

Considerable savings in fuel costs may be made by covering long lines of hot water pipe with asbestos, magnesia, hair felt, wool felt, or any other good heat insulation. Standard practice in one case calls for coverings at least ¾ inch thick, protected with a waterproof jacket over which is pasted a canvas jacket and the whole held with brass bands with lacquered finish. The same specification requires that fittings in hot water pipes are to have a plastic covering containing not less than 50% magnesia, finished with a hard, smooth surface that comes flush with the pipe covering. Hot-water storage tanks should be insulated with similar materials, but the thicknesses should be from one to three inches.

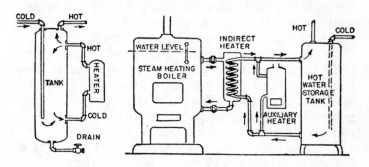

Fig. 142.—Water Circulation with Separate Heater.
Fig. 143.—Indirect Heater from Steam Boiler and
Auxiliary Heater Connected to a Single Hot Water Tank.

The principal parts of a heater with internal fire space are shown in Fig. 141. The cold water supply enters at the top and the pipe continues downward almost to the bottom of the tank. This prevents mixing of the entering cold water with the heated water which rises to the top of the tank.

A hot-water storage tank, with separate or external heater, is shown by Fig. 142. There are five threaded or tapped openings; one at the top for entering cold water, another at the top for hot water drawn off, two in the side for heater connections, and one at the bottom for a drain. The water connections have 1-inch pipe threads, into which may be screwed *boiler couplings* (a type of reducer) having a 1-inch male thread on one end and either a ¾- or ½-inch female thread on the other end to which the water pipes are connected. *Boiler elbows* may be used instead of the couplings. These elbows, a type of street elbow, have 1-inch male thread on one end and either ½- or ¾-inch female thread on the other. The cold water pipe may have a small hole through it just inside the point where it enters the tank. When the cold water supply pipes are drained, this hole will admit air and prevent siphoning water out of the tank below its level.

Heaters with automatic control of temperature have capacities as small as 15 gallons for single-family supplies, but generally are used in 20- or 30-gallon capacities. The capacity of a storage tank generally is figured at about seven gallons per person per day when water is heated to 150°.

Fig. 143 shows two heaters connected to a single hot-water storage tank. One heater, called an indirect heater, is attached to a steam heating boiler so that hot water from the upper part of the water space in this boiler flows to the upper end of the indirect heater, and so that cooler water from the bottom of the indirect heater flows back to the steam boiler as shown by arrows. Within the indirect heater is a coil of copper tubing connected to the hot water storage tank. In parallel with the coil in the indirect heater is an auxiliary heater, which may be run with gas, coal, oil or electricity. The connections of the coil in the indirect heater and of the auxiliary heater to the hot water tank are the same as in Fig. 142. Water is heated from the steam boiler while the building is being heated in cool weather, and by means of this auxiliary heater at other times.

CHAPTER 18

CARE OF PLUMBING SYSTEMS

Protection Against Freezing.—Piping which may be exposed to freezing temperatures under any conditions must be protected against such temperatures to prevent bursting. Some pipes are so located in unheated portions of the building, in exterior walls, or even outside the walls, that they must be covered with heat insulating material.

Indoor piping may be protected with various kinds of commercial coverings. A typical product consists of a layer of wool felt and one of hair felt in 3-foot lengths, split open on one side so that they may be slipped over the pipes. The covers are held in place as shown in Fig. 144 with wire, with straps of thin brass, or with tape. A quite effective covering may be made up by first wrapping the pipe with a layer of tar paper or building paper, then a layer of felt an inch or more thick, and covering the whole thing with a jacket of heavy fabric, such as canvas, which is treated with waterproof paint. An emergency covering may be made by winding the pipe with layers of cloth alternating with newspapers to make a total thickness of four or five inches. This covering may be wrapped with strips of burlap such as used for packing furniture.

When any of the coverings just described are to be used out of doors, they should have an extra outer protection of one or two layers of roofing paper held in place with copper wire or other non-rusting fastenings. Exposed pipes may be protected with a water-tight box of wood which is filled with excelsior, dry wood shavings, sawdust, or chopped straw. More effective protection for a given thickness is afforded by packing with mineral wool or other commercial insulation.

It should be remembered that water supply pipes filled with water will suffer more damage from freezing than will wastes and drains which are only partly full at most. Therefore, water pipes should be given careful attention. Copper tubing will expand without bursting when water freezes within it, but each time the tubing freezes its diameter will become permanently greater and if freezings continue the copper eventually will split.

When a building is to remain unoccupied in a climate where freezing weather may be expected the entire water supply and drainage system should be emptied of water. This includes all the pipes, all tanks, and all the fixture traps. So that the traps will continue their function of keeping sewer air out of the building they should be refilled with some anti-freeze solution. Anything suitable for use in automobile radiators for a given outdoor temperature is equally suitable for filling traps when the same temperatures are to be guarded against. Any of the glycol preparations are effective, as are also mixtures of glycerine and water, of alcohol and water, or of calcium chloride and water. Alcohol will evaporate from its mixture with water after a short time and leave the traps subject to freezing. Evaporation does not occur with glycerine or glycol solutions.

Traps fitted with cleanout plugs are easily drained by removing the plug. Those having no cleanouts may be emptied with a suction pump, by using a small hose attached to a bulb syringe, or by siphoning the water with a small rubber hose. To siphon a trap the hose is filled with water and both ends pinched closed while the hose is taken to the trap. One end must be inserted into the trap as soon as released and before the water runs out of the tubing. The other end then is held at a point as far as possible below the water in the trap and released, whereupon water from the trap will be drawn out through the tubing.

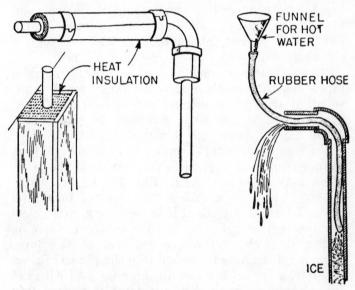

FIG. 144.—Protecting Pipes Against Freezing.
FIG. 145.—Thawing a Pipe with Hot Water.

Thawing Frozen Pipes.—The only way to thaw water frozen in a pipe is to apply heat, but there are many ways of applying the heat. A common method, but a dangerous one because of fire risk, is to play the flame from a blowtorch or even from a candle or burning paper on the outside of the pipe. A safer way is to wrap the pipe with cloths and pour boiling water upon them. An electric flat iron often may be used to advantage. Heat applied to a frozen pipe must be applied first at one or both ends of the section which is frozen. If applied at or near the middle of the frozen part, the expansion of melted and heated water against the remaining ice may burst the pipe. When thawing a water supply pipe, commence at the supply end and work toward the faucet, which should be kept open. When thawing a waste or drain, work from the sewer end toward the fixture. Boiling water poured into a fixture, or poured into a fixture drain through a cleanout, often will thaw a frozen drain pipe.

Chemical cleaners such as used for opening clogged pipes generate much heat when they reach water, so often will prove effective in opening a frozen drain or waste line when put into the pipe in the same manner as though it were being cleaned.

Frozen water supply pipes located where heat cannot readily be applied to the outside of the pipes often may be opened as in Fig. 145 by hot water poured in through a rubber hose inserted inside the pipe. To use this method it is necessary, after closing the service valve, to remove a faucet, valve or fitting that closes the exposed end of the pipe. Then a rubber hose is pushed into the pipe as far as possible, a funnel inserted in the hose, and with the funnel held up high, boiling water is poured into it. As water flows into the pipe through the hose, it will come out of the opening where the hose is entered and usually must be caught in a pail or otherwise to prevent damage.

The end of the flexible rubber hose often may be worked around one elbow by twisting and pushing, but to get farther it is necessary to remove some of the fittings and pipe lengths. As soon as water flows from the supply, the hose may be pulled out, but the service valve should be left open enough to maintain a small flow of water while parts are reassembled. If the flow is stopped immediately, the pipe is likely to freeze closed before entirely cleared of ice.

Even the most inaccessible pipes may be thawed with the electrical outfit pictured in Fig. 146 provided points may be reached on both sides of the frozen portion of the pipe. A pipe thawing transformer is attached to any alternating current electric outlet, such as a lamp socket. The ends of heavy cables from the transformer are clamped to the pipe on opposite sides of the frozen section, and the current turned on. The transformer takes relatively

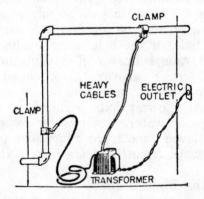

FIG. 146.—Pipe-thawing Transformer in Use.

small current at high voltage from the supply line, and sends a very large current at low voltage through the pipe. This large current produces heat in all parts of the pipe between the clamps. For a frozen underground pipe the cable clamps may be connected to the service pipe within a building and to the street valve. For pipes frozen within walls the cables may be attached at the service entrance and to an outlet in any room of the building, just as long as electric current is forced to flow through

the frozen section of the pipe between the cable
clamps.

Draining a Plumbing System. — The complete
plumbing system sometimes must be drained of all
water to prevent freezing, while at other times some
parts need draining while repairs or adjustments
are handled. To drain the water supply piping the
service valve is closed where the service pipe enters
the building. This valve may have its own handle, or
may require using a wrench. Many service valves,
or else the shut-off valve, have a drain hole through
which will run water from the building pipes when
the valve is closed against the supply pressure. All
the pipe water may be allowed to escape through
this drain hole, or the hole may be plugged while
most of the water is drawn off through the faucets.

With the service valve or shut-off closed, the highest faucet on the system should be opened to admit
air, while the lowest fixture faucet is opened to
allow escape of water. After water ceases to come
out of the lower faucet, the remainder may be allowed to escape from the drain hole in the shut-off
valve.

Unless the highest faucet is opened, or unless
the system is equipped with an automatic vacuum
breaker, the closing of the service valve and opening of a faucet near the bottom will cause formation
of a vacuum in the upper parts of the piping. This
vacuum may draw water into the supply piping
from water closets whose valves are operated by
movement of the seat, or by water pressure, also
from any fixtures having faucet openings below the
upper edge of their rim. Some plumbing systems
have a special air cock at the highest point. Opening
this cock prevents formation of a vacuum. Unless
the cock is closed before the pressure is again turned
on, the results are likely to be damaging.

For complete drainage, closet tanks and traps must be emptied. Closet tanks are emptied by flushing, and water remaining below the outlet is removed with a sponge or cloth. Water may be forced out of closet traps with a force pump, or most of it gotten out with a plunger cup such as used for removing obstructions. The remaining water may be removed with a sponge attached to the end of a wire.

Hot water tanks and water heaters may be emptied only after all fires are out. These tanks have a draining valve or plug at the bottom, and usually a cock in the opening near the top through which air may enter while the water flows out.

Steam heating and hot water heating systems are drained after all fires are out and fuel supplies shut off. With the service valve or main shut-off closed, boilers are drained by opening a special drain or draw-off cock at the lowest point. The water supply valve for the boiler should be opened, so that no water will remain in the pipe back of this valve. Steam radiators will drain when all the steam valves on the radiators are opened and when the air valves near the tops of the radiators are opened. Hot water heating radiators and piping should be emptied by opening the air valves first on the highest radiators. Then, as the water level falls, the air valves may be opened on radiators lower down in the system. If the lower valves are opened first, water will issue through them from the higher parts of the system.

When a heating system has been drained it is essential to attach to the furnace or boiler, and to all fuel supply valves and controls, large tags warning that no fires are to be lighted until the system is re-filled with water.

Clogged Drains and Traps.—When waste pipes from sinks, laundry trays, bathtubs and lavatories are correctly sized and correctly sloped, and when standard traps are installed, this part of the drainage system will not become clogged with grease, lint, hair, and such materials if correctly used. Most clogging results from particles of food, lint and hair which are allowed to collect on and in the strainers. Thus the rate of discharge is reduced to a sluggish flow which allows foreign matter to settle in the horizontal pipes rather than being swept on through.

Sink drains are least likely to clog with greasy deposits when the pipe from the trap to the vertical waste or drain is short and direct, and when this pipe is well washed by discharges from other fixtures back of the sink. When a back vent is connected close to the sink on the horizontal waste pipe, the flow of water through the pipe will be rather sluggish and will allow deposits of grease. Such a vent should be omitted if this does not conflict with local regulations.

Traps fitted with cleanout plugs are easily opened by taking out the plug, pulling grease and dirt through with a bent wire, and then flushing the trap with hot water allowed to flow into a pail before the plug is replaced.

Traps of all kinds, including those in water closets, often may be opened by using a rubber force cup such as illustrated in Fig. 147. The fixture should be partly filled with water, then the cup should be worked up and down while held over the outlet opening.

Water closet traps may be cleaned with a tool called a *closet auger* whose appearance and operation are illustrated in Fig. 147. The auger consists of a long coiled steel spring with a sharp hook on its lower end, mounted within a metal tube and attached to a crank handle. The overall length is from five to six feet. The end of the spring is inserted into the closet bowl and trap as shown, then the crank is turned. Such an auger will clear or pull out rags, pieces of paper, toilet articles and other solid matter, as well as garbage and other deposits. Similar augers, but with lighter or thinner wire coils, called *drain augers*, may be used in sinks, lavatories, bathtubs and similar fixtures where they will pass into and through the trap and on into the waste pipes.

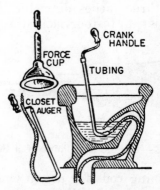

FIG. 147.—Tools for Opening Traps and Drains.

Cleaners for long waste pipes are made of coiled steel springs in outside diameters from $\frac{3}{16}$ to $\frac{5}{8}$ inch and in lengths from six to one hundred feet. These cleaners usually have a slightly enlarged part and an open twist or hook at the entering end. The cleaner spring coil passes through a hollow handle which is clamped near the hooked end when the spring is first inserted, then loosened and slid back to convenient positions as the cleaner is pushed into the drain being cleaned.

Sewer Rods.—House or building drains and sewers are cleaned or "rodded" with a sewer rod consisting of a long length of flat spring steel which is fed into the pipe while turned and twisted to clean the interior. The entering end is fitted with an oval or ball-shaped projection and a spear head such as illustrated in Fig. 148. A handle with an automatic grip or one locked with a screw is slid along the rod as it is pushed into the pipe. These spring steel rods may be had in widths of $\frac{1}{4}$ to $1\frac{1}{2}$ inches, thicknesses of $\frac{1}{16}$ to $\frac{1}{8}$ inch, and lengths from 25 to 100 feet. The quarter-inch width is suitable for pipes up to $1\frac{1}{2}$ inches in diameter, the half-inch width for pipes up to three inches diameter, and a $\frac{3}{4}$ inch width for pipes up to four-inch size.

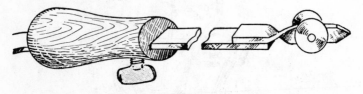

FIG. 148.—Handle and Point of a Sewer Rod.

Sewer cleaning rods for use in long lines of clay tile often are made with three- or four-foot sections of ash or hickory about one and one-half to two inches in diameter fitted with a hook on one end and a socket on the other end of each section. Cleaning tools such as shown in Fig. 149 are attached to the end of one rod, which is pushed into the sewer and another rod hooked on, proceeding thus for any length required. The rod and attached tool may be moved back and forth and twisted around as required to remove the obstructions.

Drain Pipe Solvents.—Caustic potash or potash lye (potassium hydroxide) is the chemical compound most often used for loosening deposits of grease and waste matter in drain pipes when the water commences to run away more slowly than usual. When caustic potash combines with fats the

result is a soft soap which easily flushes away with
either cold or hot water. The heat formed as the
potash reaches water helps to soften the greasy
deposits.

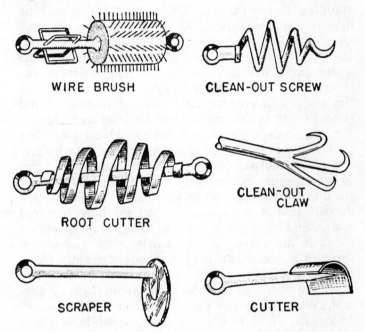

WIRE BRUSH   CLEAN-OUT SCREW

ROOT CUTTER

CLEAN-OUT
CLAW

SCRAPER   CUTTER

Fig. 149.—Sewer Cleaning Tools.

Deposits often may be softened by heating the
pipes from the outside with any of the methods
used for thawing ice. Unless the drain is completely closed, the caustic potash may well be pre-
ceded by a thorough flushing with boiling water or
the hottest water available. The potash should be
allowed to remain in the trap or drain for several
hours or overnight, then flushed out with hot water.
This chemical will not harm iron, steel, brass, copper or lead pipes, but it will damage aluminum,

porcelain and all enameled finishes, consequently must be kept away from such parts.

The caustic potash usually is poured into the drain or trap after having removed any excess water standing in the fixture. The chemical also may be dissolved at the rate of one pound to two or three quarts of hot water, and the solution poured into the clogged drain. When the potash is added to the water there will be much sputtering, which makes it imperative to keep hands, eyes and other parts of the body well covered to avoid serious burns and sores. Caustic soda should not be used as a cleaner for greasy deposits since it forms a hard soap that probably will make the clogging worse than before.

Scale Removal.—Scale and corrosion which form in water pipes will greatly reduce the rate of flow for a given pressure or pressure loss. There is more deposit in hot water pipes than in those for cold water, and in case a hot water pipe should be closed to such an extent as to nearly stop circulation through a heater, an explosion might result. Comparing a slightly caked ¾-inch pipe with a new pipe, the flow will be reduced to about 75% of normal. When badly caked and roughened the flow will be less than 50% of the original rate, while very bad caking and great roughness drops the flow to one-fourth the original amount. Scale formation is increased by some kinds of water and by methods of water softening which employ lime.

If both ends of a corroded and scaled pipe may be opened, much of the deposit may be removed by pulling a length of small chain back and forth through the opening. The chain may be passed through the pipe by attaching one end to a stiff steel wire. Instead of using a chain as long as the pipe, it is enough to use a foot or two with stout cord tied at each end, the pulling being done from the ends of the cords. A small, stiff, wire brush attached to a stiff handle may be effective if it can be gotten into the pipe far enough to reach the scale.

Limestone scale, such as formed by most waters, may be softened by soaking it with muriatic acid diluted with water. Other deposits, such as gypsum scale, are affected but little by this solution. One part of commercial muriatic acid should be diluted with from five to seven parts of water, the thicker the scale the stronger the solution. Using this mixture warm will make the action more energetic.

In iron or steel pipes the acid mixture may be allowed to remain over night, after which the pipes must be flushed with water running for some time in order to remove the softened scale and all remaining acid. The same solution will remove scale and rust deposits from water heating cavities, such as water backs, made of cast iron. To clean copper heating coils and brass connections the acid solution should be poured through the length of pipe into a basin, and this operation repeated until the deposit is softened and washed away. The parts then must be thoroughly flushed with plenty of hot water to remove the acid and remaining scale.

Cleaning Discolored Fixtures.—Fixtures such as closet bowls which have become discolored usually may be cleaned with any fine-grained cleaning powder, with a strong soap and water solution, or with kerosene on a cloth. Scouring soaps, acid preparations, salt, and gritty powders will roughen the surface and make it more than ever liable to catch and hold dirt.

Badly discolored bowls may be cleaned and freshened with sprinkling a small quantity of chemical drain cleaner or closet cleaner into the water, letting it stand for several hours, and then scrubbing with a brush or broom while the fixture is flushed.

CHAPTER 19

PLUMBING REPAIRS

Repairing Water Faucets.—When a compression faucet such as shown in Fig. 84 first commences to drip while closed, it may be repaired by merely replacing the disc washer with a new one. If the dripping is allowed to continue, the flow of water at high pressure between disc and seat will cut the seat and necessitate reaming or grinding. Disc washers may be flat, as in Fig. 84, or may be conical on the side which is to come against the seat. Flat washers may be replaced with conical ones, sometimes with good results, sometimes with poor. Washers most generally used have outside diameters of $\frac{1}{2}$, $\frac{9}{16}$, $\frac{5}{8}$ and $\frac{3}{4}$ inch. Leather and fibre washers are satisfactory for cold water, but composition materials generally last longer on the hot water side.

To replace the washer, water should be shut off from the faucet supply, the handle turned to open the faucet, and the cap nut unscrewed by means of a wrench while protected against marring by a piece of cloth. After the cap nut comes free, the threaded spindle may be turned upward out of the body to expose the washer. A screwdriver for removing the brass center screw must fit the screw head snugly, since these screws often stick. Tapping the screw head lightly, or applying a little light oil or kerosene will help to loosen it when stuck. A screw with damaged head or slot should be replaced with a new one. If the head breaks, the slot may be deepened with a hack saw to allow a new grip. With the screw removed the old washer may be lifted out with a knife tip, the new one put in place, and the screw securely tightened.

If the faucet leaks between the cap nut and spindle stem it may be that the cap nut needs turning down, but as a general rule the packing washer should be replaced. To replace this washer it is necessary to take off the cap nut, unscrew the spindle, and remove the handle from the top of the stem. A temporary repair may be made with a piece of valve stem packing, which is fabric cord impregnated with graphite and oil, or with candle wicking well oiled or covered with tallow. The cord or wicking may be wrapped around the stem and the cap nut replaced. This nut must not be screwed down so tight as to bind and possibly cut the stem. If thin brass or steel washers are used above or below the packing, these washers must be correctly replaced.

The top packing often may be replaced without shutting off water from the faucet. The spindle is turned down to close the faucet and the handle held in its closed position while its screw is removed. Then the cap nut is loosened, the handle removed and the cap nut taken off. The faucet is held closed by a small wrench on the top of the stem while the handle is off.

Dressing the Seat.—When the ground seat in a compression faucet has become pitted, grooved or notched, a new disc washer will last for only a short time before the faucet again develops a leak. In this case the seat should be dressed down true. One style of faucet seat dresser is shown in Fig. 150. This tool consists of a hand wheel attached to a spindle on which slides a threaded steel cone. Onto the bottom of the spindle is screwed a hardened steel cutter of a size suitable for the faucet. Below the cutter is screwed a brass guide which enters the flow opening in the faucet. The tool is inserted in the faucet and the threaded cone pressed down into the body opening and turned to the right, thus centering the spindle and cutter in the faucet. Using only moderate downward pressure, the handwheel is rotated to the right with the longest possible sweeps. When the tool turns smoothly the seat will be found smooth and true. Other tools doing practically the same work have different forms, such as a hollow inverted cone that fits over the outside of the faucet body.

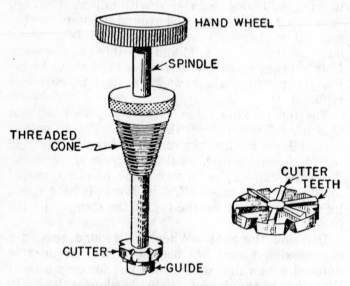

FIG. 150.—Faucet Seat Dresser.

To replace the ball in the Fuller faucet illustrated in Fig. 85 the water should be shut off and the main body of the faucet unscrewed from the part that fits the supply pipe. It may be necessary to hold the supply end with a wrench so that it won't unscrew from the piping. The stem nut now may be removed, releasing the brass cap and rubber ball from the stem. Put on a new ball no larger than the one originally used. Red rubber usually is used on hot water faucets and black on the cold water side. Parts are replaced by performing these operations in the reverse order. Leakage between the cap nut and stem of this faucet may be prevented in the same way as for the compression faucet.

If the plug sticks in a ground key stop cock or waste cock of Fig. 86 so that the handle cannot be turned, slightly loosen the nut at the small end of the plug and tap it lightly with a hammer. Leakage of these cocks often may be repaired by cleaning the plug and inside the body with very fine sandpaper, or even with a coarse cloth. If this remedy fails, the valve should be replaced with an entire new one, since the price hardly will pay for the work of regrinding. If a new cock is not available, the regrinding may be done by taking the cock apart, placing a little valve grinding compound on the plug, and rotating the plug back and forth in the body with very light pressure until the surfaces appear smooth when washed off with gasoline.

It may be mentioned that noises which occur when faucets are operated almost always are caused by loose parts in the faucet, even though the noise may travel through the water piping. The faucet should be opened and loose parts tightened.

Closet Flush Tank Repairs.—Parts required for replacement and repair of flush tanks such as pictured in Fig. 18 include the rubber ball stopper, leather washers to go under the rubber ball, brass or china seats on which the ball rests, and copper, brass, hard rubber or bakelite floats. These parts may be installed with no other tools than a small monkey wrench, screwdriver, and pair of pliers.

The rubber ball should be cleaned, which may cure any leaking. If the ball has lost its shape and no longer fits snugly into the cup-shaped seat, the

ball should be replaced. To replace the ball, close
the shut-off valve or hold the ball cock valve shut
by placing a support underneath the float. Then
take the ball off the bottom lift wire and put on the
new one. The ball seat should be examined and
cleaned. The seat metal may be dressed off with
emery or sand paper. The seat washer may be replaced, and also the seat itself if it is removable.

While the parts are being inspected the lift wires
and their slip joint should be checked. The wires
should be straight so that they slide easily and so
that the ball seats squarely. The lower wire and the
position of the ball over its seat may be adjusted
after loosening the wire guide.

If the float fails to rise with the water level it
will not close the ball cock tightly enough to completely stop flow of water into the tank. Sometimes
the fault is in a bent float rod rather than in the
float itself. The rod may be carefully bent back to
the correct shape. Bending the rod down prevents
water from rising so high in the tank, while bending it upward allows a higher water level before the
ball cock is closed. A leaky metal float may be
heated to drive out any water from the inside, then
soldered. However, the low cost of a new float makes
this hardly worth while.

The operation of one style of float and ball cock
mechanism is shown in Fig. 151. When the float
rises it raises the rod and lever. The lever, pivoted
at A, moves the link downward so that the cross bar,
pivoted at B, moves downward and presses upon
the plunger. Within the ball cock body is a seat
much like that in a compression faucet, and on the
lower end of the plunger are a disc and washer
which close the flow opening when the plunger is
pressed down. When the float drops, these motions
are reversed and the ball cock opens. To make re-

placement of the ball cock washer or to dress the seat in the valve, the cross arm is taken out after withdrawing a pin at either end. Then the cap nut around the plunger may be unscrewed, and the plunger with the valve washer removed. Details of these mechanisms vary, but nearly all the valves themselves are of the compression type.

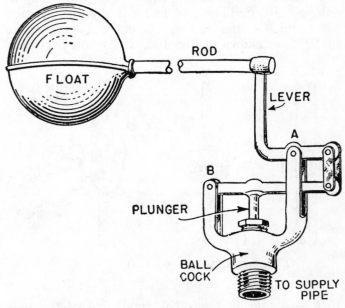

FIG. 151.—Float and Ball Cock Mechanism.

Troubles which cause continual leaking of pressure flush valves like the ones shown in Figs. 19 and 20 generally include dirt or sediment on the main or auxiliary valve seats, seats that are worn or pitted, lifeless rubber in diaphragms or washers, and clogged water or air passages. These small passages may be cleaned with a wire. Valve constructions differ, but with many of them the covers or caps may be unscrewed after the water is shut off, whereupon most of the assembly may be examined.

Repairing Leaks.—Various styles of repair plugs, washers and clamps are available for closing leaks in either pipes or tanks. When these parts are used according to the instructions which come with them the results will be satisfactory.

A hole in a tank having fairly thick walls may be enlarged by drilling and using a tapered reamer, after which a pipe plug may be entered and screwed up tight, as shown in Fig. 152. If the hole is reamed

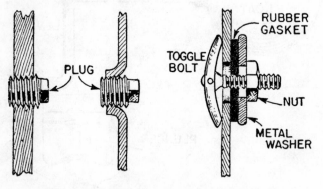

FIG. 152.—Repairs for Leaking Tanks.

to a size that just lets the small end of the plug enter, the plug usually will cut its own threads. It is safer to tap or thread the hole with a regular pipe tap of correct size. When a leak develops through thinner walls of a tank, the edges of the hole may be turned inward by carefully driving a tapered punch into the opening, then the hole closed by screwing in a pipe plug.

As shown also in Fig. 152, a hole may be closed with washers and gaskets held in place with a toggle bolt. The hole must be drilled, filed or reamed until large enough to pass the toggle through it. Then on the outer end of the bolt is placed a gasket of rubber or rubber-fabric composition through which the bolt must be a press fit to insure tightness. Outside the gasket is placed a steel washer held snugly with a nut as shown.

Attempts to calk a leak that occurs along the seam in a tank of ordinarily thin metal seldom are successful and usually make the leak worse, or else the metal is peened so thin that the joint soon opens up.

Cracks and small holes in iron or steel pipe often may be repaired by first shutting off the water pressure, then carefully cleaning the opening with some kind of scraping tool, and filling it with iron cement such as may be obtained from supply houses. The instructions which come with the cement must be followed exactly. Sometimes the cemented area is covered with a piece of sheet metal cut to size and held in place with a pipe clamp or heavy hose clamp. Cracks and small holes may be calked with lead after being cleaned out. The lead should be covered with a piece of sheet steel cut and formed to shape, and held with a strong clamp. Successful calking is more difficult than using the iron cement.

Leaks frequently develop around the threads where a pipe enters a fitting, this being the point at which corrosion first becomes noticeable in wrought iron and steel pipe. The leak sometimes may be stopped by tightening the joint with a pipe wrench, although in a line of assembled piping, tightening one joint will unscrew one adjacent unless there is a union which may be loosened. Furthermore, in the case of old piping, there is great danger of breaking the pipe and possibly the fitting. A repair may be made as shown in Fig. 153 where a piece of sheet brass or copper has been formed into a slightly tapered tube or collar around the pipe, then flanged over at the larger end which is toward the joint. Iron cement mixed to a stiff paste is packed around the threads, then the collar is pushed against the cement and held in place with a strong clamp as shown. If the threads are well cleaned where they enter the fitting, and the surrounding surface of the fitting is clean, this repair should hold.

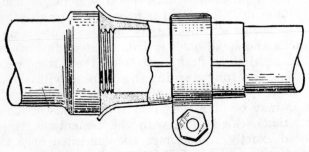

Fig. 153.—Repair for Leak at Threads.

A temporary repair of a hole or crack in piping may be made with a tight wrapping of several layers of electrician's rubber tape or else with a patch cut from an automobile inner tube. The rubber is held in place with a wrapping of friction tape, around which is placed a band or sleeve of sheet metal clamped tightly at one or two points with hose clamps. As with all pipe repairs, water pressure must be shut off and the pipe preferably allowed to drain before commencing the work.

Holes in cast iron pipe sometimes are closed by first drilling and reaming the opening, then tapping or threading it to take an ordinary iron or brass pipe plug. There is the danger that when a hole has developed, other parts of the pipe or the whole length may be so weak and thin that drilling and tapping will cause further breakage.

Cracks in laundry tubs and similar fixtures may be closed by cleaning and scraping the surfaces, then using a chisel-shaped stick or a knife blade to work the crack full of a thick paste made with powdered litharge mixed with a little glycerine. A paste of Portland cement and water may be used in the same manner.

CHAPTER 20

SEPTIC TANKS

A septic tank installation is a means for disposing of household sewage when there is no public sewer or other equivalent means for removing sewage from the property. The septic process consists of two distinct steps. First, the sewage is deposited in a septic tank and retained there until decomposed to the greatest possible extent by bacteria and fungi which reduce animal and vegetable matter to liquids. The liquids, called the effluent, flow from the septic tank to a filter bed or to a drainage field where they are oxidized by contact with air to form stable compounds which finally become odorless.

The principal parts of one simple type of installation are illustrated by Fig. 154. The house sewer empties into the septic tank. The heavier portions of sewage settle to form a sludge; grease and other light substances rise to form a scum, while relatively clear liquid remains in the space between. Bacteria of types which need no air or oxygen decompose or putrefy much of the sludge within a period of about 24 hours. Resulting gases agitate the tank contents and hasten the action.

The liquid effluent flows out of the septic tank through an outlet submerged to a depth that avoids scum at the top and sludge at the bottom. The effluent leaving the tank is foul and dangerous, oftentimes more so than the entering sewage, and must be led away from wells, springs and other water supplies until it reaches the portion of the installation where oxidation takes place.

In Fig. 154 the oxidizing process, often called the

filtration, occurs in the earth where the effluent is discharged through open-joint tile drains or through perforated drainage tile. With other types of installation the filtration takes place in specially prepared beds of broken stone, screened gravel, coarse sand or coke, retained by embankments or by ma-

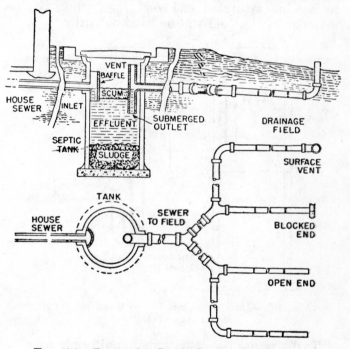

FIG. 154.—Parts of a Septic System Employing a Single Tank and a Drainage Field.

sonry enclosures. With any system there must be a tight-jointed sewer from the house to the septic tank and from the tank to the drainage field or filtration bed.

Siphon Discharge.—With the simple tank of Fig. 154 discharging directly to the sewer for the drain-

age field the flow into the field tiles will be at the
same rate as flow from the house sewer into the
tank. Since this rate is slow, at most only a few
gallons at a time, the discharged effluent will seep
away into the earth chiefly from the first few feet
of drainage tile. This portion of the field will tend
to become saturated and very foul, while the remainder of the field will be used but little.

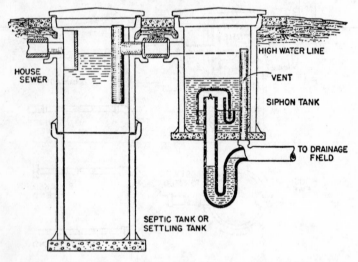

Fig. 155.—How a Siphon Is Used for Intermittent
Discharge of Effluent.

To distribute the effluent more uniformly over the
entire drainage area it is common practice to place
a siphon in a separate tank or separate compartment located between the septic tank proper, now
called the settling tank, and the sewer leading to
the drainage field. One such arrangement is illustrated in Fig. 155.

As liquid effluent passes slowly from the settling
tank into the siphon tank, the level of liquid grad-

ually rises in the siphon tank. The higher the liquid level the greater becomes the pressure on air
confined in space *A*, between the liquid in the siphon
tank and the liquid in the trap leading to the drainage field. The siphon is mounted at such a position
that when the liquid rises to the highwater line its
pressure or head displaces the air in space *A* and
flow commences through the siphon. Flow proceeds
rapidly until the tank level falls to the outer lower
edge of the siphon cap. The result is that there is
a sudden rush of nearly the entire contents of the
siphon tank through the sewer leading to the drainage field.

The total volume or capacity of the drainage tile
often is made approximately equal to that of one
discharge. Consequently, the entire drainage system is filled and there is escape of effluent liquid
into all parts of the earth. Then there follows a
long period before another discharge. During this
period oxygen in the air that penetrates the earth
or the filtration bed has a chance to act on the
effluent liquid, and much of the moisture dries away.
The vent in the siphon tank permits escape of liquid
should the siphon become clogged and fail to act
normally. There are various styles of siphons available for this purpose, some being suitable for installation in existing systems with only moderate
alterations.

Septic tanks without siphons frequently are used
where the sewage may not flow for considerable
periods, as at week-end or summer homes, also
where the slope of the drain tile is so steep as to
insure good distribution, or where the septic tank
may discharge into an already polluted stream or
into salt water. Two, or even three, septic tanks
sometimes are used in a series arrangement, with
one discharging into a following one and with all

of similar type, size, and construction. Otherwise the siphon system should be used in order to avoid creating a nuisance.

Septic Tank Design and Construction.—It should be noted that the action occurring in the septic tank itself is of a bacterial type that requires no air or oxygen. Consequently the septic tank need not have a vent, and never should have one if it is anywhere near dwellings.

The capacity of the septic tank below the high-water line or the level at which discharge occurs should be proportional to the volume of sewage per day. The septic action normally is satisfactory if the tank holds the volume for one ordinary day. Usually the capacity must be estimated in accordance with the number of persons served. Allowances vary from 25 to 50 gallons of sewage per person per day. For example, to serve a family of five, the capacity of the septic tank below the discharge level might be anything between 125 and 250 gallons. A gallon occupies 231 cubic inches, or 0.0134 cubic foot.

It is considered that a 12-hour period between siphon discharges is sufficient to keep the average open-tile drainage field in good condition. If the capacity of the settling tank is that required to hold sewage for 24 hours, the capacity of the siphon tank between highwater line and low level line then should be about half the capacity of the settling tank.

Tanks such as shown by Figs. 154 and 155 may be constructed with 24-inch diameter vitrified sewer pipe or may be bought ready-made in similar constructions. The bottoms are of 4-inch thick concrete. The inside of the bottom may be protected with a liberally thick coating of asphalt cement such as used for roofs. All joints must be made water-tight to prevent seepage into the surrounding earth.

Single septic tanks, also combined settling and siphon tanks, may be made of steel, brick, or concrete. A vertical section through a typical design of concrete tank is shown in Fig. 156. Depending on the capacity, vertical walls are usually made six to eight inches thick, with bottoms and tops four to six inches thick. Tops are of reinforced con-

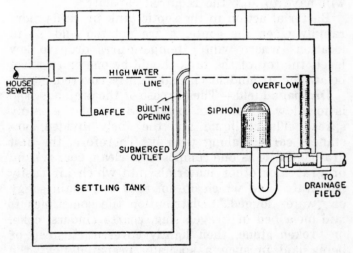

FIG. 156.—A Concrete Settling Tank and Siphon Tank Built as a Single Unit.

struction, with heavy gage wire mesh or with steel rods embedded in the concrete. The built-in connection shown between the settling tank and siphon tank is formed in the concrete wall by inserting any light-gage sheet metal pipe in the forms before the concrete is poured. Separate submerged outlets such a previously shown might be used instead of the built-in opening.

The depth of liquid to the highwater line in the

siphon tank depends on the type and size of siphon used, since it is the depth here that determines air pressure in the siphon and how the device acts. For a given capacity in the siphon tank, its length and width will have to satisfy the fixed depth to be used. Since the outer walls ordinarily are straight and continuous for the two tanks, the width of the settling tank will be the same as that of the siphon tank, so the depth and length of the settling tank will have to suit the required capacity.

Bacterial action in the septic tank proceeds more rapidly when the contents are not too cold, so in locations where winter temperatures drop to low levels the top of the tank should be one or two feet below the ground level, and tightly covered.

Drainage Field.—The purpose of the drainage field is to allow air and its oxygen to get at the thinly spread effluent liquid and the finely divided sub-stances carried along with it. Therefore, the best drainage field is one composed of clean, coarse sand or gravel or other materials into which air easily penetrates and which do not tend to remain soggy or "water logged." Distribution tile sometimes is laid on a bed of gravel, slag, coarse cinders, coke, or broken stone, then lightly covered. Instead of being laid in such a specially prepared field, the tile may be buried in any light soil that is porous for entrance of air, and well drained to avoid water logging.

Sunlight assists oxidation of the waste materials, so the drainage field should be free of trees or shrubs. The roots would tend to penetrate open joints or perforations of drainage tiles, and to cause clogging. The top cover may be protected from erosion and winds by growing any thick, coarse grass.

The drainage or distribution tile, which is perforated or which has open joints, should be buried no deeper than necessary for protection against frost in cold climates, or only enough to allow a couple of inches of top covering in warmer locations. The closer the drains are to the surface the more easily the discharge is reached by air. Before laying the tile the earth should be subsoiled, plowed or broken up, as deeply as possible to make it more porous.

The required total length of open-joint or perforated tile depends on the volume of effluent to be handled or on the total number of persons to be served, and on the character of the drainage field. In light, loose fields it is possible to have good distribution with relatively short lengths of larger tile, while for closer or more compact fields the necessary distribution area may be covered with greater length of smaller diameter tile. The following list is an approximation of common practice.

TYPE OF FIELD	FIELD AREA Sq. ft. per Person	TOTAL LENGTH OF TILE Feet per Person	
		3-in. Tile	4-in. Tile
Clean, coarse sand or gravel....	200	12	20
Light loam or fine sand..............	330	20	32
Fine sand with some loam or clay	500	30	50
Loam with some sand and clay	830	50	82
Clay with some sand or gravel	1350	80	136

For heavy clay and other soils into which air penetrates with difficulty the subsoiling or breaking up must be deeper than for any other types of field. In very close soil it usually is necessary to lay underdrains in some such relation to the drainage tile as indicated by Fig. 157. The underdrains are open-joint tile lines buried about twice as deep as the drainage tile and preferably midway between the drainage lines. The underdrain may lead to any

outlet at a still lower level, since the purpose is to
prevent saturation of the drainage area.

The open-joint or perforated drainage tile should
be laid with a gentle downward slope, say not more
than one foot in a hundred feet, to insure even distribution of liquid. The final 15 or 20 feet of each
line is preferably laid level or with a very slight

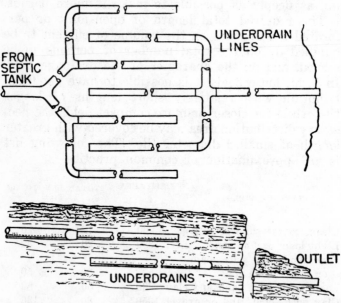

Fig. 157.—How Underdrains Are Used in Connection
with Drain Tile.

upward slope so that quantities of liquid won't collect in the ends. The ends of the tile lines may be
closed off flat with brick or a stone, but it is preferable to bring them above the surface as shown in
Fig. 154. This permits air to enter both ends of the
lines, promotes oxidation, and evaporates excess water more rapidly. Adjacent parallel runs of drainage tile should be at least six feet apart, but there

is no advantage in having more than ten feet of separation.

When the drainage field has a steep slope the lines of drain tile may be laid along the contours

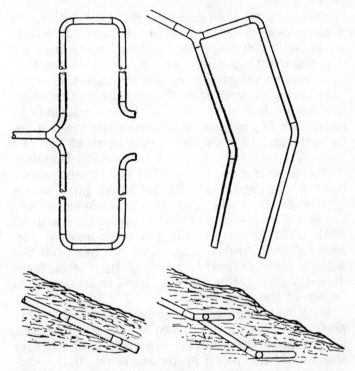

FIG. 158.—Layouts for Drainage Tile Lines on Steep Slopes.

according to some such plan as illustrated in Fig. 158. The slope of the open-joint or perforated tile then may be of the desirable small value, with the sharp drops in the connections between levels. The only requirement is that each portion of the field receive a proportionate quantity of liquid from each discharge. The fittings where tile lines diverge

should be of the V-branch type shown in the illustrations, so that the diversion is equal in both directions. With ordinary Y-branches nearly all the flow
will go through the straight leg and very little
into the side.

To insure freedom from dangerous pollution, the
first open-joint or perforated drainage tile should
be at least 300 feet from any well or spring that
supplies drinking water, and the slope of the land
must be downward toward the drainage tile.

In laying an open-joint tile line the first few tiles
are loosely butted together at their ends, and the
separation is gradually increased along the line until in the last 15 or 20 feet it may be about one-half
inch. The open joints must be protected against
dirt and other obstructions that may wash in from
the top. If the tile is vitrified sewer pipe, shown
by Fig. 80, the socket ends should be down hill and
the spigot ends centered with three or four wedges.
With plain cylindrical tile the joint may be sur-
rounded with broken stone and the top protected
with a piece of board, or short lengths of large
diameter clay gutter may be placed underneath and
on top of the open joints.

With tile made especially for drainage, having
perforations along the side to be laid at the bottom,
the joints between lengths are made with slip-over
sleeves and no special protection is required.

Sewer Lines.—The house sewer from the dwelling
to the septic tank usually is of 4-inch extra-heavy
cast iron soil pipe or else of 5-inch or 6-inch vitrified
sewer pipe. The joints must be made tight for the
whole length. The septic tank should be a minimum
of 50 feet, and preferably at least 100 feet from the
dwelling. The sewer should be buried deep enough
to protect it from frost. The minimum slope per
100 feet of run should be two feet for the 4-inch

pipe, one and one-half feet for 5-inch pipe, and one foot for 6-inch pipe.

Grease is probably the most frequent cause for clogging of the drain field tile and other parts of the system, so it is highly advisable to install a grease trap at the house end of the house sewer. Grease traps are described on page 43.

The sewer line from the septic tank to the drainage field tile should be of the same diameter as the house sewer, should have similar tight joints, and should have the same degree of minimum slope as the house sewer unless the instructions for siphon installation call for greater slopes.

Care of Septic Systems.—Relatively solid materials such as rags, heavy paper, and many kinds of garbage cannot be decomposed by septic action, so these things must not be allowed to get into the house sewer. Frequently the submerged outlet of the septic tank or settling tank is fitted with a wire screen of about one-quarter inch mesh to catch any substances that cannot be decomposed and to keep them out of the siphon or the drainage tile.

The sludge that accumulates in the bottom of the septic tank or settling tank must be removed about once a year or else it will pass through to the drainage field, clog the tile, and make it necessary to dig up and clean the whole filtration system. Sludge usually is removed by bailing or pumping. In locations where there is a nearby slope extending below the bottom of the tank it is possible to install a drain pipe from a valve placed in the tank bottom, then to drain and flush out the sludge through this outlet. The removed sludge is taken in barrels or tanks to a place where it may be buried with safety.

Scum that forms at the top of the liquid in the septic tank must be removed before it becomes so deep as possibly to go through the tank outlet.

CHAPTER 21

IRRIGATION PUMPING PLANTS

Three types of pumps are in general use for irrigation systems. They are the horizontal centrifugal, the vertical centrifugal, and the deep well turbine. At the left-hand side of Fig. 159 is a horizontal centrifugal pump, and in Fig. 160 is shown the internal construction of such a pump. Any centrifugal pump has a rotating impeller mounted inside a case, called the volute because of its shape. Fig. 159 shows an open type impeller and an enclosed type. The open impeller is used only where the water contains much trash, since the enclosed type is more efficient because of allowing less leakage between its sides and the volute.

A vertical centrifugal pump is generally similar to the horizontal type except that the shaft is vertical. The pump case is submerged in the water being lifted. The shaft extends upward to driving mechanism mounted on a rigid framework. The weight of the shaft and impeller is borne by a thrust bearing at the top of the shaft.

A deep well turbine consists of one or more centrifugal elements. The pump elements, with the discharge pipe and a central drive shaft, are joined together in a straight vertical assembly of small outside diameter. The impellers throw water outward, or outward and upward, into a surrounding bowl whose shape directs the water into passages leading to the outlet, or, in a multi-stage pump, to the center of the impeller next above.

Any type of centrifugal pump acts to create a partial vacuum, which means a pressure below that of surrounding air. Then the air pressure forces water into the pump where it is thrown outward into the volute or bowl and through the discharge opening by centrifugal force imparted by the whirling impeller. As a consequence of this action, no pump can lift water into itself from a vertical distance greater than that through which surrounding air pressure will lift the water when there is a vacuum in the pump. The distance of suction lift depends on atmospheric pressure, which is maximum at sea level

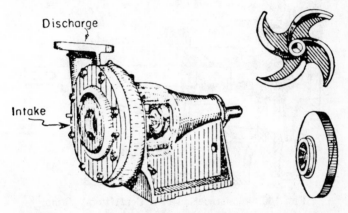

FIG. 159.—A Horizontal Centrifugal Pump. Open and Enclosed Impellers.

and which decreases with elevation above sea level. The practical lift at sea level is about 22 feet, and would decrease to about 17 feet lift at 5,000 feet above sea level.

Suction lift distance is no problem with vertical centrifugal pumps or with deep well turbines, for in these types the impellers and case are submerged. The deep well turbine, having the smallest outside dimensions, may easily be used for water which is at a level 50 feet or more below the ground surface, because it requires putting down a hole or a casing of diameter only great enough to receive the pump.

The vertical centrifugal pump requires a considerably larger opening, which costs more to put down, so is used where water level is not so far down as to require a deep well outfit.

The horizontal centrifugal pump, together with its driving motor or engine, takes up a great deal of horizontal area in comparison with the other types,

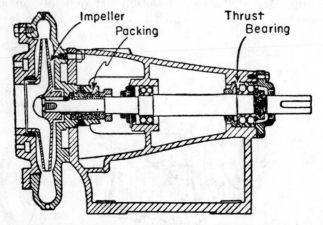

Fig. 160.—Construction of a Centrifugal Pump.

so ordinarily is used at the ground surface or in a shallow pit. The horizontal pump is not submerged, so the lowest level from which water is to be lifted into the pump may be no more than 20 feet below the pump itself. The horizontal pump is simple, efficient, and of relatively low first cost, so is used wherever the water level is not too low. The horizontal pump must be primed with water to start its action. The submerged types require no priming.

The height to which a given pump will lift water above its discharge opening depends on the impeller speed and on the power used. This height may be called the *head*, and the water delivery in gallons per minute called the *discharge*. For good operating efficiency a pump must be used with or near to the head and discharge rate for which it is designed. An increase of head will decrease the discharge, and it may take only a small increase of head to prevent pumping action. An increase of pump speed increases the discharge rate in direct proportion, it

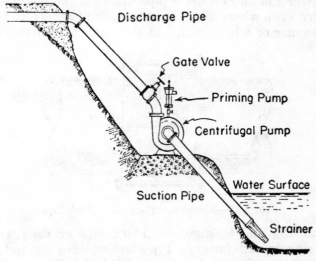

FIG. 161.—Connections and Piping for a Pump.

increases the head proportionately to the square of the speed, but the power required will increase as the cube of the speed.

The pumping plant must be located where the water is available. If water comes from a surface stream or pond, the pump should be near the edge and as near as possible to the high point of land to be irrigated. A pump so located is shown by Fig. 161. When an irrigation well is to be drilled, test borings are made and if water is available the pump is located near the highest elevation of land to be irrigated. This avoids long discharge pipes.

Piping on the suction side of the pump should be well casing or standard pipe with screw, flanged or welded joints. With welded joints a flange coupling is provided at the pump. Light weight riveted or welded pipe may rust out quickly. Almost any kinds of pipe and joints may be used for the discharge. Sewer tile and concrete pipe are used for low-pressure lines where there is no danger of severe water hammer or other shock, but these pipes are liable to

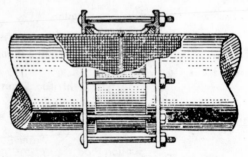

Fig. 162.—Sleeve Coupling for Steel Pipe.

cracking and leakage. Standard pipe or used well casing is satisfactory. Pipe sections are connected together with ordinary threaded couplings, with flanged joints, or they may be welded.

The most commonly used discharge pipe is light weight galvanized or black, with various types of patented slip joints or couplings. A sleeve coupling for all types of steel pipe is shown by Fig. 162. This coupling is somewhat flexible and allows for some bending. Flanged joints or unions are used where the pipe must be disconnected, as at the pump. Pipe which is not galvanized may be protected with asphalt paint or tar paint by dipping the pipe in a tank of the heated material. Added protection sometimes is given by wrappings of fabric or treated paper over the paint.

Pipe lines should have the fewest possible bends, fittings and sudden changes of direction, and should be as short as possible; thus reducing the load on the pump. This is especially true on the suction side. The suction line usually is made larger than the pump inlet. A valve such as shown in Fig. 161 should be of the gate type to reduce friction. The discharge pipe should rise no higher than absolutely necessary for the land to be irrigated, since greater rises mean more head against which the pump must work.

The accompanying table, *Discharge Pipe Capacity*, shows inside diameters of new, thin riveted steel pipe which have only reasonable losses of head. The losses are given in feet of equivalent water height per 100 feet of pipe.

DISCHARGE PIPE CAPACITY

Gals./Min. Maximum	Inside Diam.	Loss, Feet	Gals./Min. Maximum	Inside Diam.	Loss, Feet
50	3 in.	0.74	600	8	0.68
100	4 in.	.68	900	10	.50
200	5 in.	.84	1500	12	.53
300	6 in.	.74			

Power Units.—If the efficiency of the pumping plant is assumed to be 50 per cent the required horsepower may be found from the following formula:

$$HP = \frac{5.05 \times gals.\ per\ min. \times lift\ in\ feet}{10000}$$

Actually the efficiency should be better than 50 per cent. To find the horsepower required for higher efficiencies the power determined from the formula is multiplied by 50 and the result divided by the actual efficiency. For example, assuming 150 gallons per minute, a 15-foot lift, and 60 per cent efficiency, the horsepower is found from the formula to be

1.136. Multiplying this figure by 50 and dividing by 60 gives 0.947 as the required horsepower, so a 1-horsepower motor would be used.

Alternating-current electric motors are available with running speeds of 870, 1160, 1760 and 3475 revolutions per minute. Usually a motor of 1760 rpm is used, and the required pump speed is secured by suitable ratios of pulley diameters on a flat-belt or V-belt drive from motor to pump shaft. Single-phase motors ordinarily are used for loads of 5 horsepower or less, while polyphase squirrel cage motors are used for greater loads provided three-phase power is available for their operation. Motors may be equipped with a push-button starter, and always should have automatic overload and low voltage cutouts. Motors exposed out of doors should be of weatherproof types.

Internal combustion engines may be used where electric power is not available. These engines may be of types which burn gasoline, natural or mixed gas, kerosene, or, in oil engines and Diesels, the heavier grades of fuel oils. Diesel engines ordinarily are used only when running time will be about two hours per day and where long engine life is required. Engines in service are operated at speeds below the ones at which maximum power is delivered, so the expected output should be little more than half of the rated maximum. Most gasoline engines may be adapted to operate on natural gas. Automobile engines and tractor engines used for driving pumps must have provision for adequate cooling when operating with a maintained steady load for rather long periods.

Windmills sometimes are used when the required water flow is 50 gallons per minute or less, and when the total lift is not more than 50 feet. The discharge from a windmill pump varies about as the square of the wind velocity, consequently may be decidedly variable. The size of the mill and the dimensions of the pump cylinder must be chosen to suit the required discharge and the velocity of prevailing winds. For best results, there is provided a small reservoir into which the windmill may pump whenever it runs, and from which water is drawn for irrigation.

If pump speed and speed of a motor or engine are equal, the pump may be direct driven through a coupling. This is the most efficient drive. Unequal speeds are handled by belt drives. Flat belts require pulleys of liberal diameters and plenty of center-to-center distance between pulleys if slipping is to be avoided. V-belts are more efficient than flat belts and operate well with very little distance between pulley centers. Belt size, number of belts, and pulley diameters are chosen from recommendations of the manufacturer. Gear drives frequently are used for vertical centrifugal pumps and deep well turbines. Universal joints at the ends of the drive shaft permit some relative movement of pump and motor or engine.

CHAPTER 22

PRIVATE WATER SUPPLY SYSTEMS

In localities where no public water supply is available it is possible to install a private system operating automatically to furnish water in quantities and at pressures suited to all needs of homes and farms. A private system draws water from a local source which nearly always is a well, although a spring, lake, or running stream may be used. A motor-driven pump is automatically started to deliver water when needed, and stopped when the need is satisfied. The automatic control may cause

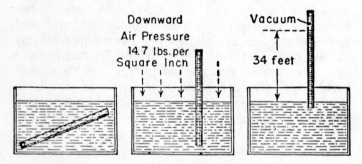

FIG. 163.—Air Pressure Causes Water to Rise in a Tube or Pipe.

the pump to run only while water is being drawn from a faucet or fixture, but it is more usual practice to provide a tank which retains enough water so that the pump need operate only a few times each day. Distribution piping for the building or buildings is connected to this tank just as such piping would be connected to a public supply.

Before considering the operation of various available pumps it is advisable to consider some of the

natural laws which limit and govern the action of
all pumps. Assume, as at the left in Fig. 163, that
there is a body of water in which is immersed a
tube about 40 feet long, open at one end and plugged
at the other. The tube will fill with water. When,
as at the center, the plugged end of the tube is
raised out of the body of water the raised end will
remain filled. Water is being pushed up into the
tube and held there by downward pressure of atmospheric air on the surface of surrounding water.

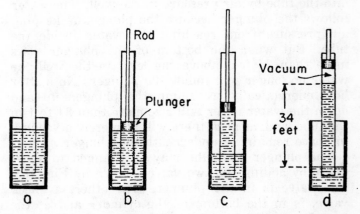

FIG. 164.—A Plunger Cannot Raise Water
More Than 34 Feet.

If the closed end of the tube is raised higher and
higher, with the open end still submerged as at the
right, water will continue to fill the tube until the
level inside the tube becomes 34 feet above the level
on the outside. Pressure of air at sea level is 14.7
pounds per square inch. A uniform column of water
covering one square inch at its base weighs 14.7
pounds when it is 34 feet high. The pressure of
air and the weight of water just balance each other.

Supposing now that the plug is removed and the
tube dipped into water in a well, as at a in Fig. 164.

Air pressure on water in the well is 14.7 pounds per square inch, and, since the top of the tube is open, air pressure on water inside the tube is likewise 14.7 pounds per square inch. With equal pressures the water level is the same inside and outside the tube. Next, as at *b*, we may place inside the tube a snug fitting plunger attached to a long rod. Pressure inside the tube now acts on the top of the plunger instead of directly on the water. If the plunger is raised, as at *c*, water will be pushed up into the tube by air pressure in the well. The water follows the plunger because the plunger is keeping air pressure from reaching the water inside the tube. But when the bottom of the plunger rises more than 34 feet above the level in the well the water no longer will follow the plunger. No matter how energetically we pump the plunger up and down the water never will rise more than 34 feet in the tube, and, as at *d*, there will be merely a vacuum in space remaining underneath the plunger.

The plunger and tube may be changed to a *lift pump* by adding the two valves shown by Fig. 165. One valve is in the plunger. The other, a check valve, is in the bottom of the cylinder and at the top of a pipe leading down into the well. When the plunger is raised the plunger valve drops closed and the check valve is opened by water being forced up from below by air pressure in the well. Water flows through the check valve into the cylinder. When the plunger moves downward the weight of water closes the check valve, pressure exerted by the plunger on the confined water opens the plunger valve, and water passes above the plunger. On the next upward movement of the plunger the water above it is lifted out of the discharge spout while more water comes into the cylinder from the well.

Were all of the atmospheric air pressure available

for lifting water during up-strokes of the plunger, the top of the pump cylinder could be as much as 34 feet above water in the well. But some of the air pressure is used to force water through the check valve, which is not an unimpeded opening, and more is used in overcoming friction of water moving

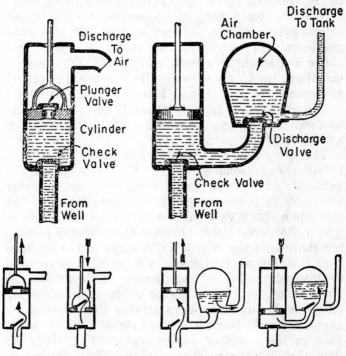

FIG. 165.—Principle of the Lift Pump.

FIG. 166.—Principle of the Force Pump.

through the piping, and still more might be used in getting water through a strainer fitted to the bottom of the well pipe to exclude foreign matter. All of these losses in pump, fittings and piping, plus slight leakage at the plunger and valves, reduce the

possible *suction lift* to about 22 feet from the bottom
of the pump cylinder to water in the well.

Any pump having a plunger working back and
forth inside a cylinder may be called a *reciprocating
pump*. If the cylinder of such a pump is more than
22 feet above the water level, as an average safe
figure, there can be no pumping because there won't
be enough atmospheric air pressure to raise water
to the cylinder. The 22-foot suction lift is a safe
maximum for elevations up to about 1,000 feet
above sea level. For each additional 1,000 feet of
elevation, up to about one mile, the maximum lift
is reduced by one foot. Thus, at 5,000 feet the
maximum lift will be only about 17 feet. All of this
assumes a pump in good condition, with tight valves
and close fitting plunger.

The lift pump of Fig. 165 will raise water only
to its open discharge spout. Fig. 166 shows the
principle of a *force pump* which will raise water
above its cylinder. There is no plunger valve, but
there is a check valve at the bottom of the cylinder
and a discharge valve between the cylinder and an
air chamber from which a discharge pipe runs to a
tank. Action of the force pump during upward and
downward strokes of the plunger is shown by the
small diagrams. When water is forced into the air
chamber during downward strokes the confined air
is compressed. During upward strokes the air pressure in the chamber forces water to continue its
flow through the discharge pipe. Thus the pulsa-
tions of flow are made less noticeable.

The bottom of the cylinder of the force pump
must be no higher above the water level in the well
than that of the lift pump, but the additional height
to which water may be forced depends entirely on
the mechanical power applied to the plunger during
down strokes and on the tightness of plunger and

valves. The total lift may be much greater than the suction lift.

A pumping outfit includes a cylinder within which is the plunger, and, in addition, some kind of driving unit for moving the plunger up and down. The drive unit may be nothing more than a pivoted handle as used on many yard pumps and household cistern pumps, or it may be a windmill, or a gasoline engine with suitable gearing. But for most automatic water systems the drive unit includes an electric motor with suitable belting or gearing, or both, between the motor and the plunger rod.

Types of Wells.—Fig. 167 shows several types of

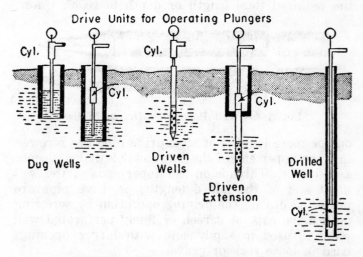

Drive Units for Operating Plungers

Cyl.   Cyl.   Cyl.   Cyl.

Dug Wells   Driven Wells   Cyl.   Drilled Well

Driven Extension   Cyl.

FIG. 167.—Wells Used for Private Water Supply Systems.

wells classified in accordance with the method of sinking them. At the extreme left is a well a foot or more in diameter dug through the soft upper soil and often through clay, shale, or loose gravel. The sides are lined with concrete, tile, or other masonry. The cylinder of the lift pump or force pump is at the ground surface, with a drop pipe extending down below the lowest water level. Since the lowest water level must be no more than 22 feet below the pump cylinder it is common practice, where water is 28 or 29 feet below the surface, to use a pump with its cylinder at the bottom of an extension pipe. This is shown by the second diagram. A rod for moving the plunger passes from the drive unit down through the extension pipe to the cylinder.

A driven well is sunk by forcing into the earth a piece of perforated steel tube two or three feet long, tipped with a sharp point. Such pieces, called *well points*, are illustrated in Fig. 168. To provide the required total length or depth to reach water,

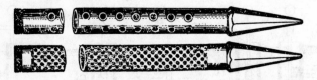

FIG. 168.—Well Points for Driven Wells.

one or more lengths of steel drive pipe are screwed into the upper end of the point as it is driven deeper and deeper. Threads on the upper ends of the well point and of the added lengths of drive pipe are protected during the driving operation by screwing on a drive cap. A screen or finely perforated well point is used in sandy soil, with larger openings used in loose rock or gravel.

When a dug well becomes dry due to dropping of the water table in surrounding earth a driven extension sometimes is used as shown in Fig. 167. Then the pump cylinder is placed near the bottom of the dug section and water may be raised from a level not more than 22 feet below this cylinder. Water from the cylinder is forced upward through a pipe within which is the plunger rod connected to the driving unit at the surface.

Wells which are dug or driven are classed as *shallow wells*. They reach only to the upper levels of ground water. Ground water is the great mass of water which has percolated downward and which saturates layers of sand, gravel, and porous rock lying above the much deeper solid rock which is impervious to water. This underlying rock, which is non-porous due to great pressure which has acted on it, supports the mass of ground water. The highest level of ground water is called the *water table*. The water table may be as high as the exposed ground surface or may be far below the surface.

When a dependable supply of ground water cannot be reached with a shallow well it becomes necessary to sink a drilled well as at the right in Fig. 167. Such wells are sunk by professional well drillers, and may go down hundreds of feet if necessary. The well is lined all the way down with a tubular casing which is two to five inches in diameter for most wells. This casing is furnished and installed by the driller.

Near the bottom of the well casing, and never more than 22 feet above the lowest water level, is placed the pump cylinder containing the plunger and valves. Extending upward from the cylinder, inside the casing, is a well pipe usually one to one and one-half inches in nominal diameter. Inside this well pipe is the rod connecting the plunger with the drive unit up above. The cylinder is preferably placed below the lowest water level. If above this level there is a suction pipe extending from the bottom of the cylinder to below the water level.

Drilled wells are classed as *deep wells*. Ordinarily they extend down through one or more layers of rock. The rock layers help exclude surface water which may be contaminated by drainage or sewage, and they filter water which does come down through them. Shallow wells are not thus protected. Water level in deep wells is little affected by seasonal variations of rainfall, and during dry seasons the supply is more dependable than from shallow wells. The top of the casing of a deep well always is capped to keep out foreign matter. Dug wells always should be provided with a well-fitted cover for the same purpose.

To insure that the pump cylinder will be within 22 feet of the lowest water level it is essential to accurately determine this level by inspection or expert advice. Seasonal changes of level must be allowed for. It is necessary also to allow for dropping of the level during periods in which pumping is proceeding at the maximum capacity of the pump.

Shallow-well Reciprocating Pump.—Fig. 169 shows typical construction of a power operated double-acting plunger or piston pump such as often used with shallow wells. The drive wheel, rotated by a belt from an electric motor, turns the eccentric to move the piston rod and piston back and forth. The crosshead and pitman rod change rotary motion of the drive wheel to lengthwise motion of the plunger. These drive parts are within a closed housing containing a supply of lubricating oil. Escape of oil around the plunger rod is prevented by a packing at the crosshead end of this rod. A packing gland around the piston rod where this rod enters the water chamber prevents leakage of water.

In the water end of the pump, toward the left, is the plunger which moves back and forth inside an open-ended cylinder. The left-hand end of this cylinder communicates with the suction valve and discharge valve at the left. The right-hand end

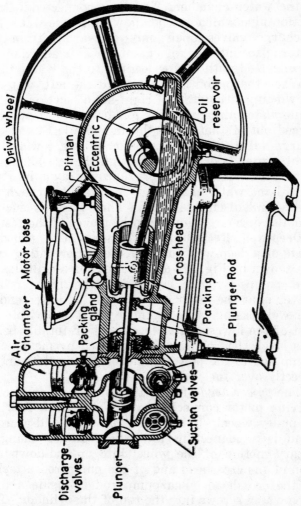

FIG. 169.—A Horizontal Reciprocating Pump
for Shallow Wells.

of the cylinder communicates with the two valves
at the right. The suction valves open only **inwardly**

to the water chamber. They are connected with a suction pipe which extends down into the well. The discharge valves open only outwardly from the water space into the air chamber. This air chamber is connected with a pipe leading to the water tank.

When the piston moves toward the left, water is drawn in through the right-hand suction valve, while water already in the left-hand water space is forced out of that space through the left-hand discharge valve. When the piston moves toward the right, water is drawn in through the left-hand suction valve while water previously drawn into the right-hand water chamber is forced out through the right-hand discharge valve. Thus there is suction and also discharge during both strokes of the piston.

Deep-well Reciprocating Pumps.—The principal parts of a deep-well pump of the reciprocating type are shown by Fig. 170 as installed for a drilled well. The pump cylinder containing the plunger and valves is at the lower end or near the lower end of the well casing. The cylinder must be within 22 feet of the lowest water level, and preferably below this level. The plunger is connected by means of a pump rod to the power head located at the surface directly over the well.

The *power head* of Fig. 170 consists of an electric driving motor connected by a V-belt to a flywheel or pulley wheel. Between the flywheel and a crosshead is a connecting rod which allows changing rotary motion of the wheel into up-and-down motion of the crosshead and of the pump rod attached to the crosshead. The pump rod is inside a drop pipe which screws into the top of the cylinder. This pipe extends upward to the pump discharge space of the power head, from which water is delivered to a tank. To prevent leakage of water a stuffing box is used around the rod connecting the crosshead and pump rod. This stuffing box may be much like the packing glands used around the stems of valves illustrated by Figs. 87 and 88 in an earlier chapter.

The simple style of power head shown in Fig. 170 would be suitable only for pumps of small capacity operating at high speed in strokes per minute. The high speed would result from the facts that speed reductions with V-belt drive cannot be more than six or eight to one, and that most electric motors of moderate price run at about 1,750 revolutions per minute. This combination would give a pumping speed of 200 to 300 strokes per minute. Pumps used in wells which are 50 to 300 feet deep usually are designed to operate at something like 50 to 100 strokes per minute. With a motor running at 1,750 revolutions per minute such pump speeds would require a speed reduction of 18 to 1 up to 36 to 1. Consequently, deep-well power heads usually contain various types of speed reducing gearing between the motor or pulley and the crosshead.

Typical constructions for cylinders with plungers and valves are shown by Fig. 171. A non-leaking fit between the outside of the plunger and the cylinder walls is insured by providing the plunger with from one to four cup-shaped members made of leather or other semi-flexible material and by making the inside of the cylinder very smooth. The cylinder usually is made of brass or of steel with a brass liner. Plunger valves and check valves which are flat or disc-shaped may be faced with leather, rubber, or other composition materials. Valve seats are of brass, bronze, or glass. All-metal ball-shaped valves are used in some pumps.

Valves in slow-speed shallow well pumps may close by their own weight assisted by downward pressure of water above the valve. Valves in the deep well cylinders of Fig. 171 are closed by these same forces, but closing is made to occur more quickly and with less backward leakage by small coiled springs. Such springs are shown on the bot-

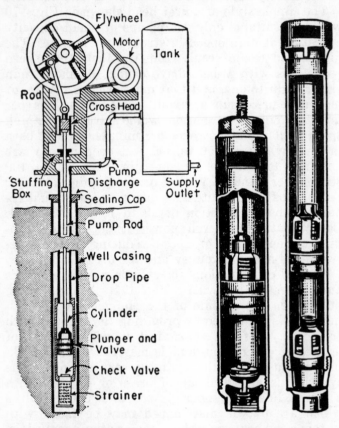

FIG. 170.—Principal Parts of a Deep-well Reciprocating Pump.

FIG. 171.—Closed and Open Cylinders for Deep-well Pumps.

tom of the check valve in the left-hand unit, and on the tops of all the other valves in both units.

The cylinder at the left in Fig. 171 is a *closed*

cylinder with the plunger rod extending upward through a guide hole at the top. Such cylinders are used with drop pipes whose diameter is less than that of the cylinder. To replace pump leathers or valve facings in a closed cylinder it is necessary to raise the entire cylinder out of the casing.

The cylinder at the right is an *open cylinder*. This type is used with drop pipe whose diameter is greater than that of the cylinder. To get at the plunger and check valve of an open cylinder the plunger first is pushed all the way down and turned until female threads on the bottom of the plunger engage male threads of an extension on top of the check valve housing. Then the pump rod is pulled up, bringing with it both the plunger and the check valve while the body of the cylinder remains in the casing. An installation of given capacity costs more with an open cylinder because of the larger diameter drop pipe and somewhat higher cost of the cylinder itself in comparison with a closed cylinder.

Sections of drop pipe and of pump rod are of equal lengths so that their couplings between sections will come at the same points, and may be screwed together at the same time during installation. The pump rod may be of small diameter galvanized steel pipe or else it may be of wooden sections having metal screw couplings on the ends. The wooden rod resists shock and corrosion better than the steel rod, consequently lasts longer, and the wooden rod operates more quietly inside the casing. Tendency of a steel pump rod to slap from side to side in the drop pipe may be lessened by using special couplings which have projections fitting rather closely inside the drop pipe while allowing free passage of water between these projections.

Fig. 172 shows how a *differential cylinder* may be used to make the work of the drive unit more uniform during up- and down-strokes of a reciprocating pump. Consider first the action of the pump cylinder alone, commencing with diagram *a*. The plunger is moving upward, with the plunger valve closed and the check valve open to allow filling the space below the plunger with water. At *b* the plunger is moving downward. The check valve has closed and the plunger valve has opened, allowing the trapped water to pass into the space above the

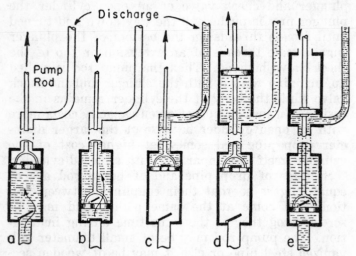

FIG. 172.—Operation of a Differential Cylinder.

plunger. At *c* there is another up-stroke. Water which was drawn into the cylinder at *a* now is being forced up through the discharge pipe by the rising plunger, while additional water is being drawn in underneath the plunger. Thus, during the up-strokes the pump is lifting water from cylinder to drive unit and is also raising water through the discharge—a double load. During down-strokes, as at *b*, no water is being raised and very little work is being done.

In diagram d there has been added at the upper end of the drop pipe a differential cylinder and plunger of the same capacity as the pump cylinder down below. The two plungers are fastened together and move up and down together. As the plunger in the differential cylinder rises it draws into this cylinder the water being elevated by the pump plunger; water which in diagram c was being forced through the discharge pipe. Water is being lifted only from pump cylinder to differential cylinder, where it is retained. This lessens the work during up-strokes.

At e, with both plungers again moving downward, water from the differential cylinder is being forced through the discharge pipe. This occurs because the pump cylinder and drop pipe are full of water drawn in during preceding strokes, and because the check valve is closed to prevent water from going downward. Now the work of forcing water through the discharge is handled during down-strokes, while raising water as far as the differential cylinder is done during up-strokes.

When the capacity or volume of the differential cylinder is equal to that of the pump cylinder we find that the work of raising water above the power head is handled only during down strokes. If the capacity of the differential cylinder is half that of the pump cylinder the discharge load will be equally divided between up- and down-strokes. Then the rate of discharge will be fairly steady.

The water handling capacity of any reciprocating pump may be found from this formula.

$$\begin{matrix} Gallons \\ per \\ hour \end{matrix} = \left(\frac{cylinder}{diameter} \right)^2 \times \begin{matrix} strokes \\ per \\ minute \end{matrix} \times \begin{matrix} length \\ of \\ stroke \end{matrix} \times 0.204$$

Diameter and length of stroke are measured in inches. As an example, assume a cylinder 2 inches in internal diameter with the plunger making a 5-inch stroke at the rate of 70 strokes per minute. The strokes are "pumping strokes" only, and with the usual single-acting pump would be only the up-strokes.

$$\frac{\text{Gallons}}{\text{per hr.}} = (2)^2 \times 70 \times 5 \times 0.204 = 285.6$$

This formula assumes the ideal conditions of no leakage past the plunger or the valves, when closed, and instant closing of the valves. Actually the capacity of a pump in average good condition will be about $\frac{9}{10}$ of the computed value. Using a factor of 0.18 instead of 0.204 will give average capacities.

Centrifugal Pumps.—Centrifugal pumps are illustrated in Figs. 159 and 160 of an earlier chapter, and are described in connection with those figures. Simple pumps of this type are not in common use for domestic water systems. Types having closed impellers may have about the same suction lift as reciprocating pumps, 22 feet, but open impeller types have maximum suction lifts of only 15 to 16 feet. In the simple centrifugal pump there are no valves to retain water. Consequently, when such a pump is used above the water level all of the water runs back into the well as soon as the pump stops, and it is necessary to prime the pump before it will again operate. Some centrifugal pumps are constructed with check valves to obviate the need for priming every time they are started. Others have water traps on the casing to retain enough water to start pumping after an idle period.

If a centrifugal pump is operated at constant speed but with different suction lifts the capacity in gallons per hour decreases as the lift becomes higher. If a given centrifugal pump is used with different total heads (suction lift plus discharge pressure) it will be found that the capacity decreases only slightly as the head is increased up to some certain value, but thereafter falls off more and more rapidly with still greater heads, and eventually becomes zero.

Rotary Pumps.—The construction principle of the rotary pump or gear pump is illustrated by Fig. 173. The shaft of the driving gear is connected exter-

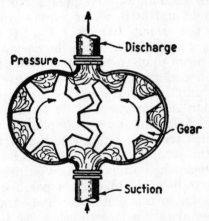

FIG. 173.—A Rotary Gear Pump.

nally to the motor. This gear meshes with a driven gear inside the pump housing. The housing fits closely around the outer ends of the gear teeth, and also against the flat sides of the two gears. As the two gears rotate in directions shown by arrows they draw water from the suction opening into the spaces between teeth, and carry this water around to the discharge side. Since the gears mesh closely in the center of the housing it is impossible for water to pass back to the inlet side, and it is forced out of the discharge opening. Rotary pumps are in common use for general utility work around country homes and farms, often being portable, but seldom are employed for domestic water supply systems.

Rotary pumps are capable of handling suction lifts up to 20 or 22 feet, and of providing a pressure head of 60 to 80 pounds on the discharge side. Rotary pumps provide positive suction and a positive discharge pressure. Their capacity is little affected by changes of discharge load, or by changes of suction head when the limit in feet is not exceeded.

Deep-well Jet Pumps.—Jet pumps are in common use for home and farm water supply systems with well depths to about 100 feet. Fig. 174 shows a deep-well jet unit lowered into the casing until this unit is no more than 15 to 20 feet above the lowest water level, and preferably is below this level.

The jet unit includes a nozzle through which is forced water at a pressure of 20 to 30 pounds per square inch. This water is supplied through the pressure pipe from a pump above the surface. Surrounding the jet is a doubly tapered tube called the *Venturi tube*. The bottom of the Venturi communicates with well water through a passage and pipe running down to the foot valve and strainer unit. The strainer always is located below the water level. The foot valve is a check valve which retains water to or above the Venturi while the pump is not operating.

When water or any other fluid is forced through the contracted throat of a Venturi at high velocity there is a lowering of pressure at this point. The drop of pressure allows atmospheric air pressure in the well to force water up from strainer to Venturi. This water then is forced on upward by the powerful jet which mixes with water coming up from the well. In the enlarged upper end of the Venturi the water slows down, but the pressure increases. That is, the force which gives velocity or speed changes to the force which we call pressure.

The greater the pressure in the pressure pipe and nozzle, and the greater the resulting velocity from the nozzle, the more water can be raised in proportion to the quantity coming through the pressure pipe, or the higher the water can be driven above the Venturi. In a typical system with supply pipe pressure four times as great as the pressure against which water is raised there will be one extra gallon raised for each gallon supplied. If supply pressure becomes nine times the pressure against which water is raised there will be two extra gallons for each gallon supplied.

Water at high pressure for the jet usually is supplied by an arrangement such as illustrated by Fig. 175, where are shown the upper ends of the pipes through which water comes up from the Venturi and goes down to the nozzle. The pump which supplies pressure here is a centrifugal type with its impeller mounted directly on the motor shaft.

The pipe from the Venturi leads to the center of the impeller, which allows water to be drawn into the pump from this pipe. Part of the water thrown from the outer ends of the impeller blades goes through the discharge pipe to the tank, but the remainder of this water goes back through the pressure pipe to the jet. The centrifugal pump supplies all of the force for lifting water from the well and raising it to the tank. Part of the force developed by this pump is utilized in the jet for bringing water up to the pump. Other types of pumps, including the reciprocating type, may be used to supply jet pressure. The rate of pumping may be varied by adjusting the rate of water flow or pressure supplied to the pressure pipe and jet.

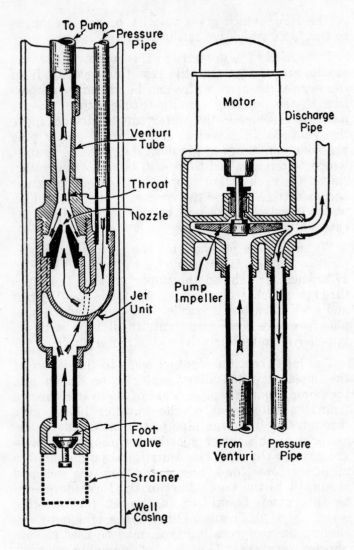

FIG. 174.—Jet Unit of a Deep-well Jet Pump.

FIG. 175.—Centrifugal Pump Used with a Deep-well Jet Unit

The pumping capacity in gallons per hour of a deep-well jet pump decreases when there is an increase of the distance from the centrifugal pump unit down to the water level. For example, a given combination of motor, centrifugal pump, and jet unit might handle 1,500 gallons per hour with the pump 20 feet above water. The same outfit would handle about 1,150 gallons per hour at 40 feet above water level, 750 gallons at 60 feet, 500 gallons at 80 feet, and 300 gallons at 100 feet between centrifugal pump and water level in the well. Capacity decreases also with increase of discharge pressure or with increase of height to which water is raised above the motor and pump unit.

Shallow-well Jet Pump.—Fig. 176 shows a combination of jet and centrifugal pump in a single unit as used for shallow wells in which the lowest water level is no more than 22 feet below the pump unit. Instead of the suction pipe from the well going directly to the center of the pump impeller, as with a simple centrifugal pump, the passage from this pipe is carried around outside of the jet and through the Venturi tube, thence to the pump impeller. Part of the water thrown off from the impeller blades goes through the discharge pipe to the tank, while the remainder goes back through the nozzle and Venturi tube. Whereas a simple centrifugal pump would have a suction lift no greater than 15 to 16 feet, the centrifugal-jet combination will handle suction lifts as great as 22 feet.

The pumping capacity of the shallow well centrifugal-jet pump decreases quite rapidly with increase of suction lift. A typical pump capable of handling 500 gallons per hour with 5-foot suction lift will pump 430 gallons with a 10-foot lift, 360 gallons with a 15-foot lift, and only 300 gallons per hour with a 20-foot lift. As with all jet pumps, the capacity decreases also with greater heights to which water is raised above the pump, or with increase of discharge head.

The shallow well jet pump requires only a single well pipe and so may be used for dug wells or driven wells pictured by Fig. 167. The deep-well jet pump, with two pipes leading to the jet unit, requires a

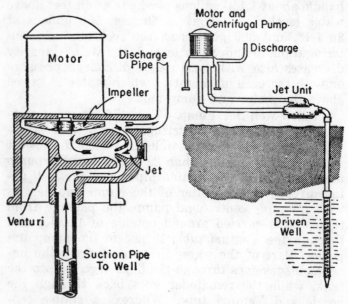

FIG. 176.—Jet Pump for a Shallow Well.

FIG. 177.—Double-pipe Jet Used with Single-pipe Well.

well casing of 3-inch to 5-inch diameter, according to pump size or capacity.

A double-pipe type of jet pump sometimes is used with a single-pipe well in some such manner as shown by Fig. 177. The jet unit is placed at the top of the well pipe, and the single well pipe is connected to the jet intake. The pressure pipe and the pipe between the jet and centrifugal pump are run entirely above the ground surface and outside of the well.

Pressure Tanks.—Most automatic water supply systems are equipped with air-tight tanks having capacities of from 12 to 100 gallons of water, with a 42-gallon size being in general use. Fig. 178 shows such a *pressure tank* and control which starts and stops the pump motor in accordance with changes of pressure in water and air inside the tank and connected piping.

In the automatic switch unit is a flexible diaphragm exposed to water pressure which acts against tension of a coiled spring. Decrease of pressure allows the spring to move the diaphragm and an attached arm downward. The arm engages a pivoted lever carrying one of a pair of switch contacts, with the second contact mounted in a stationary position. Downward movement of the arm moves the lever to close the contacts and start the motor.

In the upper part of the pressure tank is trapped a considerable volume of air. When the motor runs the pump to force additional water into the tank this trapped air is compressed to increase its pressure. Increase of pressure in the air and on water inside the tank is transmitted to the diaphragm of the automatic switch, and raises the diaphragm against spring pressure. Sufficient pressure raises the diaphragm and arm enough to separate the switch contacts and stop operation of motor and pump. The automatic switch usually is adjusted to start the motor and pump when tank pressure drops to 20 pounds per square inch, and to stop the pump when pressure has been raised to 40 pounds. Actual construction of the automatic switch is not so simple as shown by the diagram, which shows only the principle.

When any tank is originally full of air at atmospheric pressure this air will be compressed to about 20 pounds per square inch when the tank is pumped somewhat more than half full of water, and to 40 pounds when somewhat less than three-fourths full. The quantity of water which may be withdrawn

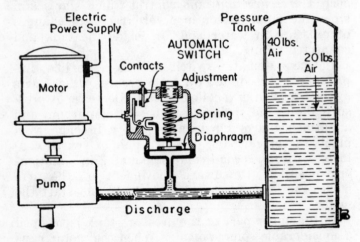

Fig. 178.—Automatic Switch Used in Connection with a Pressure Tank.

from a tank between the two pressures of 40 and 20 pounds per square inch will be about ⅙ of the total tank capacity. With a 42-gallon tank about seven gallons of water may be used before pressure drops from 40 to 20 pounds, and before the motor and pump are started to again bring the pressure back to 40 pounds.

Air in the pressure tank is gradually absorbed by water passing through the tank. Unless absorbed air is replaced there will not be enough in the tank to compress and expand, and smaller quantities of water may be withdrawn between periods of pump operation. The system is said to be water-logged.

Air may be replaced by emptying the tank of water, which lets it fill with air at atmospheric pressure, then pumping in a normal supply of water. A small hand-operated air pump sometimes is used. It is more satisfactory to automatically maintain the necessary quantity of air by means of any of numerous devices.

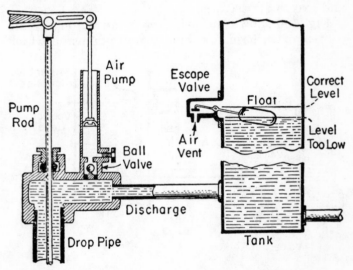

FIG. 179.—Pressure Control by Means of an Air Pump and Escape Valve.

In the power head of most deep well reciprocating pumps there is an extra air pump such as shown by Fig. 179. The air pump plunger moves up and down with the pump rod. During each down stroke a small quantity of air is forced into the discharge passage and to the tank. Somewhat more air than needed for replacement is thus forced into the tank. The excess is allowed to escape through some type of automatic valve. One method is shown in Fig. 179, where an air vent is uncovered by dropping of a hollow metal float which rests on the surface of water in the tank. With water at the correct level the float is high enough to keep the vent closed. This correct level is that at which water should stand when pressure drops to 20 pounds per square inch. When too much air has been pumped into the tank the water level drops, the float opens the vent, and excess air escapes.

Fig. 180 shows the principle of an automatic air control often used for shallow well pumps on which

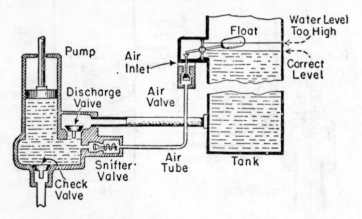

FIG. 180.—Pressure Control by Means of a Float Valve and Snifter Valve.

there is no auxiliary air pump. The correct water level shown in the diagram is that to which water should rise for maximum pressure, usually 40 pounds. If there is not enough air in the tank the water will rise too high and will lift a float whose arm passes through a flexible water-tight diaphragm to the stem of the air valve. Upward movement of the float presses the valve stem down and opens the valve so that air may come in through the inlet opening and go to the air tube. The air tube leads to a snifter valve connected to the bottom of the cylinder in the water pump. When the pump plunger rises it produces a lowering of pressure or a suction which allows the snifter valve to open and admit air which comes through the air tube, valve, and inlet so long as the float and the water level remain too high. This air mixes with water in the discharge and thus passes into the tank. When enough air has been added to drop the water level to the correct point the float valve closes and remains closed until more air is needed.

Water Requirements.—Following are usual allowances for water consumption, as used in determining the required pumping capacity.

	GALS. PER DAY
Each person; bath, closet, cooking, laundry, etc.	35 to 40
Chickens, per 100	10 to 12
Cows (milk), each	25 to 30
Cows (dry), or steers, each	10 to 12
Hogs, each	2
Horses, each	10 to 15
Sheep, each	2

Having computed the probable total gallons per day by adding together all the requirements it is next in order to decide on how many hours per day the pump is to operate. A common figure is 4 hours per day. Then the total number of gallons per day is divided by the number of hours of pumping per day. The result is the required pump capacity in gallons per hour. This capacity must not be less than the peak demand, which usually occurs around mealtimes or first thing in the morning. As much as one-third of the total daily requirement may be used within an hour, which means that the pump capacity in gallons per hour should be no less than

⅓ of the daily gallons under such conditions. Lawn or garden sprinkling with a ½-inch hose requires a pumping capacity of 200 gallons per hour, and with a ¾-inch hose requires 300 gallons per hour.

Pump Location.—When choosing a location for the pump it is well to keep in mind the following points. The suction line of a shallow well system should be as short and straight as possible. Ample protection should be provided against freezing. The pump should be kept easily accessible for oiling and repairing. Good drainage for excess water should be provided. Allowance should be made for ventilation because excess moisture may cause motor trouble and stretching of drive belts. Dirt and rubbish should be kept out. The pump should be located high enough that flood water will not rise above it. The pump should be placed where it will be least affected in case of fire. The pump should be elevated above the floor level on a rigid base. The pressure tank should be raised enough to permit air circulation over the entire bottom of the tank.

Installation of a shallow well pump or a jet pump in a dry, well ventilated basement with a gravity drain to the ground surface is satisfactory. A long suction line from well to basement sometimes is a limiting factor, although this may be offset to some extent by the fact that the pump usually is three or four feet lower than ground level, if it is on the basement floor, and this provides some advantage for the suction lift. Either kind of pump may be mounted on wall brackets if floor space is limited.

A level concrete block six to twelve inches high is desirable for mounting both the pump and the tank. This height permits easy oil drainage, the pump may be repaired without too much difficulty, and the whole assembly is not likely to be reached by scrub water or debris which may collect near it. A deep well pump cannot be satisfactorily installed in a basement because the distance between floor and ceiling is not enough to allow removal of the drop pipe.

A basement extension may be used for any type of pump, but is particularly well adapted to deep well systems. The extension usually is about six feet square and about six feet deep. The floor should be of concrete and the walls of concrete or any other material impervious to water. The top may be concrete if provision is made for a covered hatch opening immediately over the drop pipe. It is possible also to use a removable sloping wooden platform over the entire extension. The whole platform may be set to one side for removal of the pump or drop pipe.

Unless the extension is completely walled off from the basement there will be enough ventilation without any special provisions. If there is a separating wall, openings several inches in diameter should be near the top and near the bottom to permit air movement. Drainage usually is directly into the basement. The pump should be mounted on a concrete base. The pressure tank may be in either the extension or the main part of the basement.

Pumps quite often are placed in pits, which have the advantages of eliminating an extra building or an extension, and of giving adequate protection against freezing. Pits dimensions must be suited to sizes of pump and tank, with ample room for easy access during installation and for repair work. Additional room may be provided for a larger pump which may be needed later on. Pits usually are five to eight feet square and about six feet deep.

Most pits are of poured concrete, which forms a solid floor and walls. A few have concrete floor with

walls of tile or concrete blocks, stone, or brick. The
walls should be watertight. The floor should slope
to a drain. Walls should rise a few inches above
surrounding ground level to keep out surface water.
The floor drain preferably opens into a tile line leading to some point of ground surface which is below
the pit floor level. Otherwise the drain may open
into a sump below the floor level, filled with gravel
or other coarse stone that will permit escape of
water. A sump may be used only where the ground
is loose enough to take water, and where the water
table remains well below the pit floor level.

A pit may be ventilated by means of two pipes
passing through the roof or cover. One should extend nearly to the floor of the pit and the other only
a short ways below the pit roof. Downspout or other
large diameter piping may be used. The pump should
be on a concrete base slightly elevated above the pit
floor. The well casing should extend a few inches
above the floor.

For installation of a deep well piston pump a pit
sometimes is provided to place the discharge head
and all the water connections at a point below the
frost level, with the pump head mounted above
ground in a small shelter house. This allows easy
access to the pump head and the driving motor or
engine. A pit of this type sometimes is constructed
as a basement extension.

Pit installation of the complete pump mechanism
often is undesirable because there is little or no
drainage. Water wasted from the pump and
gathered from seepage through walls and floor may
rise to the level of the well casing and get into the
well. There is difficulty also in keeping out surface
water, dirt, and rodents. Ventilation often is unsatisfactory. There is more likelihood of neglecting

a pump installation which is in a pit than one more easily accessible.

A completely separate pump house is desirable for many reasons. Although a good pump house has advantages over a good pit, there is little difference in cost. The pump house is easily ventilated, it can be well drained, the pump is easily accessible for maintenance and repair, and the well is easily protected from entrance of surface water.

Possibly the chief disadvantage of a pump house is the danger of freezing in localities which experience low winter temperatures. In such places the entire pump house must be of tight construction. Thermal insulation may be required for walls and roof. Details of construction and protection depend entirely on climate of the region where the installation is made.

Wherever possible the pressure tank should be set close to the pump. A pump installed in a basement or a basement extension usually presents no problem, for nearly always there is ample room for the tank. The tank may be set with the pump in a pit or in an insulated pump house. This arrangement has the advantage of helping maintain temperature above freezing since water in the tank is periodically replaced with comparatively warm water from the well. If, however, the tank capacity is 80 gallons or more, it would be necessary to provide a relatively deep pit or large pump house. This problem may be overcome by burying a horizontal tank in the ground adjacent to a basement or a pit, so that one end of the tank extends through the wall. To this exposed end may be connected the pressure gage, air regulator, and pressure switch.

Soil around a tank tends to promote corrosion of the metal, even though the tank is galvanized. Application of a thick coat of hot asphalt or of some good preservative paint before placing the tank in position will retard corrosive action and lengthen the life of the tank.

The suction line for a shallow well system always should be installed level or with a slope draining toward the well. Any high point in the piping, with lower sections on both sides, will trap enough air to limit or completely stop the water flow. Air traps should be avoided also in the discharge line. When the piping is correctly installed the slopes will be such that the entire system may be drained should this be necessary to prevent freezing.

CHAPTER 23

SWIMMING POOLS

In a swimming pool, whether public or private, the water should be circulated and filtered, purified and clarified with various chemical treatments, occasionally drained, refilled and controlled as to water level. All this requires a variety of piping, valves and connections as well as tanks and certain mechanical equipment.

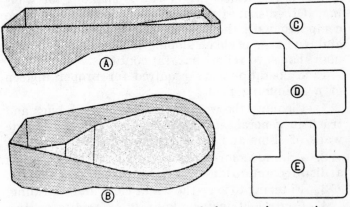

Fig. 181.—Outdoor swimming pool shapes and proportions.

The pool itself may be constructed of any of a rather wide choice of materials. Among the more common are reinforced concrete poured in place, also welded or riveted steel or aluminum plates for the entire pool or else for the sides when there is a concrete bottom. Other popular constructions include fibreglass sides with a concrete bottom, concrete or Gunite sprayed onto forms with a gun, and precast concrete sections or blocks.

Pools most often are rectangular in surface outline, as at *A* of Fig. 181. Water depth in the wading section may range from about 3 to 5 feet, with a gradually sloping bottom. This section may comprise as much as 80 per cent of total pool area. At the deep end of the pool water depth may be 8 to 10 feet when a diving board one meter high is provided, 9 to 12 feet for a three-meter board, and 12 to 16 feet or more for high diving.

Because it is desirable to have much greater wading space than that for diving, pools may be of fan shape as at *B* of Fig. 181, or of some modification as at *C*. The wider, larger end is shallow, for wading, Other shapes which allow shallow areas large compared with the diving section are shown at *D* and *E*. Large pools on sloping land may be of irregular shapes to follow natural contours.

Five operations are required for proper upkeep of a swimming pool.

1. Cleaning the water surface of leaves, bugs and trash in general, also cleaning the bottom and side walls of slime and sediment.

2. Adding chlorine or bromine to the water as a disinfectant to destroy harmful bacteria.

3. Filtering to keep the water clear and sparkling.

4. Control of water alkalinity or acidity to prevent irritation of eyes and mucous membranes of bathers, also to help in chemical treatments of the water.

5. Algae reduction to prevent either clouding (turbidity) or a greenish cast in the water.

Cleaning.—Cleaning may be done by hand. Floating debris of all kinds is removed with skimmers having long handles on one end of which is an aluminum frame carrying a screen or open bag of fibreglass mesh, plastic mesh or of perforated bronze. A rake, somewhat similarly constructed, may be used to drag the bottom of the pool. Walls and bottom may be cleaned with a wire brush or with a nylon bristle brush on a long handle. This work is done also with common highway brushes 18 to 24 inches wide, with long handles and with weights at the brush ends to hold them in contact with pool lining surfaces.

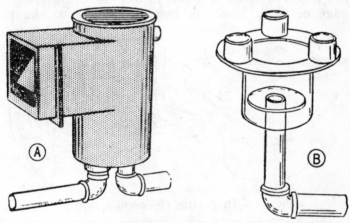

FIG. 182.—Automátic skimmers.

In a pool having water recirculated by a pump, which usually is part of the filter system, the surface may be kept free of floating trash with an automatic skimmer. Two styles are illustrated by Fig. 182. The type at A is built into the wall of the pool. Surface water and floating objects flow over the hinged weir in the opening at the left. This weir adjusts itself when water level changes by as much as four inches. Water thus removed goes to the circulating or filter pump while floating objects are caught by a perforated basket inside the skimmer body. An automatic relief valve connected to a point below normal water level in the pool prevents an air lock in the pump should water cease flowing over the weir.

The automatic skimmer at *B* has a lucite member which rises and falls on the central disc with changes of water level. This skimmer is connected to a suction or vacuum line.

Water Fittings. —Public pools in most localities are required to have, a few inches below the upper edge or walk level, an overflow gutter or skum

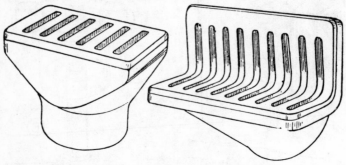

Fig. 183.—Drain fittings for overflow gutters.

gutter. Daily, or whenever excessive film or debris collects on the surface of pool water, the level is raised to cause overflow into the gutter for 10 to 15 minutes.

Floating objects or films thus are carried into the gutter and remain there for collection while overflow water is carried away through suitable drains, A drain fitting for the bottom of gutters is at the left in Fig. 183. At the right is an angle drain whose vertical openings allow escape of water even when the bottom ones are clogged. Gutters require a complete drainage system, including traps and vents to satisfy plumbing codes of the locality.

Recirculated water and make-up water are admitted to the pool through inlet fittings placed at intervals as close as 8 to 10 feet at the ends or at ends and sides. One such fitting is illustrated in Fig. 184. These inlets are submerged in the pool water, being 10 to 15 inches below the level at which the pool overflows. The center plate of an inlet fitting may be adjusted, by rotation, to regulate the

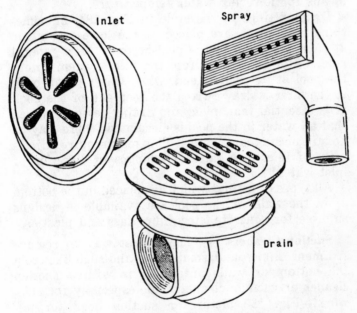

Fig. 184.—Fittings for recirculated pool water.

rate or the velocity of water flow. If not adjustable, each inlet is provided with its individual valve in connected piping.

No cross connection is allowed between a pool with its piping system and a city or other public water supply, regardless of check valves or other protective devices. Such connections and their possible effects are explained elsewhere in this book.

To avoid a cross connection, make-up water for maintaining pool level or water for filling may be drawn from a public supply into an open tank, then taken from this tank into the pool system.

Spray fittings, of which one style is shown in Fig. 184, are used to aerate pool water. During very hot weather the sprays may be operated all night as a means for lowering water temperature.

Drain fittings of the style in Fig. 184, or something equivalent, are placed at the lowest point or at each low point in the pool bottom. As a general rule, water returning from the filter system enters the pool at its shallow end, while water going back to the filter is drawn from the deep end of the pool. It is essential that inlets and drains be so arranged that all water in the pool is circulated; there may be no still or stagnant water. This may require adjustment of inlet flow rates or changes in direction of inlet water.

All types of fittings which are placed in the bottom or in the walls of the pool are available in designs suitable for concrete, steel, fibreglass and plastic.

Suction Cleaners. — The easiest way to remove sediment, slime, sand, small twigs and such like from the bottom or walls of a pool is with a suction cleaner or vacuum cleaner made especially for such work. Fig. 185 pictures a suction head for immersion in pool water and a portable centrifugal pump driven by an electric motor, all mounted on a carriage which is brought to the edge of the pool.

Suction or vacuum heads range from 7 to 24 inches wide. They rest on two or three wheels and have an adjustable brush, usually with nylon bristles, which remains in contact with the pool bottom or walls. The suction hose, of rubber or plastic, is kept from dragging and stirring up sediment by supporting the hose in water by attaching to it a suitable number of hollow floats.

Discharge water from a portable pump may go to lawns, a storm sewer or to a dry well. Pumps are available with gasoline engine drive instead of an electric motor. The pump of Fig. 185 is equipped with a strainer to catch hair, lint and other things which would clog or cause excessive wear in the pump.

Fig. 185.—A suction pump and a cleaner head for use on pool bottoms and sides.

Instead of depending on a portable pump, many pools are provided with wall fittings connected to the regular filter pump or possibly to a separate pump which provides suction. In either case there is a suction pipe line which connects to special fittings placed in walls of the pool about 8 inches below the normal surface level of the water. The hose connected to a suction or vacuum head is arranged to couple into these suction fittings.

Some pools are too wide for a suction cleaner

operated from the walk on either side to reach the center, or there may be obstructions in the way. For such conditions there are cleaners designed for use by two operators on opposite sides of the pool, one guiding the suction head by its long handle while the other pulls the head across the pool bottom. Another way is for a single operator to use a diving suit while working in deep water.

Lost hairpins, which may cause rust stains on the bottom of the pool, may be removed with a small permanent magnet on a cord attached to a fishing pole. Otherwise the hairpins may be brushed to one spot and picked out.

Sand and Gravel Filters.—The operating principle of a filter employing sand and gravel for removal of water impurities is illustrated by Fig. 186. Water from the main drain of the pool is drawn through a strainer by a motor-driven centrifugal pump and is discharged from the pump into the top of the filter tank. Pump pressure forces the water downward through a layer of filter sand possibly 18 to 20 inches deep but often 24 inches or more as required by regulations.

Below the sand is gravel, usually in four layers of differing sizes. The topmost layer consists of gravel in pieces ranging from $\frac{1}{8}$ to $\frac{1}{4}$ inch. In the next layer the gravel is from $\frac{1}{4}$ to $\frac{1}{2}$ inch in size, then comes a layer of pieces ranging from $\frac{1}{2}$ to 1 inch, and in the bottom layer the gravel is 1 inch to $1\frac{1}{4}$ or $1\frac{1}{2}$ inches. The bottom layer of gravel is about 6 inches deep, with each of the other layers 3 to 4 inches deep. From the bottommost gravel, filtered water goes through a perforated plate of bronze or fibreglass called the underdrain, thence to pool inlet piping.

The strainer, which may be a separate unit or else

built onto the pump, catches hair, lint and other foreign matter which could cause excessive wear in the pump and which, were such matter to get into

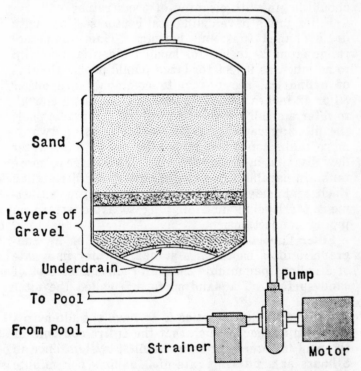

Fig. 186.—The principle of a sand-gravel filter unit.

the filter sand, could become so embedded as to be exceedingly difficult to remove with any usual cleaning process.

The top of the strainer is removable. Inside is a perforated basket of brass or stainless steel into which water flows while foreign matter is caught on the outside of the perforations. The strainer should be cleaned at least once a week, also after

each suction cleaning of the pool, and after every
cleaning of filter sand by backwashing. Investiga-
tion of any unusual drop of water flow at pool inlets
should begin with cleaning of the strainer.

Filter tanks have cylindrical center sections with
dome shaped tops and bottoms. Tank diameters
range from 20 inches for small residential pools up
to as much as 9 feet for large public pools. Heights
of cylindrical sections quite commonly are either
36 or 48 inches. A single tank may be large enough
to filter a small residential pool, but for public pools
the filtering capacity is increased by using two or
more tanks connected in parallel, with total water
flow dividing between the tanks. Two, three or more
tanks in parallel are called a battery of filter units.
Each tank may have jack legs with screw adjustment for leveling and aligning to avoid strain on
piping connections.

Filter Capacities.—Filtering capacity of a sand-
gravel unit is based on a standard water flow rate
of 3 gallons per minute through each square foot of
sand surface. The sand surface is called the filter
area.

Fairly common practice is to have the filter area
and pump capacity such that the entire contents of
the pool is forced through the filter system once in
8 hours at a filtering rate of 3 gallons per minute
per square foot of filter area. However, health department regulations may require a turnover in 6
hours or in some other time less than 8 hours.

The filter area of one tank is, of course, proportional to the diameter of the tank. Multiplying the
square foot area by 3 gives the filtering rate in
gallons per minute. Multiplying this rate by 480
gives the gallons of water passing through the filter
during an 8-hour period, which is called the turnover period.

From Fig. 187 may be read the approximate
capacity of one sand-gravel filter tank operated at a

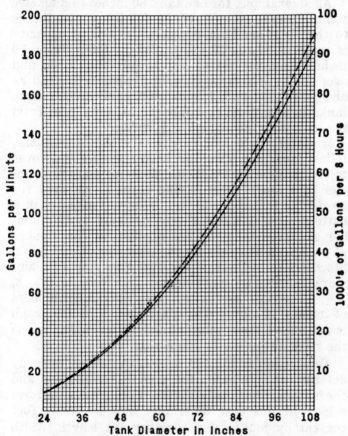

FIG. 187—Filtering rates for a flow of three gallons per minute
per square foot of filter area in sand-gravel units.

flow rate of 3 gallons per minute per square foot
of filter area. For filtering capacity in gallons per
minute use the broken-line curve and the left-hand
vertical scale. For capacity in thousands of gallons

per 8-hour turnover period use the full-line curve
and the right-hand vertical scale.

As an example, for one tank 60 inches in diameter
follow upward from 60 to the full-line curve, thence
to the right-hand scale where the 8-hour capacity
is read as about 28,300 gallons. Going from 60
inches diameter up to the broken-line curve and
over to the left-hand scale, the capacity is read as
about 59 gallons per minute. For two, three or more
tanks in a battery, multiply the capacity read from
the graph by the number of tanks.

If water content of a pool is known, in gallons,
follow from this value on the right-hand scale over
to the full-line curve, thence down to find the diameter of a single tank having capacity required for
an 8-hour turnover. If two or more tanks are in a
battery, first divide total pool contents by the number of tanks, then use the quotient as the number
of gallons in determining the diameter of each tank.
Stock tanks ordinarily are available only in diameters varying by one-half foot, such as 2, 2½, 3,
3½, 4 feet and so on, or in corresponding numbers
of inches. If a tank size determined from the graph
is not one of these values it will be necessary to use
the next larger stock diameter.

Total water content of a pool, in gallons, is easily
determined only when the pool is rectangular and
the bottom is horizontal all the way or has a uniform
slope. In this case determine first the cubic foot
content by multiplying together the length, width
and average depth in feet. Then multiply the product by 7½, which is the number of gallons in each
cubic foot.

As an example, the content of a rectangular
pool 50 feet long, 25 feet wide, with average depth
of 4½ feet would be found as about 42,200 gallons.

Fig. 187 shows that filtering this much water in 8 hours would require one tank slightly more than 72 inches in diameter. Such a large single tank would be unusual. For three tanks the pool content would be divided by 3, giving a little more than 14,000 gallons per tank. The graph shows that each tank would have to be 42 inches in diameter for an 8-hour turnover. A shorter turnover would require larger tanks.

The filter is operated long enough during each 24 hours to make pool water satisfactorily clear. If observations show that some certain number of hours per day give good results the pump drive motor might be turned on and off by an electric time clock. Greater than average running time may be required during hot weather or when the pool is used by more than the average number of bathers.

Better practice is to operate the filter system 24 hours per day during the bathing season, except during short periods for cleaning and adjustment. If filtering is stopped for any considerable number of hours there is opportunity for excessive algae to develop. The effect may show up several days later as increased turbidity of pool water. The longer the turnover period the greater is the need for continual operation of the filter system.

A common test for filter effectiveness is to drop a dime into the pool where the water is at least 6 feet deep. If, with the surface calm, it is possible to distinguish head from tail of the dime, filtering is good.

Pump motors for residential or private pool filters range from ½ to 2 horsepower and for public pools the range is from 1 to 15 horsepower. Filter tanks of large diameter require motors of proportionately large power, but one, two, three or four filter tanks of any given diameter may be operated with a pump motor of the same horsepower. In a general way, but subject to much variation with individual designs, sand-gravel filter tank diameters and powers of pump motors are about as shown in the accompanying list.

Diameter inches	Motor HP	Diameter inches	Motor HP
20 to 30	½	54	3
30 to 36	¾	60 to 66	5
36 to 42	1 - 1½	72 to 84	7½
48	2	90 to 102	10

Motors for self-priming centrifugal pumps are of greater power than for regular pumps, this being especially true when tanks are of fairly large diameter.

Floc.—Filter sand seldom removes enough of the suspended impurities to leave filtered water completely clear. Clarity is improved by forming on top of the sand an additional filter medium called floc, produced by adding alum to water entering the filter. As the dissolved alum settles in the tank it catches on top of the sand in a jelly-like mass quite like partially set gelatine. This mass retains the very fine impurities from incoming water. The alum itself is called the coagulent or the flocculant.

So far as water clarification is concerned any kind of alum may be used. However, the choice of alum has an effect on the process of chlorination for reducing bacteria. Common alum, which is potassium alum, also a kind called concentrated alum, which is aluminum sulfate, allow formation of hypochlorous acid. This acid produces a "free chlorine residual" that acts quickly and energetically as a disinfectant.

The use of ammonium alum may result in the formation of "combined chlorine" compounds which are relatively slow acting and weak in disinfecting ability, as compared with hypochlorous acid. Then more of the chlorine-forming chemicals must be used to obtain the required anti-bacterial action.

Two ounces of alum, by weight, for each square foot of sand filter area usually will produce a satisfactory floc. More alum may be required if pool water or make-up water is of exceptionally high alkalinity. Alum dosage always should be the least which allows satisfactory water clarity.

A certain length of time is required after alum is added to water for completing the formation of the jelly-like mass which is to remain on top of the sand. Therefore, the alum should be added ahead of the filter pump to allow agitation in the pump and additional mixing in piping from pump to tanks. If alum is added between pump and tanks, or if too much alum is added anywhere, floc formation still may be incomplete in filtered water going back to the pool. The result will be turbidity of pool water and possible irritation of bathers' eyes and skin.

One way of introducing alum is to put it into the strainer which is ahead of the filter pump. A better way is to use a pot type feeder such as shown later, at the left in Fig. 191. Water under pressure is fed into the bottom of the pot while the alum solution is taken from the top to a point ahead of the pump. Motor-driven chemical feeders also may be used for feeding alum solution.

Alum is added to form a new floc only after the filter has been cleaned by back-washing, which removes the old floc. Alum solution should be fed into the system over a period of 6 to 8 hours, by adjustment of valves or the feed rate, to allow fairly slow build-up of the floc. Feeder valves may be left wide open at all other times. Granulated alum dissolves rapidly in the feeder. Alum in large lumps, about the size of a walnut, dissolves slowly enough to extend the time of application regardless of valve adjustment.

Backwashing.—The sand-gravel is periodically cleaned by backwashing, which means pumping water from the pool through the filter bed in a direction opposite to that for normal filtering, and discharging the water through the waste pipe. The flow rate for backwashing is approximately four times the rate for filtering. With the normal filtering rate of 3 gallons per minute per square foot of sand filter area, backwashing will be at the rate of 12 gallons per minute per square foot. Were the total filtering rate for a certain tank to be 25 gallons per minute, the backwash rate would be 100 gallons per minute.

With only a single filter tank the pump must be capable of delivering water at the backwash rate. However, pumping power need not be four times as great as for filtering, because backwash water into the waste pipe encounters relatively small resistance to flow—the pump works against a lower head than when filtering and forcing cleaned water back to the pool.

With two or more filter tanks backwashing is done in only one tank at a time. Were backwash water delivered to all the tanks of a parallel connected battery, the tank with dirtiest filter and most resistance to flow would carry the least backwash water, while any relatively clean filter beds would get the greatest flow. Incidentally, backwashing only one tank at a time avoids need for such large pumping capacity as would be required for four times the filtering rate in all tanks together.

Filter Controls.—Fig. 188 illustrates one system of piping and valves for control of filtering, backwashing, and other operations in a system employing two sand-gravel filter tanks. Additional tanks in the battery would require only extra inlet and outlet valves for each added tank.

For normal filtering, for backwashing with pool water to the waste pipe, and for emptying the pool to the waste pipe, valves would be operated as shown by the accompanying table.

Valve	For Filtering	Backwashing Right Tank	Left Tank	Emptying The Pool
A	Open	Closed	Closed	Open
B	Closed	Open	Open	Closed
C	Closed	Open	Open	Open
D	Closed	Closed	Closed	Closed
E	Open	Closed	Closed	Closed
1	Open	Open	Closed	Closed
2	Open	Open	Closed	Closed
3	Open	Closed	Open	Closed
4	Open	Closed	Open	Closed

The pool could be emptied also by reversing the positions of valves *A*, *B* and *D* as shown in the last column of the table. Combination valves are available which control all the functions by movement of a single large handle whose pointer indicates the function performed at each of several positions. These valves have a number of ports to which connect the various pipes on the filter tanks.

One pressure gauge is connected to the inlet for the filter tanks and a second gauge is connected to their outlet side. The difference between gauge

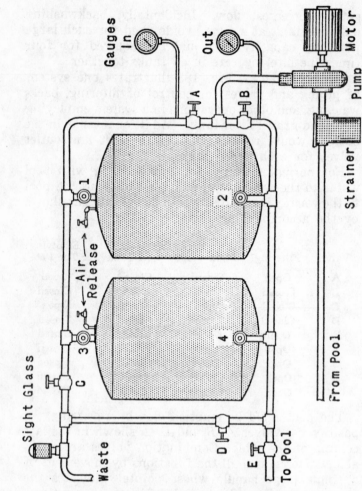

Fig. 188.—A system of piping and valves for control of a sand-gravel filter battery.

readings while the filter system is in operation is a measure of pressure required to force water through the filter beds. This pressure difference increases as the filter beds become clogged with impurities. When the difference reaches a value specified in instructions issued by the equipment manufacturer it is time for backwashing. Excessive loss of pressure in the filter tanks will lower the pressure and velocity with which filtered water re-enters the pool, this also being a signal for backwashing.

As a general rule, sand-gravel filters are backwashed when inlet pressure become higher than outlet pressure by 5 to 7 pounds per square inch. In a freshly backwashed sand-gravel filter the difference between inlet and outlet pressures may be only about 1 pound per square inch, as read from the two gauges.

When the pool is to be emptied or drained for any reason it is desirable to take all the water through the filter beds as a reversed flow for prolonged backwashing. This will improve the condition of the sand bed.

On top of each tank is an air release valve. These valves should be opened daily or oftener for escape of air which has been trapped in the water flow and which separates and gathers in the tanks. This air, if not released, greatly interferes with the process of filtration.

On the waste line is a sight glass in whose fitting or mounting is a deflector that forces part of the backwash water through the observation chamber. Backwashing should be continued until water through the sight glass appears entirely clear, then for at least two minutes longer. Valves which admit backwash water should be opened very slowly at the beginning of the process. When backwashing is complete, these valves should be closed equally slowly in order that sand may settle with its smallet particles at the top.

Since backwashing removes the layer of floc depended on for removal of finest impurity particles from water, the floc must be renewed after each backwashing. It is advisable also to clean the strainer at the same time.

Diatomite Filters. — A diatomite filter utilizes a thin layer of almost microscopically small fossil or skeleton remains of prehistoric life called diatoms. As prepared for filtering, the material is a white powder, completely odorless and tasteless. This powder is called filter aid. The diatomite filter is a type distinctly different from the sand-gravel variety.

Filter aids vary in size of particles and in degree of porosity. Various grades range from those which remove impurities so fine as to be practically invisible all the way to grades which remove only particles of relatively greater size but, of course, still very small. The filter system may be operated first with one of the finer grades, then, successively, with coarser grades until reaching the coarsest which allows satisfactory water clarity. The coarser the grade the more rapid may be the filtering and the longer will be periods between backwashing.

Filter aid action is illustrated by Fig. 189. On the perforated filter screen is first deposited a layer possibly 1/16 inch thick, which is called the precoat. To water coming into the filter is continually added a small amount of filter aid which gradually builds up on the precoat while trapping impurities to form the filter cake. Relatively smooth or hard impurities suspended in water coming from the pump and pool are stopped by the porous filter cake and precoat, while any slimy impurities tend to stick to the filter aid in the cake so that these impurities do not get into and clog the precoat.

A complete filter consists of two or three, or possibly twenty or more elements in which the filter

screens may be in the form of long cylindrical tubes
or of flat sections made from metal such as stainless steel or monel. The screens either are perforated
or formed as a mesh. Various makes of filter assem-
blies have their own special designs for elements.

The precoat is formed by mixing with water in
a separate tank 2 to 3 ounces of filter aid, by weight,
for each square foot of filter surface. Total filter

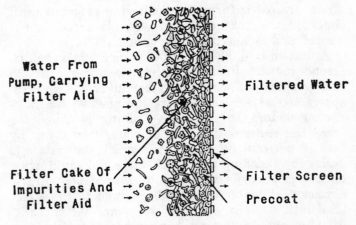

FIG. 189.—The principle of the diatomite filter.

surface in all the elements may range from about
25 square feet for a pool containing 25,000 to 35,000
gallons up to nearly 200 square feet for a pool with
300,000 gallons of water. During formation of the
precoat, water from the filter may be either wasted
or recirculated through the pool.

In filter systems for public pools it is usual practice to continually and automatically add filter aid
to water entering the filter from the pool. This mixture is called slurry. Depending on the number of
bathers and other conditions, adding from 1 to 5
pounds of filter aid per 100,000 gallons of water

circulated will make a slurry which continually forms fresh surfaces, the filter cake, to catch additional impurities.

Once a week or oftener the diatomite filter is cleaned by removing the collected filter cake and the precoat. This is accomplished by operating control valves to send water through the filter elements opposite to the direction for normal filtering, as in backwashing of sand-gravel filters. After this a new precoat is formed and filtering proceeds until time for the next cleaning. An alum floc is not needed and is not used in diatomite filters.

A diatomite filter should be cleaned when the difference between inlet and outlet pressures reaches 25 to 30 pounds per square inch as read from two pressure gauges. Some filters are equipped with a rate-of-flow meter. In this case cleaning is called for when the recirculation rate of water flow drops by 5 to 10 per cent below that for which the system is designed. Cleaning is most effective and rapid when backwash water is allowed to flow in strong surges.

Backwash water may be discharged to the waste line until a sight glass shows clear. After backwashing and applying a fresh precoat, water from the filter outlet which normlly would go to the pool may instead be recirculated through the pump and filter elements so that any suspended particles remain in the filter instead of going into the pool.

After a few months or possibly only after several seasons of operation the openings in filter element screens may become so clogged that they are not fully opened by ordinary backwashing. Then the screens should be cleaned in accordance with instructions issued by the equipment manufacturer Usually the cleaning is done with a wire brush, with compressed air, by immersion in a weak acid solution, or by some combination of these methods.

Maximum recommended rate of water flow through a diatomite filter is 3 gallons per minute per square foot of filter area. Although clear water may be had with much greater rates of flow, the greater flow rates materially reduce the time periods

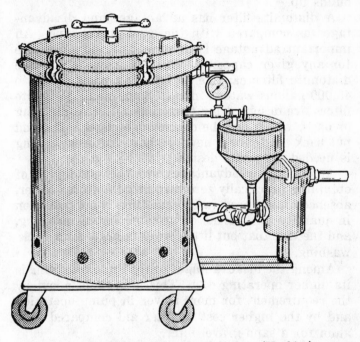

FIG. 190.—Portable diatomite filter unit. (Hopkins)

between required cleanings. Rates as slow as 1 or 2 gallons per minute per square foot allow relatively long periods. Cleaning once a day for outdoor pools is considered reasonable. Filters for indoor pools may operate satisfactorily for two to five days between cleanings.

The recirculating pump and motor for a diatomite filter must be capable of providing the required or desired flow rate against the rather high resistance which develops as the filtering cycle progresses. Some systems are provided with two pumps, one of which is used for the beginning of the cycle, with the second connected in series after filter resistance builds up.

A diatomite filter has advantages and disadvantages as compared with the sand-gravel type. An important advantage is light weight and small size for any given capacity. Fig 190 shows a portable diatomite filter capable of handling pools of up to 45,000 gallons water content. Some small diatomite filters are designed for easy removal of a filter bag or bags, which may be cleaned outside the unit and put back ready for a new precoat. No backwashing is needed with this design.

Among other advantages are the possibility of obtaining practically zero turbidity in filtered water, absence of any need for flocculating, some reduction in quantity of chlorine or bromine for disinfecting, and the fact that but little water is needed for backwashing.

Among the disadvantages of the diatomite filter is its higher operating cost. This is brought about by the requirement for more power in pump operation and by the higher cost of filter aid compared with alum for a sand-gravel filter.

Another disadvantage is the relatively short filtering cycle between cleanings, especially when filter aid is not continually added or when the system is not properly cared for. Further, the filter screens may clog and require removal for cleaning after comparatively short periods of use.

Disinfectants. —The most widely used disinfectant for water in swimming pools is chlorine, which may be added in any of various forms. One method utilizes calcium hypochlorite, a compound containing 70 per cent of chlorine by weight. It is dissolved in water for application. The powdered or granular form dissolves rapidly, the pellet form more slowly to extend the time of application. Another compound is sodium hypochlorite or chlorinated lime used in a water solution providing 12 to 15 per cent of chlorine by weight.

Chlorine gas liquefied by compression and held in a steel tank or cylinder is used in many large public pools under strict supervision and safety regulations, such as the provision of proper gas masks for use in emergencies.

Chlorine which remains in the pool water to act as a disinfectant while bathers are present is called the residual. This residual, as indicated by suitable test, is preferably as much as one part per million, which means one pound of chlorine per million pounds of pool water or 8.3 pounds of chlorine per million gallons of water. It is rather common practice, however, to maintain a free chlorine residual close to the allowable minimum of 0.3 to 0.4 part per million or something between this and about 0.6 part per million.

Chlorine may be added manually by pouring enough of the sodium hypochlorite solution into the water around the edges of a pool. This is done during early morning or evening hours, when there is little or no direct sunlight on the pool.

The addition more often is made by means of a chemical feeder or chlorinator providing a positive, motor-driven, and accurately measured rate of feed. Such a machine is at the right in Fig. 191. The chlorinator should be capable of feeding up to 2 pounds of chlorine per day for every 10,000 gallons of pool water, although the normal dosage will be much less than this maximum. Chlorine solution from the feeder is injected between the discharge side of the circulating pump and the inlet pipe to the tank or tanks.

Measurements of chlorine residual maintained in the pool while it is in use should be made with test sets designed especially for the purpose and by strict observance of instructions accompanying these sets.

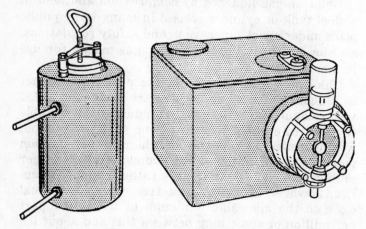

Fig. 191.—Chemical feed pot (left) and motor-driven positive feed chlorinator (right).

The test is made by adding to a small sample of pool water a pearly crystalline compound called ortho-tolidine. This compound reacts with chlorine to produce a yellow color whose shade and depth vary according to the concentration of chlorine. The resulting color is compared with standards consisting of colored glass discs or of colored solutions.

If yellow flashes up immediately upon adding ortho-tolidine the residual probably is in the form of free chlorine. But if complete development of the final color takes about 5 minutes the residual is largely or wholly in the form of combined chlorine. If coloring developes to three-quarters or more of its final value in 5 seconds the residual as determined by comparison with standards should give satisfactory disinfecting action. More precise measurements may be made by first using sodium arsenite, a very poisonous substance, to check for presence of organic matter, nitrites, iron and other substances which tend to produce false indications.

Color standards are preferably sufficient in number to allow determining residuals all the way from 0.1 to 1.0 part per million, in steps of 0.1. Measurements should be made early in the morning, again at the night closing time, and frequently when large numbers of persons are in the pool. Tests should be made where shaded from direct sunlight.

Bromine. —Bromine may be used instead of chlorine as a disinfectant. Bromine is a dark brown liquid about three times as heavy as water. Great care must be used in handling, because bromine blisters and burns the skin, and its fumes are highly irritating to eyes and lungs.

Bromine is fed by allowing water to bubble up through it, then injecting the water with its dissolved bromine into the filter system. Tests for bromine residual are the same as for chlorine. However, the yellow color always flashes up immediately when bromine is in the water. The bromine residual should be at least 1 part per million, but may be greater without causing irritation of eyes and skin of bathers.

Alkalinity-acidity Control. —Pool water should be neither excessively alkaline nor excessively acid. These qualities are measured on the Sorenson scale of numbers, whose symbol is pH. The pH for extreme alkalinity is 14.0, for extreme acidity it is 0, and for a neutral condition, neither alkaline nor acid, the pH is 7.0. Pool water should be slightly alkaline, with pH of 7.2 to 7.6.

Eyes, skin and mucous membranes of bathers are irritated if pH is lower than 7.0 or is very high. Effectiveness of normal chlorine disinfectant treatment is greatly reduced if pH is above 7.6. There is best formation of alum floc when pH is 7.2 or greater.

All chemical treatments tend to alter the pH value of pool water. Sodium hypochlorite for disinfecting tends to raise pH, while it is lowered by use of chlorine gas or pure bromine, and is lowered also by alum flocculant.

When alkalinity of pool water drops below a pH of 7.2 it usually is raised by application of a mild alkali called soda ash, which is sodium carbonate without water and is otherwise the same as washing soda or sal soda. Sometimes used is sodium hydroxide, which is caustic soda or lye, but this strong alkali attacks the skin as well as things such as woolen clothing and rubber tubing or gloves. Lime might be used to increase alkalinity but for the facts that it increases water turbidity and is likely to cause cementing of sand in filter beds.

If alkalinity of pool water goes too high, above a pH of 7.6, it may be lowered by addition of dilute hydrochloric acid or dilute sulphuric acid, but only with great care by an experienced operator. Alkalinity is lowered more safely by adding sodium bisulfate, which is sodium acid sulfate. This latter compound has the incidental advantage of acting with chlorine disinfectant in the system to loosen deposits of lime in the filter and piping.

Soda ash may be applied by suspending briquets or blocks of the substance in the pool near the outlet which is connected to the filter or pump. This need not interfere with bathing. Otherwise a water solution of soda ash may be fed to the inlet of filter tanks or to the filter pump inlet from a pot or from a mechanical feeder such as illustrated in Fig. 191.

The pH of pool water is measured by adding phenolsulphonephthalein to a sample of pool water. This chemical with the long name commonly is called phenol red. In water containing alkali it produces a red color, but no color at all if the water contains even a weak acid. The color produced is compared with color standards furnished as part of the test set. The standards should cover a pH range at least from 7.0 to 8.0, and often extend from 6.8 to 8.4.

If pool water contains a high residual of disinfectant chemical a wrong color may be obtained in the phenol red test. Disinfectant in the test tube containing the water sample may first be neutralized by adding one drop of a 1 per cent solution of sodium thiosulfate to water in the tube. A test tube used for both phenol red and ortho-tolidine should be thoroughly rinsed between tests or else both measurements will be highly inaccurate. Test sets usually are designed to make both measurements.

Algae Control. —Algae are a growth, of plant nature, which are nourished by sunlight and which multiply rapidly. They are deposited in pool water from the air, especially during rainy seasons. Free floating algae impart a greenish color to pool water, while the clinging type form slimy coatings on bottom and sides of the pool and are more difficult to treat than the floating variety.

Even before algae cause noticeable coloring or sliming in pools they cause a sudden rise in pH, possibly from 7.5 to 8.0 within a few hours. This should be a signal for immediate treatment. Uncontrolled algae make pool water so turbid that the bottom cannot be seen at the shallow end of a pool. The water may have a disagreeable odor. Bacteria then develope so rapidly as to greatly increase the amount of chlorine or bromine required to maintain satisfactory residuals. All these bad effects become worse when water temperature rises above 80°.

Superchlorination is employed to kill algae. First it must be made certain that no bathers will enter the pool. Chlorine is added or the dosage rate increased until free chlorine residual rises to at least 2 parts per million. Then the chlorinator is shut off and pool water is recirculated until the residual drops to 1 part per million. Bathers then may be allowed to enter the pool.

Superchlorination is most effective and rapid when there is first added to the pool water a wetting agent which behaves somewhat like some of the detergents used for washing clothes. This action allows disinfectant chemicals to better attack the algae. One wetting agent for pool water is a salt called quaternary ammonium halide. Very severe growths of algae often are treated with copper sulfate. Any treatment for killing algae is followed by using a brush to loosen the remains on sides and bottom of the pool, after which the job is finished with a suction cleaner.

Legal Requirements.—Design, construction, operation and maintenance of public swimming pools are supervised and quite strictly regulated by state Departments of Public Health. No public pool should be built or operated without first communicating with the controlling authorities for necessary permits and to become acquainted with reports which are required. Reports cover items such as daily tests of water conditions and chemical treatments.

Much of the information in this chapter has been obtained from publications of the Department of Public Health of the State of Illinois, but it must not be taken as a guide to requirements. Descriptions and illustrations of fittings and mechanical equipment for pools in general and for sand-gravel filters relate chiefly to products of Modern Swimming Pool Company and of Adolph Kiefer and Company.

CHAPTER 24

MOTEL PLUMBING

By far the greater portion of all plumbing in a motel consists of bathroom fixtures and piping, this because every guest unit must have complete bath and toilet facilities. While serving guest comfort to the greatest practicable degree, floor area of the bathrooms usually is kept down to the point where any-

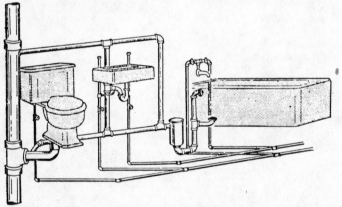

FIG. 192.—The many pipes and connections for a bathroom require a compact arrangement in order that economy of installation may be had.

thing smaller would appear cramped. It is desirable also that all parts of the plumbing installation should allow routine servicing with least disturbance to guests.

Fig. 192 shows typical supply, waste and vent piping for the three essential fixtures in a bathroom, which are a tub or shower, a lavatory and a water closet. It is plainly evident that the closer together are the fixtures the more economical will be the piping, also that having all fixtures against the same wall will greatly simplify the installation. Next best would be an arrangement with all fixtures on adjacent walls and near the corner where these walls meet.

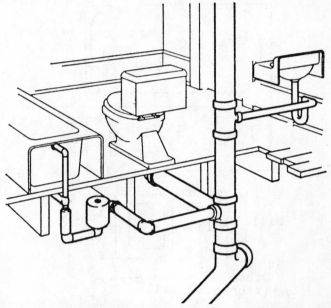

Fig. 193.—The soil stack provides venting for all the fixtures.

Another method of reducing installation costs is illustrated by Fig. 193, assuming that such a plan complies with plumbing codes. Venting is provided only by the vertical soil stack. This system operates because discharge from the closet enters the stack below the drain pipes from both the bathtub and the lavatory. Since the stack admits air after both the lavatory trap and the bathtub trap, neither of these traps can be siphoned by water closet discharges.

The minimum possible floor area of a bathroom is determined by dimensions of the fixtures and by the smallest clearances which are allowable between any two or more fixtures and between fixtures and the walls. Fig. 194 shows the least clearances which allow reasonably convenient use of the bathroom

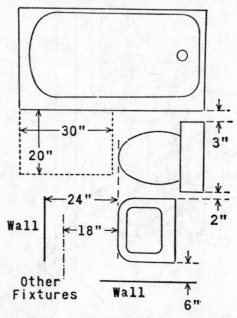

FIG. 194.—Minimum clearances which should be provided in a bathroom.

while also allowing cleaning of all exposed fixture surfaces.

Between the side of a lavatory and a water closet tank should be no less than 2 inches, with at least 3 inches between the tank and a bathtub. Along the front of a tub should be a clear space at least 30 inches long and 20 inches out from the tub. Between a water closet tank and a wall should be a minimum of 4 inches, and between the side of a lavatory and a wall a minimum of 6 inches. From the front of a water closet or a lavatory to the nearest fixture of any other kind the distance should be 18 inches or more, with at least 24 inches from the front of either of these units to the nearest wall.

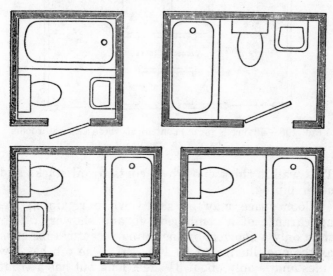

FIG. 195.—Bathroom plans for recessed tubs.

Bathroom Layouts.—Tubs most commonly are of the recessed type with overall length of about 5 feet and width of 2½ feet. The most compact arrangement of such a tub with a lavatory and water closet is shown at the upper left in Fig. 195. Inside dimensions of the room are 5 by 5 feet. At the upper right is a room with inside measurements of 5 by 7½ feet and with the same three fixtures placed for a much more economical installation of piping. The plans at the lower left and right are convenient for guest use but require more costly piping because fixturs are on opposite walls. This objection may be overcome to a large extent, as in Fig. 196, by having a common wall between the baths for adjacent guest units.

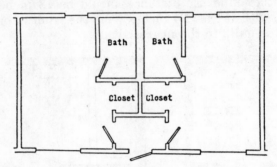

FIG. 196.—Piping is more economical where two bathrooms have a common wall.

This wall is thick enough to contain soil stacks and other piping.

Floor space may be saved while retaining the appearance of a combined tub and shower, rather than only a shower, by installing receptor tubs such as the one illustrated by Fig. 197. The tub has low sides and is only about $3\frac{1}{2}$ feet long but has a front rim wide enough to form a convenient seat. The overall floor area is much less than for a 5-foot recessed tub and only a little greater than needed for a large shower stall.

Two bathroom layouts for receptor tubs are shown by Fig. 198. Inside room dimensions at the left are 6 by 9 feet and at the right are 6 by $6\frac{1}{2}$ feet. The larger plan has ample interior space combined with the advantage of having all fixtures along the same wall. The smaller plan does not require particularly difficult piping because only the lavatory is separated from the tub and water closet.

Showers without tubs allow greatest savings of floor space, but are not so appealing to most guests and do not allow rental rates as high as for rooms

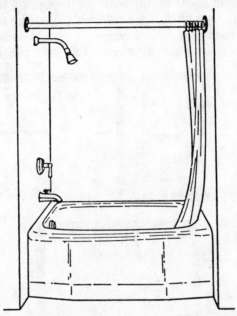

FIG. 197.—A receptor tub combines attractive appearance with minimum floor area.

having a combined tub and shower. Built-in shower stalls usually are about 3 feet square or only slightly

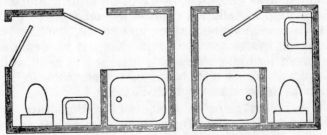

FIG. 198.—Bathroom layouts for receptor tubs.

less. Anything smaller makes it difficult for guests
to avoid the spray while soaping. The bottom of a
shower, in which is the drain, may be of terrazzo,
concrete or sheet metal with a low rim of the same
material. This part of a shower is called the receptor.

A cabinet shower is a complete unit which may be
installed in an existing room. The unit consists of a

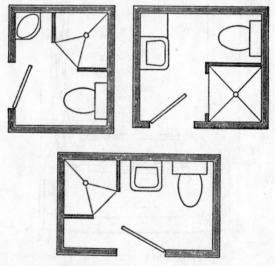

FIG. 199.—Bathroom plans for showers without tubs.

receptor, side walls, a door or a curtain hanger, the
shower head and valve, also a drain grating and outlet fitting. Installation requires assembly of the walls
on the receptor and making pipe connections for hot
and cold water and the drain. No part of a cabinet
shower need be permanently attached to room walls
or floor. Inside dimensions of cabinet showers are
about the same as for built-in types.

Bathroom plans with showers but no tubs are
shown by Fig. 199. Inside room dimensions at the

upper left are only 5½ by 5 feet, and at the upper
right are 5⅓ by 6½ feet. The smaller floor space is
made possible by using a shower with a diagonal
corner door and by using a corner lavatory. Room
size for the bottom plan is 4½ by 8 feet, practically
the same square foot area as at the upper right, but

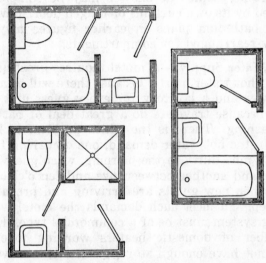

FIG. 200.—Dividing the bathroom into two compartments allows
two persons to use the facilities at the same time.

with the advantage of having all fixtures along the
same wall.

Motel guests, who usually are in a hurry to get
away in the morning, can save time if the bathroom
is arranged for use by two people at the same time
with reasonable privacy. This is allowed by dividing
the bathroom into two compartments separated by
an inner door. Such arrangements are illustrated
by Fig. 200.

The arrangement at the upper left is desirable
because the separated lavatory provides the advan-

tage of a small dressing room. The plan at the right is good because the water closet is separated by the inner door. The tub is at least partially screened from the lavatory by shower curtains or, better, by sliding shower doors. At the lower left the lavatory is in the same compartment with the lavatory, which is desirable, while the shower may be completely screened by its own curtains or hinged door. Several of the bathroom plans in earlier figures may be slightly rearranged for compartments.

Hot Water Supply.—A motel requires great quantities of hot water, partly because there will be a tub or shower and a lavatory for every guest unit and partly because travelers do a great deal of bathing and washing. There is the added problem of high peaks in the hot water demand, one occurring from seven to nine-thirty in the morning, when guests are leaving, and another between five and ten o'clock at night when new guests are arriving and preparing for sleep. To meet such demands the motel water heating system must be of a commercial type. Even a number of domestic heaters working together would not have enough storage capacity nor would their recovery rates be enough to keep up with the load.

Commercial water heaters may use gas, electricity or oil, but gas usually is preferred. The gas may be natural, manufactured, mixed or bottled, the latter being called liquid petroleum or *LP* gas. For motels with 100 or more guest units the heating unit and hot water storage tank nearly always are separate. The separate storage tank may hold only a few hundred gallons or several thousand gallons.

The recovery rate of a water heating system specifies the number of gallons whose temperature is raised a certain number of degrees within one hour.

For any given recovery rate and temperature rise the system must be supplied with a certain quantity of heat energy which, for gas heating, is specified in thousands of Btu's per hour. One Btu is the quantity of heat energy which, were none wasted, will raise the temperature of one pound of water one Fahrenheit degree, regardless of time.

A generally accepted rule is that water reaching the short takeoffs to guest unit tubs or showers and lavatories should be at a temperature little if any below 140° F. Higher temperature is unnecessary, lower ones are not so satisfactory to guests. Another common rule is to provide 10 gallons of hot water per guest per day, but the actual use is so irregular that this average figure is of little help in selection of equipment.

Commercial water heaters with self-contained storage tanks commonly store 50 to 75 gallons of heated water and have recovery rates ranging from 60 to about 160 gallons per hour. A 50-gallon unit might have a recovery rate of 100 gallons of 140° water per hour. During a two-hour period of peak demand this unit would deliver its originally stored 50 gallons plus twice its one-hour recovery rate for a total of 250 gallons during the peak period.

Heaters designed for use with separate storage tanks may have little storage capacity in the heater unit, but recovery rates as great as five times the built-in storage capacity. For periods of peak demand there is available the large quantity of hot water from the separate tank plus the small quantity from the built-in tank.

Fig. 201 shows relations between temperature rise, recovery rate in gallons per hour, and heat input. As an example in using this chart, assume that water entering the heater is at 50° F., and output temperature is to be 150°. Then the temperature rise is the difference, or 100°. Assume also that the recovery rate is to be 125 gallons per hour. Following downward from the intersection of the 100° temperature line and the horizontal line for 125 gallons per hour shows that heat input must be 150,000 Btu's per hour.

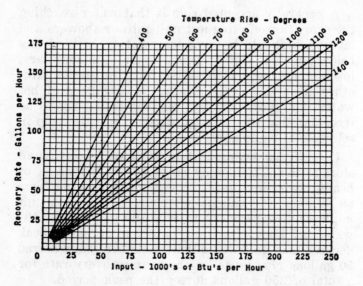

Fig. 201.—A chart allowing determination of required heat input for any recovery rate and temperature rise.

The recovery rate in gallons per hour, plus the number of gallons stored at the required temperature, must at least equal the peak demand for hot water during any one hour. Some excess capacity should be provided. The chart is based on standard thermal efficiency, which means that 70 per cent of the heat input is effective in raising water temperature. Approved heaters will not fall below this efficiency. Many high quality units exceed it.

Water temperature is limited by a thermostat or aquastat which cuts off the heat source when temperature rises to the value for which the control is adjusted. These controls limit maximum temperature but can have no effect when hot water is used at a rate greater than the recovery rate. A safety control shuts off the heat source in case water temperature exceeds the maximum value for which the thermostat or aquastat may be adjusted. A drain or discharge valve is automatically opened should tank pressure exceed a safe value, as might occur with clogged piping and boiling of the water.

Electric heating for water is satisfactory where the rates are low enough to make it economical and where electric power wiring can be made of sufficient size or current capacity to carry the load. Dividing the required Btu's per hour by 3415 gives the electric power rate in kilowatts. In the earlier example calling for 150,000 Btu's per hour this would mean an electric power rate of close to 44 kilowatts, which is equivalent to about 59 electrical horsepower.

Motel water heating equipment often consists of two or more units, each having its own heat source and storage tank. Suitable piping connections force each unit to deliver its proper proportion of water into the distribution piping. The total recovery rate of several heaters working together usually is so much greater than that of a single large unit that storage capacity for heated water may be much less than for the one larger unit.

Because hot water is costly, no matter how it is obtained, the heat loss from piping should be reduced as much as is economically possible. All hot water lines, or at least the longer ones, should be insulated as explained elsewhere in this book. Many motels are designed with four or more guest units in each

of a number of separated buildings. Each building
may have its own water heating and storage facilities of capacity sufficient only for the number of
units. Otherwise a central water heating and storage system may be used, with piping run to the separate buildings.

Fig. 202 illustrates a method of running piping
between buildings in a manner which reduces heat

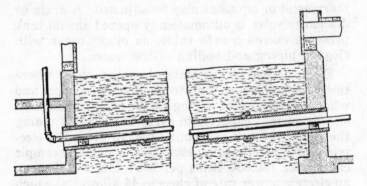

FIG. 202.—Reducing the heat loss from hot water piping
run between buildings.

loss. The enclosure consists of ordinary sewer tile or
of impregnated fibre tile, with joints not cemented,
laid below the frost level. One end is lower than the
other, and open, so that condensed moisture will
escape. The pipe is supported by wooden blocks,
with air space around it acting as heat insulation.

Quick-repair Faucets.—Washers of ordinary compression faucets are quite easily replaced, and the
seats may be dressed a few times before complete
replacement of the body becomes necessary. This latter process keeps the lavatory, shower or tub out of
service for an inconveniently long time. In some
designs the seat threads into the faucet body, being

removable for replacement with a new one by using a special screwdriver or wrench.

The faucet of Fig. 203 allows removal and replacement, as a unit, of the seat, the washer and the

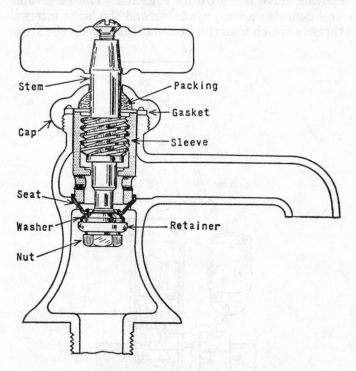

Stem

Packing

Gasket

Cap

Sleeve

Seat

Washer

Retainer

Nut

Fig. 203.—A Chicago faucet from which all wearing parts are in a single unit easily removed and replaced.

threaded sleeve. Turning the cap nut off the body permits taking out the entire replaceable section. Then, with the bottom cap nut removed, the retainer and washer are forced off by turning the sleeve After putting on a new seat and washer the sleeve is. turned back in place, the bottom cap nut is replaced and the unit is ready to go back into the faucet body.

A somewhat different design as adapted to a shower valve is shown by Fig. 204. The removable unit contains a seat, a washer and the large internal threads which take the external threads on the stem.

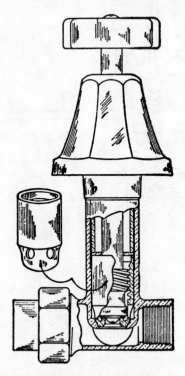

FIG. 204.—A Kohler faucet with a replaceable unit containing washer, seat and threaded sleeve.

Worn threads cause almost as much trouble as badly worn seats in ordinary faucets. An advantage of these quick-repair faucets is that a number of replacement sections or units may be kept on hand for fast correction of troubles with minimum disturbance of guests. Worn parts in the units removed may be replaced at some other time.

Vacuum Breaker.—The water supply source for a building or group of rooms often must be shut off for repairs while the distribution piping is filled. Opening a faucet on a lower level then allows water to escape and form a partial vacuum higher up. If the higher piping connects to any receptacle open

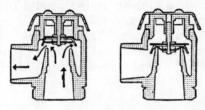

Fig. 205.—A vacuum breaker which prevents siphoning of water from open fixtures.

to air, such as a closet tank, water may be siphoned from that receptacle into the piping. This is prohibited by plumbing codes. Siphoning may be prevented by opening a faucet at the highest point in the system.

An easier way is to install vacuum breakers or siphon breakers such as shown by Fig. 205. This unit is connected into a supply faucet pipe in a position where no valve can be closed between the faucet and breaker. In the breaker unit are flexible discs above and below a shallow cup. While a shutoff valve for the faucet is open, water pressure forces the cup upward and allows free flow. But a partial vacuum in the supply piping draws the cup down and prevents flow of water from the faucet into the distribution piping.

Utility Tunnels.—All of the main water supply, drain and waste piping lines for a motel may be made easily accessible for servicing and repair by placing them in what is called a utility tunnel. This is a walled trench or excavation at least two feet wide and four feet deep run underneath hall and passageway floors or immediately outside an exterior wall. An outside tunnel must be protected from rain and snow. Conduit and boxes for electric wiring, also gas piping, often are run in the same space.

So far as possible the piping should be arranged to require only short and fairly straight runs to fixtures in the guest units. Then cleanouts located in the utility tunnel allow routine servicing with minimum labor and no inconvenience to patrons.

INDEX

INDEX

INDEX

INDEX